The Labour Party and the Struggle for Socialism

DAVID COATES

Lecturer in Politics, University of York

CAMBRIDGE UNIVERSITY PRESS

Published by the Syndics of the Cambridge University Press
Bentley House, 200 Euston Road, London NW1 2DB
American Branch: 32 East 57th Street, New York, N.Y.10022

©Cambridge University Press 1975

Library of Congress Catalogue Card Number: 74-19526

ISBNs
0 521 20740 1 hard covers
0 521 09939 0 paperback

First published 1975

Printed in Great Britain
at the University Printing House, Cambridge
(Euan Phillips, University Printer)

Contents

Socialists in the Labour Party have been afraid, far too long, of describing it as it is. There has been a continual breeding of illusions and false hopes. In so intractable a problem, with so much at stake, there is of course no easy answer. But the only possibility of an answer comes from telling the truth: describing the incorporation, in terms of policy and of procedures; refusing those spurts of temporary confidence which would show it other than it is; and then, in that mood, following the argument through, taking the necessary action, wherever it leads.

R. Williams *et al.*, *May Day Manifesto 1968*

Preface

This book is preoccupied with a single question - of the role, if any, which the Labour Party can play in the creation of a socialist society in Britain. To answer that question involves the consideration of many subsidiary themes. It requires an assessment of the Party's programmes and practices over the years, and of its periodic promise of socialist change. It requires a discussion of the nature of Labour Party leadership in both Parliament and Government, and an assessment of the forces that act upon men and women working within those institutions. It requires consideration of the role of left-wing activists within the Party, and of the consequences of the Party's performance in office for its own electoral viability and for future socialist advance. But throughout, in discussing these themes, my purpose will not simply be to provide yet another history of the Labour Party. It is rather that I wish to relate that history to, and assess it within the context of, the long-established struggle to create a socialist society out of the degradation and human waste created by capitalist modes of production. And because that is my purpose, I would like in this preface to discuss some of the responses that are likely to be made to an exercise of this kind.

Let me first indicate briefly the nature of the argument that will run through the book. I will argue that the Labour Party has periodically claimed to be engaged in the creation of a democratic socialist Britain, and that even when it has not been so bold, its leaders have invariably promised that if elected to power they would introduce major programmes of equalitarian social reform of a scale and character sufficient to alter qualitatively the lives of the many poor and dispossessed in our midst. And as a result, the Labour Party has always appealed for the support of working people and their families, and has offered itself as the natural home for socialist militants in the labour movement.

Yet I shall argue that so far at least Labour Governments have systematically failed to live up to the promises of the Party in Opposition. I will argue that Labour Party politics cannot, and will not, culminate in the creation of a genuinely socialist society; and that, on the contrary, the Labour Party and its claims are a major blockage in

the struggle to create the kind of party and the kind of labour movement that the struggle for socialism requires. I shall argue too that
there is now very little hope that Labour Governments can deliver
substantial and sustained packages of social reform; and that far from
embodying in its political practice the actual interests of its predominantly working class electorate, the Labour Party when in power seems
fated to come ever more into conflict with groups of workers who are
forced to defend their living standards, job control and even job
security *against* the policies of the very Labour politicians that they
helped to elect into office. And so, I will argue, and as far as I can tell,
the Labour Party is in deep and permanent crisis, standing ever more
visibly in a bankrupt tradition of working class politics that is in need
of criticism in theory and of replacement in practice.

But lest it be thought that what follows will therefore be yet another
exercise in the predetermined condemnation of Labour Party politics of
the conventional sectarian kind, the reader should perhaps realise that
this study was begun in an attempt to assess, and hopefully to find, the
Labour Party's road to socialism. In the event, and with great reluctance,
it became obvious as the preliminary work progressed that the road did
not exist, and that the revolutionary socialist alternative offered what
hope there was of transcending the irrationalities of capitalist
production and the alienation of human labour that is at that system's
core. So what follows is not, I hope, an exercise in condemnation by
dogma, and will not indulge in the 'death by categories' substitute for
analysis that turns so much of left-sectarian writing into a private
dialogue intelligible only to those long schooled in the language of
Marxism. Instead, the study will proceed historically, using terms that
hopefully make sense to most if not to all of us, in order to explain
how and *why* Labour Party politics fail to achieve their periodic
socialist promise, and how in the process the Party's leaders undermine
the interests of the working people that they claim to represent.

Nonetheless, in being so critical of the Labour Party, a study of this
kind will, I hope, attract detailed and cogent defences of Labour Party
potential, and even of past Labour Party practice. Such a response
might at least rekindle the debate on the possibilities of Parliamentary
Socialism in Britain, and in the process hopefully clarify those issues on
which the interested reader has to come to a decision before beginning
active political work. Certainly if that debate did begin, then it would
seem to me to make publication of this book worthwhile. But even if it
does not, the reader should realise from the beginning that what follows

is far from being a conventional analysis of Labour Party politics. Within its design lie firmly held views on the crucial issues that divide the Left: on the degree of capitalist instability, on the limits of state power under capitalism, and on the problem of working class consciousness. These are issues which have long been subjects of dispute, and on which vast literatures already exist. I will not always be able in this book to explain in detail (though I hope that I will make clear in general terms) why I believe capitalism as an international system of labour exploitation to be inherently and increasingly unstable, why I reject the view that the state in a modern industrial society has a great degree of manoeuvre and power even against the collective interests of industrial and financial capital, and why I am not impressed by those who argue that the Western European working class has visibly lost whatever revolutionary socialist potential it might once have had. I have preferred here to focus the argument on the Labour Party alone, in the hope that my views on the three issues just mentioned would offer insights into Labour Party practice that writers more sympathetic to the Party systematically miss; and that in the process the credibility of this argument about the Labour Party (if it has any) might then inspire the reader to pursue on his own the more general questions of capitalist stability and socialist change. To that end, I have tried to indicate in the footnotes and in the text those points at which my interpretation of events differs markedly from more conventional ones, and have mentioned there alternative reading for those who would like to see those interpretations for themselves. It would be nice if this book stimulated debate. It would be sad if it simply helped to establish a 'left-orthodoxy' that went without challenge. So let me begin that debate here by considering briefly three of the major points of criticism that my kind of analysis of the Labour Party seems invariably to attract.

There is firstly that body of argument that says that the British working class is very conservative in its politics, and whilst it might tolerate and even support programmes of social reform, it has inherited no revolutionary tradition from its pre-industrial forebears, nor shown any propensity to engage in revolutionary socialist activity. And that accordingly, Labour Party moderation can best be seen as a response to this wider, and prior, moderation in its own class base. Now it is certainly the case that for the bulk of the Labour Party's history its working class base has been apparently content with constitutional forms of politics, in that it has been unwilling to give mass support to organisations (like the Communist Party) which offered more radical political perspectives. But this is also true of most Western European working classes for most of their histories, for capitalism could hardly survive for a day if it lacked those material and ideological mechanisms through which to prevent its labour force from being in perpetual revolutionary ferment. Capitalism rather, as Westergaard has suggested,[1] seems even in its periods of greatest stability and material affluence to leave simply a 'counter ideology' of disaffection, dissatisfaction and hostility in the bulk of its labour force, whose crystallisation into a revolutionary class consciousness requires a complex historical conjuncture of changing material circumstances, intensifying industrial struggle and revolutionary political leadership.

In other words, men's consciousness of the socially-contingent nature of the conditions under which they live, and their familiarity with alternative conditions and the means of attaining them - all this clearly varies over time and circumstance, and is determined by many factors, one of which at least being the kind of political leadership that is present at moments of particular class tension. And as can be seen from even a cursory survey, there have been such moments in twentieth century British labour history (1911-14 was perhaps one, 1918 another, 1926 a third) when large numbers of working people might well have responded to very radical political leadership indeed.

So the arguments that say that the pattern of Labour Party politics is best explained as a simple reflection of patterns of moderation among sections of the British working class have at least to recognise that the Labour Party over the years has been a major influence shaping that moderation, by offering to its electorate time and again a coherent definition of 'politics' and 'working class interests' that associated both with Parliamentary tactics and with social reform. Indeed the responsibility which the Labour Party has for shaping its own electorate seems to me to be an enormous one. For it has been at times of mass working class despair and militancy that the Labour Party has always found it electorally expedient to promise its vision of a socialist society - to make, that is, the promise of a qualitatively higher form of human existence for working men and their families - a promise which, once in office, Labour leaders have either failed to deliver or have quite simply forgotten. Consider for a moment the memoirs of James Griffiths, deputy leader of the Labour Party under Hugh Gaitskell. In his *Pages from Memory*, he described a visit by Ramsay MacDonald to the destitute mining valleys of South Wales in 1924.

When the time arrived for the meeting to begin, the hall was packed
to suffocation and the street outside was crowded with people,
many with tickets, who had failed to get in. When Ramsay arrived
the vast audience inside - and outside - joined in the singing of one of
their favourite hymns - the bard Watcyn Wyn's vision of the day
when every continent 'neath the firmament would hail the Nazarene.
The address was in tune with the hymn - with peace on the horizon
if only we had the courage to reach out. The crowd was thrilled and
after the Prime Minister had gone on his triumphant way to Aberavon
the streets rang with shouts and songs till the early hours of Sunday.
There is nothing here to suggest that the growing conservatism of the
Parliamentary Labour Party under Ramsay MacDonald owed much to
working class conservatism. People do not sing 'till the early hours of
Sunday' in the hope that unemployment will grow, and their poverty
with it. But that is what in the end they experienced under a Labour
Government led by the man 'to whom we had vouchsafed our trust
and whom we had saluted as our hero'.[2] What has to be explained is
why the Labour Party has so systematically disappointed its supporters,
and what has to be assessed are the consequences that might flow from
the repeated experience of that disappointment for future patterns of
working class political action. And that certainly requires a detailed
look at the Labour Party itself, and at the logic of its own political
development since 1900.

Which brings me to the second body of potential response to the
argument in this book - that which says that the Labour Party has never
been a socialist party in the 'continental' or 'Marxist' sense, but only a
social democratic party, a coalition of various interests stretching all the
way from left-wing idealists and Christian socialists to piecemeal
reformers and social engineers. Then to discuss the Labour Party in the
context of the struggle for socialism - so the argument so often runs - is
really to criticise the Labour Party for failing to be something that it has
never attempted to be, and as such, is illegitimate and misleading. To
which the reply must be made, I think, that the Labour Party is
certainly a social democratic party, as that term came to be understood
after the split in the international working class movement brought
about by the Russian Revolution;* and it is with the logic and limits of

---

* The meaning of the term 'social democratic' is closely tied up with the
development of the international labour movement. For as Western Europe
and Russia industrialised after 1870, working class parties emerged, invariably
subscribing to some variant of a Marxist philosophy, and so, at the level of

social democratic politics that I will be concerned here. But as a social democratic party, the Labour Party has in the past (and most recently, at its 1973 conference) claimed to be a democratic and a socialist party, with the creation of a socialist Britain as its goal. Moreover, even in its more moderate periods, the Party has always claimed to seek substantial reforms, and has always insisted that as a result, political parties offering alternative routes to socialism should be rejected as both irrelevant and actually damaging to working class interests. This has been the Party's attitude to syndicalists, to communists, and even to the tiny Trotskyist sects operating to its own left. That is, the Labour Party has always offered itself as *the* one party on the Left that is capable of resolving the problems of capitalist society to which communists and Trotskyists have offered more radical solutions. It is therefore surely both legitimate and essential to consider the nature and potential of the Labour Party's 'socialism', to assess the possibilities of successful social reform under its leadership, and to question the degree to which its claim that its politics render more radical parties irrelevant is justified. All that the text will do.

There is yet a third body of potential response that I would like to consider before beginning the text, namely that which asserts that the problems of the Labour Party are as nothing compared to those associated with more revolutionary politics, and that consequently criticism of Labour Party behaviour and potential should best wait until the revolutionary alternative has become clearer. Yet it seems to me that amongst the largest of the problems facing those who would win large numbers of workers to a genuinely revolutionary socialist movement is the widely held illusion that the Labour Party offers a safer way

---

their rhetoric and programme at least, revolutionary. They came together in a loose confederation - the Second International - which from the late 1890s regularly met together in congresses to discuss major problems of socialist strategy and tactics. With this Second International, in which all parties tended to call themselves 'social democratic', the Labour Party had only a tenuous connection (through the Independent Labour Party). Hence perhaps one reason for its reputation of being 'different' from 'continental' and 'Marxist' working class parties. However the Second International split under the impact of the First World War and the Russian Revolution, to leave a third, Communist International, made up of national Communist Parties loyal to Moscow and initially at least seeking working class revolutions in Western Europe on the Bolshevik model; and a *Social Democratic* International, made up of parties seeking socialist change through constitutional channels. The Labour Party has always subscribed to, and operated within, the theory and practice of the post-1919 social democratic Labour and Socialist International, of which from the beginning it was a leading member.

to the same goal. These illusions of Labourism have to be shed before
alternative sources of political loyalty can grow; and I hope that this
book will be of some assistance to those seeking to demonstrate to
workers and their families that the Labour Party is not, sadly, to be
taken seriously as a representative of working class interests, as a bearer
of major social reforms, or as a route to a genuinely socialist society.

Of course, all university academics who write glibly about 'revolutions' from the safety and relative prosperity of a Western university
fall into the sin of 'armchair Marxism'; and this issue troubles my
conscience and presumably ever will. Yet the choice for my generation,
and for my children's, does seem to be that which Marx and Engels once
put, between socialism and barbarism. To avoid having to live under an
increasingly barbaric social order with intensified human alienation and
misery, the weapons with which to build a genuinely socialist society
must be forged. It may already be too late in the West to do this, as the
cynics say; but it seems to me that the rich human potential which such
a movement requires exists still in abundance. The task is clearly
difficult. To be a revolutionary socialist, even in the relatively liberal
environment of Britain in the 1970s, requires a personal wager of an
enormous kind - a wager that the instabilities of capitalism can be made
to culminate in the forging of a revolutionary socialist proletariat, and a
willingness to work daily to that end in the face of opposition, frustration and even danger. Only brave and dedicated women and men
make revolutionary socialists, and many of us will struggle with the
interplay of our hopes and fears to the grave. But one thing is certain.
That if that revolutionary alternative is to be forged, many people will
have to break with the illusions of Labour Party politics, and dissociate
themselves even from those left-wing activists within the Labour Party
who repeatedly struggle to pull the leadership back to the Party's own
'socialist' promise. I shall argue in chapter 7 that this Labour Left must
always fail, and in chapter 8 that the revolutionary Left need not. The
tragedy for our children will come, it seems to me, only if, in this
generation, neither variant of socialist succeeds.

Which brings me to the question of socialism itself, and to the
political perspective that underpins the analysis that follows. For the
dream of creating a socialist society that would tap the immense potential for human freedom and self-development offered by industrialisation
has inspired the noblest sections of each generation of the politically
active on the Left since capitalist industrialisation began. But like all
dreams that can be realised, between the aspiration and the achievement

have lain all the problems of analysis, mobilisation and action; and these problems have divided socialists as bitterly from each other as from their common capitalist opponent. Indeed the politics of the working class in Western Europe since the 1870s have been dominated in large part by precisely these internal disputes: of what socialism is, of how it can be achieved, of what kind of political party its achievement requires, and of how socialist movements are to relate to the social and political forces that stand in their way.

Now within the Labour Party, as we shall see, socialism has traditionally been understood, from 1918 at least, as involving a mixture of extensive public ownership, democratic state planning and substantial welfare provision; though from the 1950s many within the Party came to prefer a definition of socialism that focused on the theme of social equality, and which downgraded public ownership to simply being one means (and not normally a very good one) to its attainment. To the debates around this, we will come in chapter 4. But this book is written, as I have said, from a standpoint outside and to the Left of the Labour Party, from a perspective which rejects both these visions of socialism as inadequate and which says of the Labour Party that it could not attain them anyway. Socialism, as Marx defined it, involved a qualitative transformation in human experience, and a break for all time with the alienation of human labour associated with capitalist modes of production and their associated class systems of domination. To achieve socialism, he argued, required a total break with the system of free wage labour on which capitalism is built, through the dismantling of the system of property relations (and associated systems of industrial management and political authority) that are prevalent in bourgeois society. Nothing that I see around me persuades me that what Marx said a century ago has lost any of its force, or its possibility of attainment. Nor is what I take to be his vision of socialism, of a system of workers' control at the point of production that is accompanied by the dismantling of the superstructure of bourgeois legal, political and cultural forms, any less telling. But on one thing Marx was clear, that this emancipation of the working class would involve the mobilisation of the whole working class in a revolutionary upheaval. Rare indeed are Marx's references to the possibilities of Parliamentary Socialism, and the bulk of his writing seems to preclude peaceful and gradual change to a socialist society. In my experience, the only political group operating in Britain which comes anywhere near to such a perspective is the International Socialists, and it is to their publications and activity that the reader might turn if he finds the analysis that follows convincing.

I recognise that there are many gaps in what follows, and that these reflect both my own lack of knowledge and the still underdeveloped state of working class studies in this country. In particular, I will not discuss the Communist Party, and its decline from its initial revolutionary promise. There is still a great need for an adequate analysis of its politics, in spite of recent publications on its record. Nor has anyone yet written for the post-war working class the kind of study that E. P. Thompson wrote on the two generations of workers who experienced the worst rigours of early nineteenth-century industrialisation.[3] And that is a great lack. Nor have we yet seen a definitive study of changing trends in Western capitalism since 1945. Until all these studies are completed, our understanding of the total state of working class politics in Britain must remain very limited indeed, and studies of this kind on the Labour Party can only hope to be tentative and partial. Even so, I hope that what follows will make some contribution to our understanding of an important part of working class political experience, and in the process be one building block on which wider studies can later be based.

This work has taken a long time to prepare, and many people have given time and assistance in its preparation. Its argument draws heavily on earlier writings by Ralph Miliband, as its notes will show. It also reflects years of teaching with Robert Looker at the University of York, and it is a matter of personal sadness that, in the end, he was not more directly involved with a work on which he has had such an enormous influence. The Labour Party was discussed endlessly, and the text read repeatedly, by Lewis Minkin and by Jim Jupp, both of whom gave great help whilst systematically disagreeing with the book's central thesis. Indeed, given that disagreement, it is perhaps more than ever necessary for me to make clear that responsibility for what follows is mine and mine alone. I cannot even divide that responsibility with Dorothy, with David or with Joan, even though they have lived with this work for so long. Perhaps they will find it enough if I simply dedicate the book to them, in deep and lasting affection.

York
July 1974

Glossary of abbreviations

B.M.A.   British Medical Association
C.B.I.   Confederation of British Industry
C.L.P.   Constituency Labour Party
C.N.D.   Campaign for Nuclear Disarmament
D.E.P.   Department of Employment and Productivity
E.E.C.   European Economic Community
G.A.T.T.   General Agreement on Tariffs and Trade
G.N.P.   Gross National Product
I.L.P.   Independent Labour Party
I.M.F.   International Monetary Fund
I.R.C.   Industrial Reorganisation Corporation
L.R.C.   Labour Representation Committee
N.A.S.D.   National Association of Stevedores and Dockers
N.A.T.O.   North Atlantic Treaty Organisation
N.B.P.I.   National Board for Prices and Incomes
N.E.C.   National Executive Committee
S.D.F.   Social Democratic Federation
P.L.P.   Parliamentary Labour Party
T.G.W.U.   Transport and General Workers Union
T.U.C.   Trades Union Congress
V.F.S.   Victory for Socialism

1. The socialist promise

When the Labour Party met in conference in October 1973, the democratically elected Marxist Government of Salvador Allende had just been overthrown in a bloody military coup in Chile. Alvaro Bunster, Allende's ambassador, came to the conference and received full public support from Labour leaders for his call to resist the Junta that was already torturing and killing Chilean socialists in their thousands. Yet six months later, when the new Labour Government had been in office for only six weeks, the Labour Foreign Secretary allowed warships to be handed over to the new Chilean authorities, and successfully resisted a campaign against his decision that was waged by the Party's General Secretary, by left-wing junior Ministers, and by trade union leaders. Concessions were made by the Labour Government to this pressure from within its own ranks: the sale of spare parts, and the overhaul of engines for military aircraft already sent was banned, and the Labour Government opposed plans by a major engineering consortium to build a copper smelting plant for the new military regime. But the warships that the Chileans had ordered, and which had been the focus of the left-wing campaign, were sent.

This sharp reversal of policy was important in its own right, for it involved a Labour Government in allowing arms to be sold to a regime which had already murdered men and women holding similar political views to those found in the rank and file of the British labour movement. But it was important too because it raised in sharpest relief the questions to which this book is addressed: of the relationship between the promises of Labour politicians in opposition and their performance in power, and of the seriousness of their claims to be seeking to create a new and a socialist Britain. For the Labour Party conference in 1973 did not simply discuss the events in Chile. The men and women who gathered in Blackpool that autumn also believed themselves to be committing the next Labour Government to the Party's most radical programme for at least forty years.

In that *Programme*, the Labour Party declared itself to be 'a democratic Socialist Party', prepared and determined to 'put the principles of

1

democracy and Socialism above considerations of privilege and market economics'. It promised the creation of 'no less than a new social order' through the pursuit of the Party's 'basic Socialist goals'. These the *Programme* listed, as follows.

*To bring about a fundamental and irreversible shift in the balance of power and wealth in favour of working people and their families.

*To make power fully accountable to the community, to workers and to the consumer.

*To eliminate poverty wherever it exists.

*To achieve far greater economic equality in our society - in income, in wealth, and in the living standards of everyone.

*To increase social equality by a substantial shift in the emphasis now put on job creation, housing, education and social benefits.

*To improve the environment, so that the workplace is more comfortable, our cities more inviting, and the air and water around us cleaner.

To achieve these basic objectives, the *Programme* made a long series of specific policy proposals. The next Labour Government, it said, should extend price and exchange controls, should increase state pensions, should repeal the Housing Finance and Industrial Relations Acts, should take rented property into municipal ownership, and should tax the rich to finance the extension of social services to the poor. The next Labour Government should establish a complex planning and control machinery over the giant private firms which - on the *Programme*'s own argument - dominate the economy; and it should extend the public sector into at least North Sea Oil, shipbuilding, docks and building land. The *Programme* was explicit on this need for public ownership, and in being so it broke with over twenty years of Labour Party ambivalence on what was once Labour's defining policy. To restrict Labour Government activity simply to social reforms, the *Programme* said, is insufficient. For 'even the most comprehensive measures of social and fiscal reform can only succeed in masking the unacceptable and unpleasant face of a capitalist economy, and cannot achieve any fundamental changes in the power relationships which dominate our society'. Only the use of public ownership and State planning can end 'the arbitrary exercise of economic power' and transfer social control 'from a small elite to the mass of the people'.[1]

If the Labour Government retains office in 1974, the willingness and ability of Party leaders to implement this *Programme* will soon be demonstrated, and their performance in office will show how genuine is

2

the socialist intent of a political party from which virtually all men and women of socialist principle were driven by the events of 1964-70. For there are questions which have to be put and answered before the promise of *Labour's Programme 1973* can be believed. In the short run, and for the electorate in general, Labour's new found radicalism raises again the credibility of the Party's promises, and the extent to which Labour in power can offer a genuine and more radical alternative to Conservative policies. In the long term, and for socialists of all varieties, the renewed radicalism of the Labour Party poses even more central questions, against which they will have to determine the allocation of their own political loyalty and activity in the next decades. Has the Labour Party *really* converted itself into a force that will reform capitalism out of existence, and if it has, will the promise of the 1973 *Programme* prove more successful than have similar Labour Party promises in the past? Or is it still folly to believe that the Labour Party is, or ever could be, anything more than a major blockage on the struggle for socialism, and a major threat to the industrial power, living standards and job security of workers in an advanced capitalist society?

I hope that the argument which follows will contribute to an assessment of these questions, by its interpretation of Labour Party history and by its analysis of Labour Party development. For this is not the first time that this radical appeal and socialist promise has come from the Labour Party, and so an assessment of the potential of the Party now does seem to require a prior consideration of how the Party has developed, and of what in the past it has promised and it has done. In particular, since Labour politics are *par excellence* the politics of Parliamentary action, any assessment of the potential of the Labour Party in the mid-1970s must be based on an appraisal of the kinds of Parliamentary leadership that the Party has had, and which it now enjoys. Indeed, that assessment of the possibilities of Labour socialism must go further, to an understanding of the logics, potential and constraints that have come to be associated with Parliamentary politics, and which even now shape the character of the Party's Parliamentary leadership and its own left wing.

To that end, the chapters that follow look closely at the Party's history and in particular at its two periods of office since the war. Chapter 2 considers the formation and early character of Labourism and traces its development to the General Election of 1945. Chapter 3 looks in detail at the experience of the 1945-51 Labour Governments, to see what happened on the last occasion that the Party attempted to implement a radical programme of the type it adopted in 1973, and to locate some of the problems that it might conceivably experience if it were ever to try to reform capitalism into a new social order again. Chapter 4 traces the response of the Party leadership in the 1950s to the failed promise of the Attlee years; and chapter 5 looks in detail at the record in office (between 1964 and 1970) of the men who still lead the Labour Party. Chapter 6 then attempts to explain why this pattern of conservatism and frustrated socialist promise has been so unbroken; and chapter 7 explains why the left wing of the Labour Party has so far been unable to stem the conservative tide. The final chapter then returns to the questions set here; and in drawing the strands of the argument together, argues the bankruptcy of the Labour Party's road to socialism.

2. The early Labour Party

The Labour Party, at its creation, was the culmination of a long nineteenth-century tradition of working class politics that had repeatedly sought the amelioration of working class conditions through involvement in existing Parliamentary structures, and which had consistently rejected more violent and more radical forms of political behaviour. The Labour Party grew out of this non-revolutionary tradition: one that stretched back at least to Francis Place, and which had been transmitted down the century through the 'moral force' wing of the Chartist movement, through the Reform League of the 1860s, through the Parliamentary Committee of the Trades Union Congress after 1871, and, after 1874, through the Lib-Lab working class M.P.s who followed Gladstone. Throughout the nineteenth century, these men and institutions - embodying as they did in their various generations this non-revolutionary prescription for working class politics - had participated in Royal Commissions and Select Committees, had lobbied the House of Commons, had periodically mobilised working class political energies behind moves to extend the franchise, and had latterly urged working people to seek their political salvation through the election of men of their own class to an increasingly democratic Parliament. And with such a background the early Labour Party politicians did not have to define afresh how the working class should seek its political goals; nor indeed, did they have to define the character of those goals themselves. Rather, early Labour Party leaders *inherited* a set of attitudes and practices which defined working class political goals as a set of ameliorative measures attainable within the existing social structure of property ownership and control, and which indicated that those goals could best be pursued by constitutional means. The early Labour Party, that is, inherited a set of attitudes and practices that defined 'politics' for the working class by specifying the parameters of that class's legitimate and adequate political aspirations and actions. It was these parameters to which Keir Hardie referred at the founding conference of the Labour Representation Committee (as the Labour Party was known from 1900 to 1906) when he spoke of

The early Labour Party

'Labourism': that body of working class political 'theory and practice which accepted the possibility of social change within the existing framework of society; which rejected the revolutionary violence and action implicit in Chartist ideas of physical force; and which increasingly recognised the working of political democracy of the parliamentary variety as the practical means of achieving its own aims and objectives'.[1]

It is impossible to understand the character of the early Labour Party without recognising that this was its background, and without seeing the *industrial* and *social* attitudes, practices and institutions of the working class that had come in the nineteenth century to buttress it. It was these, after all, that had provoked Marx's attack on the 'sheepish attitudes of the workers'; and drawn from Engels his famous outburst: 'the English proletariat is actually becoming more and more bourgeois, so that this most bourgeois of all nations is apparently aiming at the possession of a bourgeois aristocracy and a bourgeois proletariat as well as a bourgeoisie'. For only rarely had the separation of industrial and political institutions and activity that was at the heart of this 'Labourist' legacy of the Victorian working class been challenged in the nineteenth century. It had been questioned only by the 'physical force' Chartists of the 1840s and by the Marxist sects of the 1880s and 1890s - each of whom had, in their different ways, argued both that the working class should use its industrial power to advance its political aims, and that those aims were realisable only in that revolutionary transformation of society that was anathema to the more constitutionally minded of the Victorian working class political and industrial leaders. But these revolutionary calls had repeatedly failed to gain mass working class support; and in their failure had left ever stronger the tradition of constitutional reform politics (Labourism) that was their major competitor.

For the century which had seen - on one view of Chartism - 'the first broad and politically organised proletarian-revolutionary movement of the masses' (Lenin) left, as its legacy to twentieth-century working class politics, not the predominance of a revolutionary tradition but a constitutional reforming one. The nineteenth-century revolutionaries had failed in part, of course, because of that poor leadership, weak organisation and deficient tactics that are the curse of every failed revolutionary movement. But they failed more because they faced a working class which - after the defeat of Chartism, and in the mid-Victorian period of industrial supremacy with its Imperialist aftermath - had established those 'extraordinarily deep sociological roots of reformism'[2] that were later to buttress the Labour Party. Late nineteenth-century socialist revolutionaries, that is, faced a working class whose leading sections had already 'warren [ed capitalism] ... from end to end'; and had laid down what were to remain its characteristic institutions: not the revolutionary party but the 'trade unions, trades councils, T.U.C., co-ops, and the rest'.[3] And they faced a class which, in the process, had generated institutions and leaders who, in periods of prosperity at least, could deliver those marginal but significant improvements in wages and conditions on which support for social reform politics and class collaboration in industry could and did flourish. Moreover, in the process, these very institutions and leaders, and the sections of the class that they represented, gathered an increasing interest in rejecting and opposing political movements that might, by their radicalism, jeopardise existing gains.

In particular, 'Britain's economic dominance of the first seventy years of the nineteenth century [had] enabled skilled workers, through the scarcity of their skills and union organisation, to gain a privileged position for themselves within the labour market, and on that basis [to] dominate and control the emerging working class movement'.[4] Indeed, between 1850 and 1890 their craft unions were the major working class institutions functioning persistently on a national basis. Though the philosophy of class collaboration and reform politics within which they struggled to defend their craft privileges against the unskilled was challenged by the Marxist S.D.F. and by the unions of the unskilled that S.D.F. militants helped to organise in the late 1880s, that challenge was weakened by the twenty-five years of dominance that the crafts had enjoyed after the failure of Chartism. These unions and their members were the institutional and sociological bed-rock of the non-revolutionary tradition of working class politics; for they had much to lose in revolutionary upheaval and much to gain from a co-operative legislature. As E. P. Thompson said,[5]

> Each advance within the framework of capitalism simultaneously
> involved the working class far more deeply in the *status quo* ...
> Each assertion of working class influence within the bourgeois
> democratic State machinery simultaneously involved them as
> partners (even if antagonistic partners) in the running of the
> machine. Even the indices of working class strength - the financial
> reserves of trade unions and co-ops - were secure only within the
> custodianship of capitalist stability.

And so, although there were moments - in the 1820s, 1840s and 1880s - when the prospects for a sharp break with non-revolutionary working class politics were greater than hitherto, in the end the nineteenth-century revolutionary tradition proved weak in the face of 'the truly astronomic sums of human capital which (had) been invested in the strategy of piecemeal reform'.[6] It was from this capital that the Labour Party emerged.

2

The natural political home of working class reformers in the late nineteenth century was the left wing of the Liberal Party. 'With the exception of one or two Conservative trade union leaders, the officials of (all) the labour organisations belonged to the Liberal Party';[7] and so too, in their voting allegiance, did the majority of their members. Lancashire and Birmingham were perhaps the major exceptions to the more general rule that enfranchised workers (especially the more skilled and better organised) tended in the last quarter of the nineteenth century to give their newly acquired vote to the party of Gladstone.* And it was only slowly, and against an inherited set of ideological, organisational, political and personal links between the older trade union leaders and the Liberal Party, that this allegiance was severed and a separate Labour Party formed.

The reasons are doubtless well-known. The Liberal Party under Gladstone was increasingly preoccupied with the Irish question, to the virtual exclusion of all else; and in the Irish struggle, the political autonomy of the Irish M.P.s offered a model and a hope to those who thought separate political organisation would give the working class greater leverage at Westminster. The senior councils of the Liberal Party proved unresponsive to the trade union movement's growing need for legal protection in the face of a hostile judiciary. At grass roots level, local Liberal caucuses proved reluctant to accept as candidates aspiring politicians from the working class. And finally, for the tiny group of

---

* There was, even so, a substantial Conservative vote amongst working class electors. As H.Pelling observed: except in Yorkshire, working class voters were 'evidently subject to more contradictory pressures than the middle class voter in this period . . . ' and were consequently less prone to vote solidly for Liberal candidates. Moreover, 'the evidence of electoral behaviour suggests . . . that unskilled workers showed (even) less cohesion on class lines than those who were more skilled'. H.Pelling, *Social Geography of British Elections, 1885-1910* (London, Macmillan, 1967) p. 420 and p. 424.

socialists who formed the Independent Labour Party in 1893, the Liberal Party's commitment to private enterprise and to an inactive State clashed with their collectivist aspirations and with their search for 'the public ownership of the means of production, distribution and exchange'.

For all these reasons, and particularly the last, the I.L.P. sought separate Labour representation in Parliament through the 1890s. For all these reasons, *except the last*, the leaders of both the old craft and new unskilled unions, under pressure from socialist militants within their own ranks, came to abandon their Liberal connections as the nineteenth century closed. So in February 1900 the Labour Representation Committee was created, as yet another of the Labour Committees seeking direct working class representation in Parliament: in this case, as an alliance between the pitifully weak Socialist societies (the I.L.P., S.D.F., and the Fabians) and initially the newer and less skilled unions of the T.U.C. - 'to promote and co-ordinate plans for labour representation'. It was this body which by 1906 had changed its name to the Labour Party, had lost the support of the Marxist S.D.F., and had - in the wake of the Taff Vale judgment - won the support of the bulk of the unions affiliated to the T.U.C. Of the major unions, only the Miners' Federation retained their Lib-Lab connections; and with the affiliation of their M.P.s to the Labour Party in 1909, the Party had established itself - if only shakily - as the political voice of the organised working class.

But although the Labour Party was, after 1900, organisationally distinct from the radical wing of the Liberal Party, the aspirations of its leaders and the substance of its policies remained enmeshed in the intellectual and ideological universe of Liberal-Radicalism. It is true that there were socialists of the I.L.P. variety in the Party, and that these men played a disproportionately large part in the senior echelons of the Edwardian organisation. But from the beginning the Labour Party was a coalition, in which the socialist wing was a minority; and the I.L.P. leadership proved more committed to holding that coalition together than to inscribing socialist policies and aspirations on an organisation which would doubtless have split under the strain. They settled instead merely for an agreement[8]

> establishing a distinct Labour Group in Parliament, which shall have
> their own whips and agree upon their policy, which must embrace
> a readiness to co-operate with any party which for the time being

may be engaged in promoting legislation in the direct interest of
labour.

That, in the context of pre-1914 British politics, meant an alliance with
Liberal policies and with the Liberal Party; and the I.L.P. knew it.

For in a real sense, I.L.P. socialists had no choice if the Labour Party
was to avoid internal schism and electoral annihilation. The only way in
which the I.L.P. leaders of the Parliamentary Labour Party could retain
the newly won allegiance of the trade unions was to restrict the Party
to a programme of discreet social reforms acceptable to union leaders
who were - in the main - merely 'loyal but disheartened Gladstonians'.[9]
Nor could the Party adopt a more socialist programme if it was to avoid
electoral defeat at the hands of a working class electorate steeped in
this same Gladstonian liberalism; and it was to avoid such a slaughter at
the polls that Ramsay MacDonald (the I.L.P. secretary of the Labour
Representation Committee) signed the secret electoral pact with the
Liberal Party in 1903. This too bound the early Labour Party to
Liberal-Radicalism. For though in the long run - and with the benefit of
hindsight - it is clear that the Labour Party was the greater beneficiary
of this agreement to prevent Liberal and Labour candidates running
against each other in the 1906 General Election, in the short run it tied
the hands of the tiny Party to the support of 'the general objects of the
Liberal Party'.* It meant that at local level the Labour Party had to
select candidates whose moderation would neither alienate the Liberal
vote nor drive the local Liberal caucus to break the agreement and run a
separate candidate. At national level it kept the Parliamentary Labour
Party as a loyal vassal of a Liberal Government which it dared not
offend, lest the pact between them be abandoned and the Labour Party
run the risk of almost certain electoral defeat.

But it must not be thought that even I.L.P. M.P.s found this close
proximity to the Liberal Party irksome. On the contrary: one of the
first L.R.C. M.P.s defected to the Liberals within twelve months of his
election; and the rest of the early Labour Party M.P.s remained bound
by close personal and ideological ties to the radical wing of the Liberals.
After all, men like Hardie, Henderson and Shackleton - who all led the
Labour Party at various times in its early years - had initially thought of

---

* Under the agreement, 'the Liberal leaders agreed to use their influence to
prevent local Liberal opposition to any L.R.C. candidate who supported 'the
general objects of the Liberal Party'; in return the L.R.C. was to 'demonstrate
friendliness' to the Liberals in any constituency where it had influence'.
R. Miliband, *Parliamentary Socialism* (London, Merlin Press, 1973) p. 20.

entering Parliament as Liberal Party candidates in the late 1880s or 1890s, and had come to the Labour Party only when that avenue had proved unsuccessful. Hardie in particular, though he had no love of the Liberal Party, retained a strong affinity with the radical wing of Liberalism. Moreover a sizeable proportion of the Parliamentary Labour Party after 1909 were Miners' M.P.s who brought to the Party a long tradition of Liberal perspectives and Liberal Party allegiances.* And it is clear that, in the case of MacDonald at least, the experience of this close working relationship with the Liberal Party rapidly mellowed his socialism to a point that left him ideologically indistinguishable from many of the radical Liberal M.P.s. As he told the Liberal Chief Whip in 1903, the majority of L.R.C. candidates 'were in almost every case earnest Liberals who would support a Liberal Government'[10]; especially one which, under Campbell Bannerman and Asquith after 1906, was engaged on a major programme of reform legislation. It was not just the electoral pact which bound the early Labour Party to Liberal-Radicalism: the Party 'was not an ideological butterfly struggling in vain to free itself from the restricting chrysalis of the Liberal connection, but rather a tick carried along on the Asquithian sheep'.[11]

It was within this Liberal orthodoxy that the Labour Party grew; and within which its first critical generation of Parliamentary leaders learned their politics. The L.R.C. successfully captured two seats in the 1900 General Election, and acquired three more in by-elections in 1902 and 1903. In 1906, amid the Liberal landslide, all the major Parliamentary figures of the early Labour Party were returned to the House; and their twenty-nine M.P.s that year included MacDonald, Henderson, Hardie, Clynes, and Snowden. The Miners' Federation M.P.s joined the Party in 1909; and in the two elections of 1910 this strengthened Labour Party won first forty and then forty-two seats, though it was down to thirty-seven by the outbreak of war. As a small ginger group on the left of the Liberal Party, these early Labour M.P.s acted 'above all to protect the unions as industrial organisations and to promote a brand of social reform compatible with capitalism and with the

---

* And drove even Hardie to despair. As he wrote to Bruce Glasier in 1908, 'I grow weary of apologising for a state of things for which I am not responsible and with which I have scant sympathy. Then when the miners come in the Annual Conferences will be controlled by Coal and Cotton, and . . . that means more reaction. There are times when I confess to feeling sore at seeing the fruits of our years of toil being garnered by men who were never of us, and who even now would trick us out.' Quoted in H. Pelling, *A Short History of the Labour Party*, (London, Macmillan, 1972) p. 21.

piecemeal social reform of the Radicals'.[12] They successfully pressed
for the repeal of the Taff Vale judgment in the Trades Disputes Act of
1906. They raised the problem of the unemployed. They pressed for
workers' compensation, and for Factory Act reform. They urged the
introduction of old age pensions. They gave loyal support to the reform
measures of the Liberal Government: its Wages Board Act, its Labour
Exchanges Act, its 1909 Budget, and its decision in 1911 to establish a
system of health and unemployment insurance. And they were solid
Liberal supporters on the critical issues of Free Trade and Irish Home
Rule.

In all this, they came under attack from a number of quarters. They
were attacked from outside Parliament, by the Syndicalists and Marxists,
for failing to connect with and offer leadership to the growing wave of
industrial unrest that swept Britain in the years before 1914. And they
were criticised within Parliament - by I.L.P. dissidents in particular - for
their low Parliamentary impact and their continuing subservience to the
Liberal cause. Yet to both sets of critics, the Parliamentary leadership
offered no ground at all. MacDonald especially, as 'the main architect
and the most articulate advocate of the politics of manoeuvre and
compromise',[13] consistently defended the Parliamentary and the
constitutional road to political power against those who suggested more
violent and more industrial means; and defended the Parliamentary
Labour Party's record as all that could be achieved in a political
universe dominated by a Liberal electorate. Nor would the Party leadership frame and adopt a systematic programme, though they were
consistently urged to do so by the Party's socialist wing. For neither the
political sympathies of the bulk of the Parliamentary Party, nor the
political convictions of the Party's trade union backers and electorate,
made this a viable proposition before the changed conditions of 1918.
Rather the Labour Party went into the First World War as it had been
formed: as a Parliamentary expression of trade union aspirations which
involved no coherent programme and no officially accepted socialist
commitment.

3

It was the mass working class radicalism engendered by the senseless
slaughter of the First World War that led the Labour Party to commit
itself publicly to a comprehensive programme whose implementation
would create 'a new social order' that might transform capitalism into

socialism. The war had initially split the Party leadership; and in doing
so had regained for Ramsay MacDonald the reputation of a radical and
a socialist which his Parliamentary moderation before 1914 had done
much to undermine - a reputation on which he would successfully
regain the Party leadership in 1922. Meanwhile, and amid continuing
Party dissension, leading members of the majority wing of the Parliamentary Labour Party eventually joined Lloyd George's Coalition
Government in 1916; but they remained there only with increasing
difficulty as working class militancy grew. Indeed, Henderson and
Clynes apart, the Labour Party representatives in Lloyd George's
coalition eventually severed their connection with the Party, rather than
accept a conference instruction to withdraw into opposition in 1918.*
For in the interim, sections of the Labour Party leadership had learned
again the rhetoric of international socialism; and in its 1918 programme
(*Labour and the New Social Order*) the Labour Party appealed to its
working class electorate for the first time in its history as a socialist
party: one, that is, that claimed to be in battle not simply with discreet
problems but with a total social *system* (capitalism) which it aimed to
transform into a new and socialist order by the deployment of a
Parliamentary majority once won. The rhetoric of that programme
marked a sharp break with all that had gone before, and it set the
terms of reference within which 'the socialist generation' of the Labour
Party played out its politics. It is therefore worth pausing, to look at it
in detail.

The new programme, and the new party constitution of 1918, were
part of an attempt by Labour Party leaders - and in particular, by men
like Henderson and Webb - to establish the Labour Party as an independent force in British politics, by breaking distinctly with a Liberal-
Radicalism that was no longer appropriate to the class militancy of
post-war Britain.† In the reforms of 1918, the Party structure was
completely altered: with the trade union movement replacing the
socialist societies as the major institutional power centre within the
Party's Conference and National Executive Committee; and with local
Constituency Labour Parties being created to replace the pre-war
dependence on local I.L.P. branches. In both these changes, the I.L.P.
was the loser; and yet in this hour of its ejection from the senior

---

* Henderson had already resigned, in 1917, after the famous 'door mat incident'.
† Thus Henderson in 1917: 'some sort of Socialist faith was the necessary basis
for the consolidation of the Labour Party into an effective national force'.
Quoted in S. Beer, *Modern British Politics*, (London, Faber, 1965) p. 149.

decision-making centres of the revamped Labour Party, it saw that Party publicly commit itself to the very programme that the I.L.P. had long existed to achieve. Clause Four of the Labour Party's new constitution committed the Party 'to secure for the workers by hand or by brain the full fruits of their industry and the most equitable distribution thereof that may be possible, upon the basis of the common ownership of the means of production'. It was as a party committed to socialism that the Labour Party in 1918 drew up its new programme.

The promise of that programme, *Labour and the New Social Order*, was enormous, and its rhetoric radical and uncompromising. In it, the Labour Party rejected any attempt to reconstitute private capitalism.

The individualistic system of capitalist production . . . with the monstrous inequalities of circumstances which it produces and the degradation, both moral and spiritual resulting therefrom may, we hope, indeed have received a death-blow. With it must go the political system and ideas in which it naturally found expression. We, of the Labour Party, whether in opposition or in due time called upon to form an Administration, will certainly lend no hand in its revival. On the contrary we shall do our utmost to see that it is buried with the millions whom it has done to death.

Rather the Labour Party looked to the creation of a 'new social order'.

We of the Labour Party . . . must ensure that what is presently to be built up is a new social order, based not on fighting but on fraternity - not on the competitive struggle for the means of bare life, but on a deliberately planned co-operation in production and distribution for the benefit of all who participate by hand and brain - not on the utmost inequality of riches, but on a systematic approach towards a healthy equality of material circumstances for every person born into the world - not on an enforced domination over subject nations, subject races, subject colonies, subject classes, or a subject sex, but in industry, as well as in government, on that equal freedom, that general consciousness of consent, and that widest participation in power which is characteristic of Democracy.

This promise of a major redistribution of class power 'in industry as well as in government' was embodied in a series of policy commitments: to maintain minimum standards of health, leisure, education and subsistence; to avoid unemployment; to so increase taxation, capital levies and death duties on the rich as to bring 'the nearest possible approximation to equality of sacrifice' between the classes; to 'progressively eliminate the private capitalist from the control of industry'; and to achieve 'the scientific reorganisation of the nation's industry on the basis of the common ownership of the means of production', by nationalising in the first instance the railways, mines, shipping, canals, electricity and industrial insurance - and, 'as suitable opportunities occur', by nationalising the land itself.[14]

The story of the Labour Party in the inter-war period is one of a retreat from and return to these aspirations of 1918, in the face of a Parliamentary leadership which, in the 1920s at least, proved reluctant when in office to make even marginal moves towards the programme's implementation. But before tracing that process in detail, we must note that even here - at its most radical point since its formation - the Labour Party was adopting a programme that was in no sense a revolutionary document. On the contrary, as much of Europe plunged into open class war in 1918 and 1919, the Labour Party committed itself to a programme that was riddled with limitations and ambiguities which would only become fully evident, paradoxically, after a second world war had taken the Party back to its 1918 radicalism. Those limitations and ambiguities were as follows.

There was firstly the anticipated manner of the programme's implementation. The man who drafted it, Sidney Webb, later spoke of a faith in 'the inevitability of gradualism' that characterised Labour Party politics even at their most radical. For if the 1918 programme promised a transformation of capitalism into a new social order, it was a transformation that would be achieved the Parliamentary way, by the capture of the democratic state, *slowly and without violence*, with all due process of law, with the consent of all groups involved, and with generous compensation for those newly dispossessed of their property and privileges. This, as we have already seen, was quite to be expected from a party inheriting the nineteenth-century tradition of non-violent working class politics; and had been made explicit by Philip Snowden even before the First World War, when he wrote;

> The transition to Socialism will be brought about with as little hardship to existing interests as can be avoided. Above all else Socialism must regard the honour and probity of the State, and must do nothing to give its citizens the impression that it cares nothing for existing rights which have been established and recognised by law ... [Consequently] compensation will have to be given in some form to the expropriated classes. The unfairness of any other method becomes more apparent when it is remembered that the transition to public ownership will be gradual, and it would be utterly

unjustifiable to take the property of certain persons without compensation and leave others still in possession of theirs. When it was thought that Socialism might come as the result of a great catastrophic event there was everything to be said in favour of no compensation. If all the property owners were dispossessed at the same moment, it would palpably be absurd to give compensation. But that is a situation which can never arise.[15]

This was the spirit of the 1918 programme; and in the optimism of their faith in gradualism, neither the programme, nor the Party, nor Snowden himself faced squarely the problem of class power that was at stake. For if the Party was to so ameliorate interests that no social group felt outraged, how radical could its social transformation be? And yet, if that social transformation was as radical as the 1918 programme appeared to anticipate, might not the Party realistically expect some resistance from those it threatened to dispossess? But the 1918 programme avoided this question of class resistance to gradualism in the ambiguity of its rhetoric; and the Party, as we shall see, was not to face the issue openly until the 1930s, and then only to disregard it thereafter.

Moreover, *Labour and the New Social Order* was ambiguous at its very heart - on the purpose and consequences of its major policy proposal, nationalisation. For when the programme spoke of democratisation 'in industry as well as in government' it appeared to promise a major shift in class power - down to the working class - at the point of production and in government. This at least was how a generation of left-wing socialists within the Labour Party was to read the promise of 1918, and how the Labour Party leadership in Opposition was prone at times to present it. And yet clearly this was not the view of the men who drafted the 1918 document, for whom any shift in class power that might result from public ownership was either undesirable, or at least was as nothing compared to nationalisation's role in serving a wider, *non-class*, public interest: by guaranteeing the 'scientific reorganisation' of industrial production and the consequent increase in national output. To the men who drafted the 1918 programme, nationalisation was the key, not to workers' control, but to national productivity. As the programme put it,

What the nation needs is undoubtedly a great bound onward in its aggregate productivity . . . what the Labour Party looks to is a genuinely scientific reorganisation of the nation's industry, no longer deflected by individual profiteering, on the basis of the common ownership of the means of production; the equitable sharing of the proceeds amongst all who participate in any capacity and only among those; and the adoption, in particular services and occupations, of those systems and methods of administration and control that may be found, in practice, best to promote, not profiteering, but the public interest.[16]

Compared to this, any interest in shifting power down to the working class was, in Webb's own words in 1918, a 'shibboleth'.[17] Yet without it, how socialist would Labour's 'New Social Order' be? No one was to know until 1945; but the seeds of the disputes of the 1950s lie here - in this ambiguity at the heart of the 1918 programme.

For even on its most radical interpretation - and Labour leaders in the 1920s were never going to give it that - the 1918 programme when implemented would still have left the bulk of the economy in private hands. Its specific proposals, as Webb himself said, were merely a summation of the specific demands to which individual trade unions had committed the Labour Party before 1914. Behind its radical rhetoric was 'an explicit affirmation by the Labour Party that piece-meal collectivism, within a predominantly capitalist society, was the key to more welfare, higher efficiency, and greater social justice. Shorn of its rhetoric, *Labour and the New Social Order* was a Fabian blueprint for a more advanced, more regulated form of capitalism.'[18] Yet other parts of the Labour Party programme of 1918 - especially those on taxation - were if implemented bound to affect, indeed to undermine, the structure of incentives (and hence performance) in this private capitalist sector. But on the problems attendant on this, the 1918 document was - in its ambiguity - silent.

So, as the Labour Party in 1918 grafted on to its pre-war personnel the more radical prospect of socialist transformation, it wrote into its later history a set of dilemmas that only the ambiguity of its rhetoric initially hid: of the danger that Parliamentary sovereignty might not prevail when the interests of the propertied class were under challenge; of the aims to be pursued when taking industries into public ownership; of the relationship to be established between a public sector and industries still in private hands; of the possibilities of maintaining a healthy private sector in an egalitarian society; and - ultimately - of what the Labour Party actually meant when it talked of socialism. These ambiguities were resolved (as resolved they had to be) only when a later generation of Labour Party leaders, after 1945, attempted to fulfill the promise of 1918. In the meantime they were masked by

17

the systematic refusal of the Party's inter-war leadership to attempt the programme's implementation when in office. In the fight against this refusal, the whole energies of the Party's socialists were focused on returning to the programme of 1918, rather than in assessing that programme's inadequacies. Those who knew how real those inadequacies were had, by the 1930s, long since left the Labour Party - so leaving the Party to fight between the wars over a constitutional route to the 'socialist commonwealth' that, after 1945, would prove to be no route at all.

4

In the 1920s within the Labour Party, the fight went badly for those seeking to realise the socialist potential of *Labour and the New Social Order*; and this can be seen in the drift from radicalism that was apparent in the programmes on which the Labour Party went to the electorate in that decade, in the attitudes of its Parliamentary leadership when in Opposition, and in their performance when in office.

The party programmes of the 1920s settled into a distinctive pattern. They did not abandon totally the radical promise of 1918. Indeed, in their preambles, they kept alive the Party's promise of total social transformation. So in 1925 the Party programme began with an assertion of socialist faith. 'National reconstruction', it ran, 'cannot be successfully undertaken under capitalist conditions. Only upon avowedly Socialist principles can the claims of the workers for a fair and decent livelihood be met.'[19] And in 1928, MacDonald, in his preamble to '*Labour and the Nation*', stressed again how different was this Labour Party from its pre-war origins. The Labour Party, he wrote, 'unlike other parties, is not concerned with patching the rents in a bad system, but with transforming Capitalism into Socialism . . . the Labour Party is essentially one of action, and it asks for power both in order to lay the foundations of a new social order and to relieve immediate distress'.[20]

Yet at the same time, the radicalism of 1918 was moderated everywhere, as the Parliamentary leadership stressed again the 'national' character of the Party and attempted to play down its 'class' outlook and image. This is clear even in the changing title of its programmatic documents. In 1918 it had at least openly talked of 'a new social order'. By 1925 is talked merely of 'National Reconstruction and Reform', and by 1927, simply of 'Labour and the Nation'. Not that this would have been more than trivial had it not also reflected a draining of the class content of the programmes themselves. By 1927 the 'socialism' which the Labour Party leadership sought to achieve was explicitly and proudly 'tentative and doctrineless', and ever more explicitly equated simply with State intervention in industry and society.* As such, of course, it was no monopoly of the Labour Party. For whatever the programme preambles said, in reality the Party offered itself to the electorate in the 1920s not so much as an alternative that was qualitatively different from the rest, but as one whose use of State power could be *better guaranteed* to bring 'the fullest utilisation of scientific knowledge and administrative skill, [and] a social order in which the resources of the community shall be organised and administered with a single eye to securing for all its members the largest possible measure of economic welfare and personal freedom'.[21]

In the process, the Labour Party programmes of the 1920s whittled down the scope, the character and the purpose of public ownership. Whereas in 1918 the Party had promised to the workers 'by hand and by brain the full fruits of their industry . . . upon the basis of the common ownership of the means of production', by 1925 common ownership had been restricted simply to 'the larger and more widely used public services'.[22] By the mid 1920s, that is, the Party had restricted its aspirations to what it termed 'foundation industries'; and had abandoned any pretence of challenging the private ownership of the profitable industrial and financial sector: chemicals, armaments, motor cars, food processing and private banking. Nor, even where public ownership was contemplated, were the Labour Party leaders now committed, as in 1918, to 'progressively eliminate the private capitalist from the control of industry'. Far from it: power in the nationalised industries would not pass into the hands of the working class. Rather, as Philip Snowden said in 1927, socialism would come 'through a public corporation controlled in the interests of the public by the *best experts and business men*'.[23] Capitalists were not to be eliminated, but to be harnessed to the socialist cause by their conversion into public servants.

By 1927 public ownership had nothing to do with the transference of class power in industry. It was, rather, part of the Labour Party's

---

* So MacDonald defined socialism as 'the idea of the political state acting more and more in co-operation with the industrial state' - a definition so vacuous as to take in the Tory party of the 1930s, Mussolini and Stalin. Quoted in A. Hutt, *The Post-War History of the British Working Class*, (London, Gollancz, 1937) p. 120.

first priority - 'the restoration of normal trade . . . the prevention, by all practicable means, of trade depression, the expansion of trade and industry'.[24] And this involved, not the confrontation of class with class, rich with poor, and unemployed with capitalist, but the co-operation of Capital and Labour in national reconstruction. So that if the preambles to the Labour Party programmes of the 1920s left the electorate in no doubt that their economic and social miseries were rooted in capitalist instabilities and in the inadequacies of capitalism as a system, the small print of those same programmes made it equally clear - at least to the discerning - that the 'captains of industry' were to remain the pillar on which socialist reconstruction under Labour would take place, if that reconstruction could reasonably be called 'socialist' at all.

This growing propensity for class collaboration in industry, and for the establishment of close and co-operative relationships with 'progressive management' as the key to economic revival, was clear too in the attitudes of the Labour Party leadership to the critical events of the period of Opposition after 1924: namely to the General Strike of 1926 and to the Mond-Turner talks of 1928. The General Strike was nothing but a complete embarrassment to the Parliamentary leadership: in part because it rendered them redundant, but more importantly because it militated against the easing of class relationships on which the Parliamentarians increasingly depended for the success of gradualism. MacDonald, for one, was highly critical both before and after the event. As he told the Commons on 3 May, 'with the discussion of General Strikes and Bolshevism and all that kind of thing I have nothing to do at all'.[25] 'The General Strike', he wrote in *The Socialist Review* in June 1926, 'is a weapon that cannot be wielded for industrial purposes. It is clumsy and ineffectual. It has no goal which, when reached, can be regarded as victory . . . I hope that the result will be a thorough reconsideration of trade union tactics. If the wonderful unity in the strike . . . would be shown in politics, Labour could solve the mining and similar difficulties through the ballot box.'[26]

However, to the Mond-Turner talks which followed, in which industrialists and trade union leaders sought a set of common interests and mutual understandings in the wake of the Strike's defeat, the Labour Party leadership gave their total support. It was J. H. Thomas, after all, a Labour Party leader as well as a leading member of the T.U.C. General Council, who pressed for talks with employers in the wake of the General Strike he had worked so hard to end: so that both sides of industry could 'promote effective co-operation in developing more

20

efficient, less wasteful methods of production, eliminating unnecessary friction and avoidable conflict'.[27] There was no echo here of the class hostility of the 1918 period, when even the Webbs had dismissed this conciliatory strategy as 'disastrous undermining of the solidarity of the whole working class, and a formidable obstacle to any genuine Democratic Control of Industry, as well as to any general progress in personal freedom and in the more equal sharing of the National Product'.[28]

For the politics of Labour in the 1920s were dominated by a search by the Parliamentary leadership of the Party for a rapprochement with those very class forces - controllers of a private capitalist economy - who had prospered amid the carnage of the First World War, and who had been so vigorously attacked as 'the Old Social Order' in the Labour Party programme of 1918. It was to these groups that MacDonald, in leading his Minority Governments in 1924 and in 1929-31, addressed his attempts to prove Labour's 'fitness to rule', Labour's 'moderation' and Labour's 'responsibility' - attempts which determined and controlled the policy initiatives of the Party in its two periods of inter-war government. Of course, the Party in each case was a minority government, dependent on the support of the Liberal Party for its continuance in office. But this alone does not fully account for the Labour leadership's refusal to attempt the implementation of even its 1923 and 1927 programmes. Rather, its minority status provided the Labour Governments with 'the great alibi'[29] behind which, through the 1920s at least, the Parliamentary leadership obscured its own growing conservatism.

For the Labour Party of the 1920s - officially committed as it was to a Socialist Commonwealth - was still led by that generation of Labour Party politicians who had created the Party in the Edwardian period, and they carried into the post-war politics of the Party sets of attitudes and aspirations formed long before. In particular, many of them carried a noticeable hostility to open class confrontation, and a concomitant sensitivity to a so-called national interest. This was evident in many ways. It had been obvious before the First World War in the Parliamentary Party's aversion to the industrial militancy of the Syndicalists: an aversion encapsulated in that classic rejection of industrial strife by the Party's post-war leader, J. R. Clynes - namely that 'too frequent strikes caused a sense of disgust, of being a nuisance to the community'.[30] It was evident too in the Labour Party's willingness in office to contemplate the use of troops as strike-breakers when sections of the industrial wing of its own labour movement and electorate refused Government calls to go to arbitration. So the first Labour Government

21

was prepared to threaten the use of troops against dockers officially on strike under the Transport and General Workers Union in 1924 and against transport workers striking under the same pro-Labour trade union leadership later in the same year. As Clynes proudly recorded, in the handling of these strikes the Labour Government played 'the part of a *national government and not a class government*, and [he was] certain that any Government, whatever it might be, could not in the circumstances have done more . . . to safeguard the public interests'.[31] Well might the Transport Workers' leader, Ernest Bevin, later tell a Labour Party conference that he knew something about 'emergency powers. The first Labour Government rushed down to Windsor to get them signed in order to operate on me . . . I do not like emergency powers even when they are operated by my friends.'[32]

But if Bevin and the Parliamentary leadership were on opposite sides in the specific industrial disputes of 1924, they shared a common aversion to the use of industrial power by the working class for political ends, and a common commitment to Parliamentary politics. This was the major legacy of the pre-war period that the Labour Party leadership carried with it into the bitter class struggles of the 1920s. When in 1920, London dockers blocked arms-shipments to the anti-Bolshevik forces in Poland, Labour Party leaders - still operating as they were against the background of a proletariat radicalised by war - only gave the most reluctant support. As the Party chairman said even in 1919:

the movement . . . to employ the strike weapon for political purposes . . . would be an innovation in this country which few responsible leaders would welcome . . . We are either constitutionalists or we are not constitutionalists. If we are constitutionalists, if we believe in the efficiency of the political weapon (and we do, or why do we have a Labour Party?) then it is both unwise and undemocratic because we fail to get a majority at the polls to turn round and demand that we should substitute industrial action. [33]

Thereafter, as their attitude to the General Strike showed, the Labour Party leadership were consistent in rejecting extra-constitutional tactics by the working class - tactics which they saw as communist, revolutionary and dangerous, not least because their use by the working class might inspire other groups to act similarly against a Labour Government, so destroying the basis for gradualism. As Clynes asked the militants in 1919,

Were they going to concede to every other or any other class the right they were claiming to exercise? Did it mean that any class

which could exercise the power should have the right to terrorise a
Labour Government by the use of any means and manoeuvre that it
could apply? . . . The blow which they were threatening would not
be a blow at a Government but a blow at democracy. It would be a
hurt to themselves, it would do greater and more permanent harm to
the true interests of the working class than to any other class in this
country . . . Millions of men in the street could not be there long
without mischief, riot, disorder, disturbance and bloodshed.[34]

Of course, what Clynes never asked was whether this example of
self-denial by the working class in its moment of strength would equally
prompt self-denial on the part of the propertied class in the event of a
Labour Government being sufficiently radical to threaten their prerogatives and privileges. Instead the Labour Party leadership spent the
1920s educating the movement in the niceties of Parliamentary politics.
This education took two principle forms. It first involved establishing
the autonomy of the Parliamentary Party from its extra-Parliamentary
organisation, by arguing that control by the latter would offend
Parliamentary privilege, would tie M.P.s to programmes that would
prevent a flexible response to unanticipatable circumstances, and would
not enable the individual Labour M.P. to represent adequately the
constituency for which he was elected.* It also involved the education
of the Parliamentary Labour Party in the procedures of Parliament, and
in the slow pace of Parliamentary change.

In both these processes of education, MacDonald, as Party leader,
played a critical role. It was he who transformed the role of party
chairman from its pre-war insignificance into that of 'chairman and
leader', and as such the personal embodiment of the Party and its
aspirations. He selected his Governments like any Conservative or
Liberal Prime Minister before him - alone, or in consultation only with
chosen advisors, and without recourse to Conference approval. He
accepted and resigned office with equal autonomy. And most crucial of
all, he was instrumental in instructing the new arrivals in the limitations
of Parliamentary Government, and in the 'wider purposes' of the

---

* This desire of the Parliamentary Party for autonomy had first come out in
1907, when the M.P.s had claimed successfully the right to determine the
'time and method of giving effect' to conference instructions. By the 1920s,
MacDonald expected much more, as was shown by his exchange with Fenner
Brockway in 1928: that, 'as long as he held any position in the Parliamentary
Party . . . they were not going to take their instructions from any outside
body unless they agreed with them'(!). This, in R. T. McKenzie, *British
Political Parties* (London, Mercury Books, 1963) p. 312.

'national interest'. Not that his leading colleagues were slow to learn. On the contrary, Clynes reported that, after less than twelve months in office, Labour 'was being converted from its former grooves to the wider view'; and J. H. Thomas, that 'men faced with these responsibilities [of Government office] can never again be the indifferent propagandists that they were in the past. They must remain for all time responsible politicians keeping only in mind the greater interests of a great country.'[35]

For the Parliamentary leaders of the Labour Party in the 1920s Socialism had become something to which lip service was to be paid for electoral purposes, but which was not to be allowed to obscure the more moderate tasks of government. Long involvement in Parliamentary politics had already softened the rigour of their class radicalism* - to that ludicrous point with J. II. Thomas in which he was prepared to win libel actions against communists by denying that he was a socialist at all.† MacDonald too had long since moderated his politics, so that Beatrice Webb could write of him in her diary that 'he is no longer intent on social reform - whatever indignation he ever had at the present distribution of wealth he has lost'.[36] And yet it was not his conservatism that she was to criticise, quite so much as his periodic indulgence in radical rhetoric. As early as 1924 she recorded,

> I do not accuse him of treachery, for he was never a Socialist, either revolutionary . . . or administrative . . . he was always a believer in individualist political democracy tempered in its expression by utopian socialism. Where he has lacked integrity is in *posing* as a Socialist and occasionally using revolutionary jargon.[37]

And though Beatrice Webb's diaries contain criticisms of MacDonald's conservatism from as early as 1912, it is clear that it was particularly between the first and second Labour Governments that MacDonald showed 'growing impatience with the moods and manners of many of his [militant] followers', and an 'increasing common ground with his Conservative opponents . . . especially [with] the young Tories who

---

* 'Old members,' Snowden recalled, 'smiled at the impatience of new members. They reminded us of the time when they first came to Parliament full of an earnest enthusiasm to achieve some good purpose; but despair had entered into their hearts and . . . they had resigned any hope of ever being able to move that cumbersome machine at any reasonable rate along the path of reform'. Quoted in Miliband, *Parliamentary Socialism*, p. 23.
† In a libel action brought by Thomas in 1921 he was asked, 'Are you a socialist?' 'No', replied Thomas. Quoted in E. Eldon Barry, *Nationalisation in British Politics* (London, Cape, 1965) p. 206.

(were, as he said in 1925) men of very great promise'. Sooner or later, he insisted, 'the partition between us and them will be so thin that they might as well break it down and come over to the Socialists' camp'.[38] In the event it was MacDonald who moved, six years later, but with hindsight we can see that this was but the culmination of a rapprochement between him and the Conservatives that was of far longer standing.

Under leadership such as this, there was never any chance that the radical promise of 1918 would be fulfilled in the 1920s. But this is not to say that the performance of the Labour Party between the wars can be explained away by the 'accident' of conservative leadership. This has been done far too often.* For the leadership, though 'conservative', was no accident. Rather the conservatism of men like MacDonald, Snowden and Thomas had been acquired through involvement in Labour Party politics over more than two decades, and was markedly intensified in the 1920s by their experience of the possibility of office when in Opposition, and by the reality of office in 1924 and 1929-31. For given the Party's refusal and inability to capitalise on the period of working class militancy immediately prior to and after the War, (given, that is, its unwillingness to forge that industrial militancy into a class weapon on which to push through a rapid social transformation) the Labour Party in the 1920s found itself placing all its faith in the reforming potential of the Parliamentary State. Yet in Government in 1924, and in 1929-31, Labour Party leaders found themselves constrained and impotent, hedged about by opponents of their radical programme, and persistently subject from many quarters to a barrage of conservative orthodoxies. In the face of this wall of well-reasoned, quietly-spoken resistance, the Labour Governments of the 1920s dithered, thought, procrastinated and eventually succumbed. Their repeated experience in office of the difficulties of radical action drove them yet more moderate and conservative. In their conservatism, they became increasingly reluctant to act; and in their inactivity their promises went unfulfilled and their supporters disappointed.

The experience of office in 1924, and again between 1929 and 1931, demonstrated for the first time a process that we will see again towards the end of the Attlee Government, and persistently under Wilson in the 1960s: namely the debilitating effect on the radicalism of the Labour

---

* So recently, Philip Snowden's policy was explained away as follows: he 'was an ignorant and stupid man, determined to be as reactionary as possible'. J. Vaizey, *Social Democracy* (London, Weidenfeld & Nicolson, 1971) p. 127.

25

leadership of their occupation of Governmental office. For between the Wars, the spinelessness of the MacDonald administrations, their passivity in the face of events, and their systematic refusal ever to attempt the implementation of the programme on which they had been elected - all these bore witness to the extent to which the already considerable pre-war moderation of the Labour Party leadership that had been acquired in long Parliamentary careers, was hardened into deep conservatism by the constraints, blockages and limited potentialities that these Labour men experienced when in office.

At their most visible, these constraints were Parliamentary ones. Both the Labour Government of 1924 and that of 1929-31 were minority Governments. In December 1923, the Party had a popular vote of 4,356,757 and 191 Parliamentary seats. In 1929, it was slightly stronger, and by now the largest Party in the House, with its 8,360,000 votes and 287 seats. But in both cases the Labour Government was dependent on Liberal support, and consequently constrained in what it could do. It was a situation welcomed particularly by Asquith in 1924, in that the installation of a Labour Government 'with its claws cut [meant that] the experiment could hardly be made under safer conditions. We still sleep', he added 'more or less comfortably in our beds. Capital steadily pursues its old routine of continuous and on the whole prosperous investment.'[39] And when in Opposition later, Labour leaders frequently used this argument of their minority position as 'the great alibi' by which they explained and justified their failure to implement their electoral promises. Yet the Party's moderation, as we have seen, ran deeper than this; and if its minority position explained much of 1924, it cannot be so used for the Labour Government's performance between 1929 and 1931. For then the Liberal Party - under Lloyd George - was *more radical* than the Labour Government, at least in its policy on unemployment and on the nationalisation of mining royalties; and was a loyal supporter of the MacDonald Government, to which it made repeated appeals for coalition. These were rejected, partly from distrust of Lloyd George, but mainly because the Labour Government rejected as 'fanciful and unworkable' the Liberals' Keynesian proposals for the amelioration of unemployment. For in both 1924 and 1929, the Labour Government could always have gone to the country again - on the basis of a radical programme rejected in Parliament - to educate its electorate and win a popular majority as urged by its left wing. But this tactic was consciously rejected, and a radical policy never attempted. Instead, legislation 'was carefully

modulated in order that no harsh note should shock the ears of its
Liberal patrons'; and policy was 'diffident, conciliatory, undramatic,
and very mild'.[40] There were good reasons for this, in that the Government's moderation reflected the Labour leadership's preference for, and
need of, class collaboration: to prove its 'fitness to govern', its
'responsibility' and its 'respectability' to the concentrations of
industrial and financial capital that it faced, and with whom it sought
a close and co-operative relationship.

For the need for class collaboration lay at the heart of the Parliamentary strategy consciously chosen by the Labour Party in the 1920s.
Its leaders had refused to create, use or sustain a radicalised working
class as an alternative ally in the implementation of its programme; and
therefore needed the co-operation of industrialists and financiers if the
Party was to obtain the full utilisation of the nation's resources, as it
repeatedly promised. It was therefore no accident that J. H. Thomas
had 'wide industrial and financial connections' through which in 1929
and 1930 he 'tried to bring industry and the City together in an attempt
to provide finance for rationalisation projects'.[41] For the Labour
Government *had* to do this, to achieve anything at all. As Thomas
himself said, 'all that government can do, when all is said and done, is
infinitesimal compared with what business can do for itself'.[42] And yet
of course, the Labour Government found that the co-operation of
industry and the City was hard to win; partly because of the Labour
Party's own radical rhetoric,* partly because of class antagonisms to
new, socially inferior and untried men. It certainly found that co-
operation was only forthcoming on terms which precluded the implementation of the Labour programme. Indeed the Labour
Government in 1929 was greeted on its arrival in office by a demand
from the Federation of British Industry that 'it take a holiday from
social legislation', and it was told repeatedly thereafter that high
taxation was crippling economic performance to such a degree that it
should be lightened. The Labour Government, told this often enough,
in the end appeared close to believing it.

For the Labour Party in office succumbed to this, as to many of the
other leading orthodoxies of the day: orthodoxies that it daily received
at first hand from its civil service, and from the senior financiers and

---

* As Skidelsky observed, 'One of the problems facing a Labour Government
was that it had to prove itself more virtuous than a Tory Government in order
to generate an equivalent degree of confidence, for it was bound to be widely
suspected of having evil designs on industry and profits.' (R. Skidelsky,
Politicians and the Slump, Harmondsworth, Penguin, 1970, p. 177).

businessmen with whom it had to deal. There is much evidence that MacDonald at the Foreign Office in 1924, Snowden at the Treasury, and Thomas as the Minister responsible for employment policy in 1929-30, fell heavily under the influence of their civil servants, and operated within the prevailing Departmental orthodoxies inherited from the Conservative administration.* J. H. Thomas in particular cut an increasingly pathetic figure in the 1929-31 Labour Government. 'Capitalism will last to doomsday,' Bertrand Russell was driven to say in 1931, 'if J. H. Thomas is all that confronts it';[43] since he was 'every capitalist's reassurance that the Labour Party did not take its socialism too seriously'.[44] Yet Thomas was less significant in this regard than the Chancellor, Philip Snowden, whose advocacy of classical Treasury economics was accepted by the Labour Government as the terms of reference within which they were obliged to operate, and whose political dominance thus crippled any move to more interventionist and more radical Government policy.

It was MacDonald and Snowden between them who were responsible for the decision in 1924 to make the search for 'sound' money and a return to the Gold Standard the fundamental aim of their monetary policy,[45] and who resisted any attempts to proliferate public works schemes that might provide jobs for the unemployed at the cost of an unbalanced budget or higher taxation. It was Snowden's Treasury orthodoxy, his 'bleak insistence on Free Trade, the Gold Standard and a balanced budget',[46] which led the Labour Cabinet to reject both Mosley's attempt in 1930 to solve the problem of unemployment by deficit budgeting and industrial protection and the Liberal Party's earlier proposal to achieve the same end by similar Keynesian means. Instead the Labour Party placed its faith in a revival of trade; and as Bevan remembered with bitterness later, MacDonald 'was waiting

---

* So although MacDonald had promised in 1923 'to end the bureaucracy of the Foreign Office, with its queer mentality and selection of subversive agents' in the end he did not. As Hutt said, 'He came to the Foreign Office, he saw, and was conquered. Those skilled dealers with men took his measure swiftly . . . "He is the easiest Foreign Secretary I have ever had to manage", was the complacent summing up of one of the most powerful of them . . . He has written his own epitaph . . . [when] he boasted naively how he - who had been sent to Downing Street to change the whole current of our Foreign policy - had preserved its continuity'. (Hutt, *The Post War History of the British Working Class*, p. 91). 'How do you like your new chief?', a Treasury official was asked soon after Snowden had succeeded Churchill as Chancellor. 'We are delighted at the change', was the reply. 'We feel we have moved from the pantry into the drawing room.' (Quoted in Skidelsky, *Politicians and the Slump*, p. 432).

anxiously for capitalism to solve its own crisis, and therefore rescue him
from his embarrassments'. 'Recovery', Bevan reported him as saying, 'is
just around the corner'.[47] In the meantime, the Labour Government of
1929-31 procrastinated, appointed a Royal Commission on Unemployment Insurance as a time-filler, and watched as unemployment rose
and the international financial crisis intensified. Unable to solve its
central economic problem, the second MacDonald Government made
precious little headway even in the detail of smaller things. Its 1929
programme promised nothing so much as surveys and inquiries: into
cotton and steel, into the reorganisation of the mines, into emigration,
and into unemployment insurance. When legislation came, it was
moderate. Part of its Coal Bill, for example, was too conservative even
for the Liberals. Other legislation - not least the promise of 1929 to
repeal the Trade Disputes Act - never reached the statute book. The
programme of public works was restricted. Committees of Inquiry,
Royal Commissions, and Committees on the state of the economy were
filled with men hostile to the Labour Party's socialism, and with
traditional supporters of Labour's opponents. Indeed in 1924,
MacDonald took substantial numbers of Liberals into his own Government, and left a major Party figure like Lansbury out altogether. All in
all, two periods of Labour Government left unaffected the massive
inequalities of wealth and income, the system of private ownership, and
the colossal deprivation of millions that the Party had promised to
alleviate. Though there were individual successes and radical initiatives
in certain areas (Wheatley's Housing Bill of 1924 is probably the most
famous if almost the only example), in general as Hutt said, 'the whole
outlook of the Cabinet was hidebound; the limits of orthodox capitalist
precept and practice were their limits.'[48]

Yet it is not simply that Labour leaders were weaklings, spineless and
easily dominated by their civil servants. Some, like Thomas, undoubtedly were. Others, like Snowden, were much more substantial
figures. As far as we can tell, he rejected the 'radical ideas' of the
Liberal economists and of the Left within his own Party not because of
some 'aristocratic embrace', but because the orthodoxies and advice
which he received from the Treasury officials were widely held in the
administrative, industrial and financial circles in which he moved,
tapped strands in his own Gladstonian background - and, most
important of all, were at one with the manner in which the deep rooted
problems and divergent interests of industrial and financial capital were

defined by their representative institutions with whom the Labour Government sought a co-operative relationship.

For the Labour Government faced a power structure, groups of men whose social position rested in their control of private industries that were in deep trouble through the 1920s, or in their control of financial agencies whose viability was seriously threatened by the ripple-effect of the Wall Street Crash of 1929. To achieve its goal of full employment, the Labour Government had to provide the environment in which these private institutions could flourish. But British capitalism in the 1920s could not revive without major restructuring, since it was dependent on industries - coal and cotton in particular - which had long since lost their competitive edge, and which were crippled by the low level of effective demand established in the Depression. Yet the men who owned these industries were slow to see, and even slower to admit, that their difficulties were more than temporary; and by the late 1920s lacked the internal capital on which that restructuring could occur. They also, of course, manifested an antipathy to State intervention by a Labour Government, and demanded a general easing of the State's financial and administrative pressures upon them. Hence the Labour Government's 'passivity'. Moreover, these industrialists faced a set of financial institutions which had vast international commitments, which had a set of interests different from their own,[*] and which possessed a far more immediate leverage on the thinking and policy of Government than either the coal or the cotton magnates. It was the financial institutions of the City, after all, which had overcome the opposition of industrialists to win the restoration of the Gold Standard from a Conservative Government in 1925, and whose commitment to the financial orthodoxy of the balanced budget argued against any programme of deficit budgeting that could have alleviated at least the worst excesses of untrammelled Depression.

The Labour Government of 1929-31, in succumbing to these orthodoxies, was in reality succumbing to this power structure whose perception of its own interests the prevailing orthodoxies embodied and helped to define. As Skidelsky said, the prevailing economic orthodoxy in the 1920s 'was not the creation of contemporary economists; rather

---

[*] 'Nowhere else would the leaders of high finance be able to pursue their own narrow and selfish aims of financiers while recklessly damaging the productive capital of the nation, for nowhere else are the two separate, and nowhere else has finance such unrestricted power over the minds of Government and the civil service'. (S. Pollard, quoted in R. Harrison, 'Labour Government: then and now', *Political Quarterly*, vol. 41(1) January - March 1970, p. 25.)

it was the product of traditional views held by the most powerful
institutions and interests in the economic community concerning their
own functions and the proper role of Government.'⁴⁹ To understand the
politics of the Labour Government in 1931, it does not matter whether
those economic orthodoxies were right or wrong. It matters only that
they were almost everywhere taken to be right, that the major industrial
and financial agencies believed them to be right, and that to run
Government policy in contradiction to their policies was to invite
counter-moves from a private power-structure whose confidence such
radicalism would undermine. At the heart of that power structure stood
the financial agencies of the City, and of the international financial
community. The Labour Government had to follow orthodox economic
policies because financiers expected them to; and if they did not, men
like Snowden believed that international loans could not be procured,
foreign currency would leave the country, and trade and employment
would be further depressed.* As Harrison said, 'what enslaved [the
Labour Government] was not so much a decrepit orthodoxy as . . . the
bearers of that orthodoxy: the Treasury, the bankers, the financial
authorities. What was impressive about these gentlemen was not so
much the cogency of their arguments as the extent of their institutional
resources and the place that they occupied within established patterns
of power.'⁵⁰ It was they who insisted in August 1931 that the Labour
Government reduce unemployment benefits by 10% before loans
would be forthcoming to maintain the pound; and it was they, in doing
so, who provided the issue on which the Labour Government broke and
fell.

The events of August 1931, when MacDonald agreed to lead a
National Government (of predominantly Conservative Ministers) that
was willing to reduce unemployment benefit and defend the Gold
Standard in the face of opposition from a Labour Party driven from
office, provided the Party in the 1930s with yet another myth, that of
the 'great betrayal'. Yet in a sense, MacDonald's willingness to reduce
unemployment benefit and to introduce widespread wage cuts was a
logical consequence of the type of politics that the whole Labour Party
had played through the 1920s: namely that of a search for

* When Snowden met the T.U.C. General Council in August 1931, he 'said that
if sterling went, the whole international financial structure would collapse,
and there would be no comparison between the present depression and the
chaos and ruin that would face us in that event. There would be millions more
unemployed and complete industrial collapse.' (Quoted in A. Bullock, *The
Life and Times of Ernest Bevin*, vol. 1 (London, Heinemann, 1960) p. 484).

accommodation with the private concentrations of industrial and
financial power, whose co-operation and commercial viability were
essential if Labour was to achieve its promise of a full utilisation of the
nation's resources (including labour) in an economy that was still
predominantly in private hands. Hence it is significant that the Labour
Cabinet in August 1931 were slow to dispute with MacDonald the *need*
for the cuts. As Bassett said, 'at the time of the crisis, no question was
raised within the Cabinet about the possibility of going off the Gold
Standard'. On the contrary, 'such a step was apparently regarded as
unthinkable . . . and as Henderson said [later], they were in absolute
agreement that the Budget must be balanced'.[51] Opposition to the cuts
came from outside the Parliamentary Party, and in particular from the
General Council of the T.U.C. Even here, the opposition of the General
Council 'was not of course the result of a sudden conversion to the Left.
What it represented was a last minute disassociation from the logical
outcome of a trend of policy they had, until then, been willing to
endorse. But it was the *outcome* of a trend of policy that was being
rejected, and not the trend itself.'[52] As for the Parliamentarians, their
opposition from within the Labour Cabinet was less about the cuts than
about whether they should be the people prepared to initiate them.
MacDonald's sin in 1931 - as far as the majority of the Parliamentary
Labour Party was concerned - was not a sin against the working class
and the unemployed, but a sin against the Party. 'MacDonald broke
with his colleagues not over policy but over primary loyalty',[53] and the
perspectives of Labourism that his policies had embodied remained
firmly entrenched in the Party that he left behind.

Yet the events of 1931 were a trauma for the Labour Party. Three of
their leading Parliamentary figures (MacDonald, Snowden and Thomas)
had turned against them. A Labour Government had been bundled from
office in the face of demands from American bankers; and in the subsequent General Election, the Parliamentary Party was virtually annihil-
ated, as the number of M.P.s dropped from 289 to 52.* Two periods of
office had culminated not in socialism, as anticipated in 1918, but in
betrayal; and in the process most of the early leaders of the Party had
either defected or been electorally defeated. And of course the
Depression remained, and intensified. It was with this as the background
that the Parliamentary leadership of the Party shifted to a second
generation of men: to men who had learnt their Labour politics after

* The Labour vote fell less sharply, and remained at 6,600,000.

1918, within the socialist rhetoric of *Labour and the New Social Order*, and who had no strong and direct links with the Liberal roots of the pre-war period. In the event, these men were to carry much of the hesitancy and all of the constitutionalism of MacDonald with them into their own period of political domination. But they were not entirely of MacDonald's making; and it was under their leadership, and with strong grass-roots pressure from within the Party's conference, that the Labour Party after 1931 sought again its socialist potential.

5

It is conventional on the Left nowadays to play down the significance of policy shifts within the Labour Party after 1931, and to stress instead the continuity of policy in the inter-war period as a whole.[54] This is clearly preferable to taking at face value Herbert Morrison's sudden discovery in 1931 of the 'need to put Socialism first', and Clynes' admission that 'Socialism had not failed. We had never yet begun to try even a little part of it.'[55] In fact, as we shall see, the points of continuity across 1931 are strong and important. But it is not necessary either to deprecate totally the commitment of the post-MacDonald generation of Parliamentary leaders to the need for radical social reform - a commitment reflected in the policies they adopted in the 1930s, in the speeches that they made, in the books that they wrote, and in the legislation upon which they embarked in the immediate wake of electoral victory in 1945. For if the Labour Party has ever had a generation of leaders that was genuinely concerned to achieve a total social transformation, then this was it; and if their socialist aspirations were hedged about by the legacies of attitude and policy acquired in the MacDonald period, they were no less genuine for that.

The pressure to adopt more radical programmes, and to prevent the worst excesses of the MacDonald period, undoubtedly came initially from outside the Parliamentary Party, and was in the main opposed by certain remnants of the old leadership. Henderson in 1932 insisted 'that nothing [had] happened either to the Party or to (its) electoral position to warrant any scrapping of our programme or policy or the revolutionising of our methods'.[56] But the Party activists did not agree, and the early 1930s were marked by innovations in policy from the floor of conference and from the Party's N.E.C. that were accepted by the Parliamentary leadership in the 1934 programme *For Socialism and*

Peace, and which shaped the legislative initiatives of the new Party leadership under Attlee after 1945.* Those policy innovations took a number of forms.

At one level they were concerned to prevent future Labour Governments systematically disregarding Party programmes in the manner of the Governments of 1924 and of 1929-31. So in 1933 the Party conference committed the next successful set of Labour leaders to consult widely in the Labour movement before accepting office, and to holding a special conference of affiliated organisations before taking power as a minority government. It also committed a future Labour Prime Minister to consultations with elected representatives of the Parliamentary Party before selecting his Cabinet; and the Cabinet to regular liason with the Parliamentary Labour Party while in office. And, most important of all, it insisted that the policies to be pursued by future Labour Governments should be those 'laid down in resolutions of the Annual Conference and embodied in the General Election Manifesto'.[57] To this last requirement at least, the 1945 Labour Government was to remain remarkably loyal.

It was in those resolutions that the new found militancy of the Labour Party in the early 1930s found its earliest expression. The N.E.C. in 1932 brought to the conference a typically ambiguous and unspecific resolution, of the kind commonly accepted by Labour Party conferences in the 1920s: saying merely that 'a Labour Government, equipped with adequate power, would turn its immediate attention to the reorganisation of banking and finance as a public service, to the transference of the land to the nation, and to the development under public auspices of the power and transport services', with the caveat that it was 'not possible to specify exactly in advance the order in which a majority Labour Government would proceed with its measures of economic reorganisation'.[58] But this would not do for the Party activists that year. They passed without discussion a resolution that 'the main objective of the Labour Party is the establishment of socialism' and 'that the common ownership of the means of production and distribution is the only means by which the producers by hand and brain will be able to secure the full fruits of their industry'. They also

---

*   It is interesting to note that in the debacle of 1931, all but three of the
    Ministers in MacDonald's Government lost their seats; and that the three who
    survived - Lansbury, Cripps and Attlee, were by chance all on the 'left' of the
    Party. This meant that between 1931 and 1935 the power of the Parliamen-
    tary Party over the Party conference was much reduced, and that the
    leadership of the Parliamentary Party was gravitating into more radical hands.

supported a resolution calling on even a minority Labour Government immediately to promulgate socialist legislation, 'to introduce at once, before attempting remedial measures of any other kind, great Socialist Measures, or some general measure empowering them to nationalise the key industries of the country';[59] so that, regardless of all else, 'the Party shall stand or fall in the House of Commons on the principles in which it has faith'. In particular, they committed the next Labour Government to the nationalisation of the joint-stock banks, and to nationalising or controlling the finance, banking, and acceptance houses. A year later, the conference of 1933 committed the next Labour Government to the nationalisation of agricultural land, of transport and of electricity generation and distribution.

Moreover, for the first and indeed only time in the Labour Party's inter-war history, the Party conference of 1933 demanded explicitly the redistribution of class power *within* industry itself. It had been traditional for the Labour Party to envisage public ownership in the form of public corporations, answerable to a Minister in Parliament, but with a typically capitalist administrative structure headed by a board of directors appointed 'on appropriate grounds of ability'.[60] Indeed, the Labour Party's reluctance in the 1920s to challenge the need for a traditional managerial hierarchy in the public sector was at one with their overriding commitment to Parliamentarianism; since as Morrison was later to argue, 'Parliament could fix responsibility on Ministers only if they had full power to appoint at will and hold accountable for performance in accord with Ministerial directives the persons administering the nationalised industries'.[61] In arguing for this as strongly as he did in 1933, Morrison was thus fully in the tradition of the Webbs and of men like Snowden, who had long advocated the appointment of 'the best available directive ability and technical skill'.[62] For Morrison was convinced that any substantial concession to the demand for workers' control would commit the Labour Party to giving the direction of the nationalised industries to men whose managerial ineptitude would depress production and alienate the electorate from the Labour Party itself. As G. D. H. Cole had said, the Labour Government 'cannot afford to risk failure and confusion by trying to be too "democratic" at the very start'.[63] Instead, he placed his faith in 'the captains of industry', a faith which had already guided Morrison in his reform of London Passenger Transport. For the managing board of that public concern he had sought 'the best brains that we can secure for the purpose', arguing that it was 'obvious that the people in charge,

35

certainly the Chairman of the Board, must have great industrial and managerial ability', and that consequently the Labour Party 'must be prepared to pay what is necessary in order to secure that ability, if the undertaking is to be efficient'.[64]

It was on this set of assumptions that the N.E.C. in 1933 proposed to conference that worker-participation be restricted to questions of working conditions, and that the process of production be placed firmly in the hands of experts appointed directly from above on the criterion of ability. But all this came under heavy challenge in 1933, as committing the Labour Party to the creation of nothing more than 'an efficient bureaucracy'. As one speaker put it at the 1933 conference, 'the workers are looking for something more from the Labour Party than so many shillings extra in the pay envelope on a Saturday. They are looking for an opportunity, through the policies that this Party stands for, for an added dignity, for an added status, for an added opportunity of a fuller and broader life.'[65] Merely to replace capitalist management by bureaucratic management was to 'doom working people to remain hewers of wood and drawers of water under the perpetual control of their bosses' - and so to fail to gain 'the economic self-government that is the promise of socialism'.[66] The conference accordingly committed the Labour Party, in spite of Morrison's opposition, to the direct representation of the trade union movement on the boards of nationalised companies, with those trade unionists to be there as *representatives* of their members and not as ordinary managerial personnel. Indeed the conference went further, in committing the Labour Party to the view that the workers' 'right to an effective share in the control and direction of socialised industries should be acknowledged by law and that the trade unions should be represented not only on the board of direction and control, but also on other administrative bodies in the industry or service'. The Labour Party spent the rest of the 1930s committed to this ambiguous call for workers' control. As Attlee said in 1935, 'workers' control is . . . an essential part of the new order'.[67]

The debates of 1932-4 were significant. In them,
there was a bolder conception of the economic role of a Labour Government; conscious planning was now considered essential. There was a revival of socialist purpose; capitalism was not to be reconstructed but superceded. 'Gradualism' was repudiated; socialism would not come by evolution, but must be established by legislation. 'Rationalisation' was dead; nationalisation must now be

rehabilitated. In journals, pamphlets and books, and in trade union and Labour Party meetings, the problems of socialism were thrashed out: what industries and services should be nationalised and in what order; how they should be reorganised and managed; what compensation should be paid.[68]

The conclusions of that debate were summed up in the Labour Party's most radical inter-war programme, *For Socialism and Peace*, published as 'the Labour Party's programme for action' by the N.E.C. in July 1934, and ratified by that year's Party conference.

The programme offered the electorate a simple if fundamental choice: 'either a vain attempt to patch up the superstructure of a capitalist society in decay at its very foundations, or a rapid advance to a Socialist reconstruction of the national life. There is no half-way house', the document maintained, 'between a society based on private ownership in the primary means of production, with the profit of the few as the measure of success, and a society where public ownership of those means enables the resources of the nation to be deliberately planned for attaining the maximum of general well-being'. It was to create the latter society that the 'Labour Party seeks a mandate ... to establish a free and prosperous society of equals, and believes that the high road to such a society lies through the gateway of Socialism'. And the programme went on to tell 'the electors ... what the establishment of Socialism means in terms of concrete domestic measures'; namely 'great fundamental measures of economic reconstruction ... and many forms of social provision, rendered especially urgent by the failure of the present system'. But in going on to list its specific proposals, *For Socialism and Peace* was adamant 'that what the nation now requires is not merely social reform, but Socialism. That is the end for which Labour asks the mandate of the electors.'[69] Then, under a section on 'Economic Reorganisation', the Labour Party proposed,

1. To apply a policy of full and rapid socialist economic planning, under central direction.
2. To establish public ownership and control of the primary industries and services as a foundation step, including the banking system, transport, coal and power, water supply, iron and steel, and other key industries.
3. To establish public ownership of the land and its proper utilisation, including the provision of national parks.
4. To reorganise agriculture under public direction and control.
5. To apply public regulation, including enforcement of

reorganisation of industries and services not under public ownership, in accordance with general economic planning.

6. To establish the right, acknowledged by law, of employees in socialised industries to an effective share in direction and control.

7. To utilise fully the consumers' co-operative movement in national economic planning.[70]

The Labour Party also committed itself to extensive additions to the social services, to more housing, to rent control, to educational provision, to the maintenance of the unemployed, to a major programme of public works - and, to pay for all this, to a system of direct, progressive taxation that would adjust the 'burden to the backs most capable of bearing it' by taking most heavily 'from those elements in our midst which often contribute relatively little to social efficiency and who only too frequently squander their resources unproductively'. The programme also threatened to abolish the House of Lords if legislation was obstructed; and ended with an appeal to all classes, starting with 'the working classes, because they know, in the bitterness of their experience, how profoundly capitalism has failed'.[71]

This was a radical document, committing the Labour Party as it did to the replacement of one system (capitalism) by another (socialism) on the basis of a legislative programme steered through by a majority Labour Government. Yet even at its most radical, the Labour Party of the 1930s still carried ambiguities, hesitations and tendencies to moderation from its earlier period. For the programme still proposed to leave in private hands the bulk of productive industry, and to restrict itself - at least initially - to what Brailsford unkindly but accurately called, the public ownership of 'capitalism's derelict industries'.[72] And by 1937 the leadership had moderated even this, by restricting again its list of industries to be nationalised, and by altering its position on land ownership.* For the rest of the economy, the Labour Party in the 1930s merely proposed 'reorganisation'; and it was not clear just how significant this reorganisation would be. Certainly men like Maynard Keynes felt that the Labour proposals would make hardly any difference at all.† Moreover, the Party was still proposing to pay

---

* The 1937 document, *Labour's Immediate Programme*, confined nationalisation to the Bank of England, electricity and gas supply, coal mining, the railways, 'and such other transport services as are suitable for transfer to Public Ownership'; and though saying that 'the land should belong to the people', actually proposed only that a Labour Government should 'acquire such land as they need for any purpose without delay and at a reasonable price'.

† On the proposal to nationalise the Bank of England, Keynes said, 'with the

compensation to the rich industrial owners it dispossessed, even though
the economic system over which that class presided (and which the
Labour Party ostensibly sought to replace) had dispossessed millions
for generations with no compensation at all. Its criteria of nationalisation remained as ambiguous as before; and its selection of industries as
accidental. And there were in its leadership men like Morrison who were
fundamentally opposed to the transference of industrial control down
to the working class - leaders for whom 'this buses for the busmen and
dust for the dustmen stuff is not *socialism* at all . . . it's middle class
syndicalist romanticism'.[73]

And of course the road to socialism that was being proposed was
still Parliamentary, piecemeal and gradual; and committed the Party
leadership to no action (beyond Parliamentary debates and public
meetings) before it had achieved its Parliamentary majority. On this
the Labour Party leaders, challenged as they were by the I.L.P., the
Communist Party and the Socialist League, were adamant. They were
prepared to consider constitutional reform (including the abolition of
the House of Lords) to speed the constitutional route to socialism; but
they steadfastly refused to go beyond Parliamentary action and procedures, and refused to politicise a depressed and potentially militant
working class in more than the requirements and ethics of electoral
politics. Whether a more radical politicisation of the working class by
the Labour Party would have succeeded must remain an open question.
What is significant is that the Party leadership made no attempt to find
out; and in their inactivity - amid the mass poverty of the Depression
and in the face of continental Fascism - they provided their critics, both
then and later, with ground for legitimate grievance.*

Indeed by the late 1930s the Party's overriding preoccupation with
questions of domestic reform had given way to bitter disputes on
foreign policy and defence issues, in the face of the threat posed by the
rise of continental Fascism. In those debates, the bulk of the Labour
Party leadership systematically opposed the political alliances with the
Communist Party that their own left-wing supporters so ardently

personalities the same, and knowledge no greater, it might not have made
much difference if the machinery which the Labour Party desires had been in
operation during the last ten years'. (Quoted in Hutt, *The Post-War History of
the British Working Class*, p. 239).
* In this crucial respect the points of continuity in Labour Party politics across
the great divide of 1931 are marked. These new leaders, Hutt said in 1937,
'continued to take the old disastrous road that Mr. MacDonald trod before
them' (*ibid*. p. 316).

sought, and eventually gave support to the rearmament programme of the Conservative Government to which that same Labour Left were so opposed. Yet even amid these internal disputes, the commitment of men like Attlee to major social transformation under Labour Party leadership remained. For the Labour leadership in Parliament in the 1930s was not the mere mirror image of its 1920s predecessor, and this too must be recognised if the true character of the Labour Party on the eve of the Second World War is to be grasped. The Labour leaders of the 1930s were determined never to go again through the debacle of 1931, and they had learned lessons of a kind from the experience of the Party under MacDonald. True, they still waited on a Parliamentary majority, and still placed their faith in the Parliamentary route to socialism. They would have no truck with mass working class mobilisation, or with the armed seizure of State power. All this they understood as Communist politics, and to that they were resolutely opposed. Yet we must beware of reading the politics of the 1930s with the benefit of hindsights drawn from the post-war period, if that reading leads us to write off Attlee, Dalton, Morrison and even Cripps as men dedicated to their own self-aggrandisement at the expense of the working class.

For if the ambiguities of their socialism became clear and fundamental after 1945, there is no doubt that, in the 1930s, these leaders of the post-war Labour Government did see their Party's role as one of transforming one social system into another by the capture of Parliamentary power. They had not tried the Parliamentary route to socialism. They had seen the alternative Bolshevik route decline into a Stalinist terror. They were thus both wary of extra-constitutional politics, and optimistic that capitalism could be transformed the Parliamentary way. If that involved waiting until an electoral majority for socialism was won - then for them even that was a point in favour of the Parliamentary route, for it guaranteed that the socialist transformation would have that degree of popular support which alone would prevent its degeneration into Party dictatorship.[*] The Labour Party leaders of the 1930s were under few illusions about the Stalinist autocracy. What illusions they had they kept for the Parliamentary alternative.

The capitalism that they rejected was not one that - in their view - was characterised by insurmountable cleavages of interest between

---

[*] Morrison in particular was very clear on this. See below, p. 141.

classes. Rather the Labour Party leaders of the 1930s rejected capitalism as a system because of the inequalities of wealth and consumption that it engendered, and because of its manifest inability to achieve the full employment of human and material resources. And it was to be transformed out of existence, not by the bloody suppression of class by class, but by a majority Labour Government that would nationalise key industries, redistribute wealth downwards, extend social services on the principle of human need, and plan production for the 'social good'. Snowden's 'bleak insistence on free trade, the gold standard and a balanced budget' was to be replaced by a new and a *democratic socialist* trinity: of public ownership, planning, and universal social welfare.

For the Party's Parliamentary leadership had passed to new hands - to men committed to active legislation and to extensive public ownership. The next Labour Government, Dalton wrote in the 1930s, 'must start off with a well planned rush'; and he wrote of that rush extending as far as the public ownership of shipbuilding, the heavy chemical industry and electrical goods producers.[74] Nor did these men promise a repetition of the MacDonald inertia in the face of opposition. On the contrary, Attlee wrote in 1935 that 'if financial interests attempt to sabotage a Labour Government, it will unhesitatingly seek emergency powers. If any faction were unwise enough to attempt to overthrow it by force, it would use the full power of the Government to defeat it.'[75] No matter how others have seen them later, throughout the 1930s these men saw themselves as socialists, leading a Party that would transform capitalism into socialism; by taking a system of private ownership and turning it into a society in which 'the common ownership of land and capital together with a democratic form of government' would guarantee 'production for use not profit, and distribution of the product either equally to all or at any rate with only such inequalities as are definitely in the public interest'.[76] This was the Labour Party's promise of socialism, which it took with it into office in 1945.

3. The Labour Governments of 1945~51

It took the mass radicalism generated by a second world war to give the Labour Party its first Parliamentary majority, and hence its first opportunity to test in untrammelled political conditions the potential of the Parliamentary State as a mechanism for substantial social change. The Party leadership in 1945 was taken by surprise both by the achievement and by the size of its electoral victory over its partners in the war-time coalition. In a 73% poll, just under 12,000,000 people voted for the Labour Party and its programme, and the Party came to dominate for the first time the political loyalties of the major English urban centres. Even Birmingham, with its 23% swing to Labour, gave ten of its thirteen formerly Conservative seats to a Party which described itself in its manifesto as 'a Socialist Party, and proud of it', whose 'ultimate purpose at home is the establishment of the Socialist Commonwealth of Great Britain - free, democratic, efficient, progressive, public spirited, its material resources organised in the service of the British people'.[1]

For the radical promise of Labour's manifesto, *Let Us Face The Future*, tapped the aspirations of an electorate whose experience of depression and then of war appears to have left many 'eager for major, even fundamental, changes in British society'.[2] The legacy of Tory rule amid the poverty of the 1930s, the progressive rhetoric of the war-mobilisation, the experience of wartime full employment under State controls, and the personal deprivations and sacrifices of modern warfare appear to have combined not to create a potentially revolutionary situation (as arguably had occurred in 1919) but at least to break traditional voting loyalties on a sufficient scale to give the Labour Party 209 net gains, and an overall majority in the House of Commons of 146 seats.

The promise of *Let Us Face The Future* was enormous, and yet in its omissions and vagueness the manifesto was ambiguous at its critical points. In it, the Labour Party announced its opposition to, and sharp break from 'the profiteering interests and the privileged rich', the

42

'czars of Big Business', 'the hard faced men and their political friends' who had ruled and prospered amid inter-war depression, who had 'controlled the banks, the mines, the big industries, largely the press and the cinema' and in whose hands 'the concentration of too much economic power' had led to 'great economic blizzards' and mass poverty. Against the private 'chaos' of these uncontrolled 'Big Interests', 'Big Business' and 'profiteers and racketeers', the Labour Party in 1945 offered 'constructive progress' on the basis of its programme of public ownership, democratic State planning and welfare provision. The 1945 election manifesto committed the next Labour Government to the nationalisation of a specific list of industries: the Bank of England, the fuel and power industries, inland transport, iron and steel, and 'ultimately' land - industries which were said to be 'inefficient and fall[ing] down on the job' and as such 'ripe and over-ripe for public ownership and management in the direct service of the nation'. The rest of industry was to be left in private hands, but to be subject to 'constructive supervision' by the State, to prevent the abuse of monopoly power, to harmonise financial policy and to guarantee full employment.

The promise of planning and of State control was everywhere. 'For the Labour Party is prepared', *Let Us Face The Future* said, to achieve 'a great programme of modernisation and a re-equipment of . . . homes . . . factories and machinery . . . schools [and] social services . . . by drastic policies of replanning and by keeping a firm constructive hand on our whole productive machinery'. 'Labour will plan from the ground up - giving an appropriate place to constructive enterprise and private endeavour in the national plan, but dealing decisively with those interests which would use high-sounding talk about economic freedom to cloak their determination to put themselves and their wishes above those of the whole nation.' In that planning, the Labour Party promised as its priorities the achievement of maximum production, the re-establishment of the export trade, the creation of 'fair play' in consumption, and a new social contract of price-controlled housing, free secondary education for all, a wide scheme of social insurance and free medical care. The Party promised taxation that 'bears less heavily on the lower income groups', and price controls of 'the necessities of life' in the context of an economy that was to be rid of the problem of underconsumption that had bedevilled the 1930s. The Labour Party did not promise the Socialist Commonwealth in five years. 'Socialism', it reminded its electorate, 'cannot come overnight'. The Party promised simply 'a step towards that, its ultimate purpose', and in the meantime, 'a happier future', 'free from the horrors of unemployment and insecurity'.[3]

In power, the Labour Party under Attlee's leadership was remarkably true to the letter of its programme. The Administration began with great optimism: 'we are the masters now', Hartley Shawcross was quoted as saying on the morning of victory. 'There was exhilaration amongst us,' Dalton wrote, 'joy and hope, determination and confidence . . . That first sensation . . . was of a new society to be built, and we had the power to build it.'[4] To build it, the Labour Government of 1945-51 nationalised the Bank of England in 1946, and the coal industry on 1 January 1947. It placed the ownership and control of electricity generation and transmission into the hands of the British Electricity Authority by an Act of 1947, and that of gas into the British Gas Council a year later, and made both answerable to the Ministry of Fuel and Power. Its Transport Act in 1947 created a Transport Commission answerable to Parliament, and responsible for the national railway system, 76 wharves and docks and 1600 miles of canals and internal waterways, plus the entire London transport system of buses and underground railways, and later long distance road haulage and road transport terminals. At the very end of its period of office, the Labour Government nationalised the iron and steel industry in the face of intense Conservative political and industrial opposition, and ended its period of office having in addition 'nationalised parts of such industries as ordnance, engineering, building materials, hotels, restaurants and catering, wholesaling . . . land, housing, theatres'[5] and telecommunications and cables. A little over 20% of the national economy was in State hands by the time that the Labour Party lost office in 1951, and 2,000,000 people were employed in the new State industries.

Over the 80% of the economy still in private hands, the Labour Government maintained its complex machinery of State planning and control. The Labour Government inherited in 1945 a situation that was particularly well-suited to this aspect of its politics, namely as Bevan said, 'a system of wartime controls and disciplines which could not have been realised in normal conditions without something approaching a revolution'.[6] 'Most of the controlling departments, agencies and committees had been established during the war, and were [simply] retained afterwards. Similarly the system of controls or methods by which the controls were operated, originated, to a considerable extent, with the Coalition Government.'[7]

At the centre of the entire planning mechanism were the Labour Cabinet, and the Cabinet subcommittees through which more detailed planning policy was evolved. At civil service level four interdepartmental committees were established, to consider programmes for manpower, materials, balance of payments and capital investment. After 1947, a Central Economic Planning Staff was appointed (of civil servants and economists, headed by a Chief Planning Officer, and answerable first to Herbert Morrison and later to Sir Stafford Cripps) 'to develop a long term plan for the use of the country's manpower and resources' and to liaise with the various Government Departments. Surrounding this central machinery were national advisory committees on industrial production and on labour questions, an Economic Planning Board and a Dollar Export Board, through which Government Ministers and senior civil servants liased with senior representatives of industry, commerce, finance and the trade unions. The machinery was completed by a series of regional boards for industry, by industry-wide committees on specific topics (on science and technology, production, investment and industrial research), and by general and more specialist advisory committees linking individual industries to their 'sponsoring' Government Department. There were a hundred or so such committees that advised the Labour Government, 'the most important [being in] engineering, machine tools, vehicles, electrical plant, building and shipbuilding'.[8]

Through this machinery the Labour Government applied a large number of financial and physical controls, including price control and taxation, materials control, building control, machinery and exports control. Throughout the period of the Labour Party in power, no factory building or repair work in excess of £1,000 could be undertaken without a license, and requests were rigorously vetted for building projects well in excess of this figure. The Labour Government used its Capital Issues Committee to direct the flow of new capital investment by approving or vetoing new issues on the capital market, and new issues were in fact directed almost exclusively to industries which were export-earning or import-saving, at the cost of those supplying less essential goods to the home market. Distribution, entertainment, insurance, hire-purchase and banking were all starved of new issues in this period. Government Departments kept tight control over both the volume and source of imports, and purchased themselves as

much as half of all the goods imported even as late as 1951.* Private
importers were subject to tight Board of Trade scrutiny, and required
import licenses which indicated both the amount and the value of
goods they could buy abroad in a specified time period. Once imported,
the industrial consumption of foreign raw materials was tightly
regulated by an allocation system which, in the early years of the
Labour Government at least, extended to a vast range of imported
goods. Home domestic consumption was also rationed, not least to
free as much as possible of domestic production for export purposes;
and 'in a few cases . . . home consumption was totally prohibited' to
allow all domestic output to be sold abroad. Finally, behind these
physical controls, the Central Economic Planning Staff issued periodic
'surveys' (sets of targets for industrial production, consumption, investment and crucially, for manpower use) as a guide to resource allocation
and investment; and the Government applied its whole set of
budgetary powers to maintain full employment and to encourage and
direct the pattern of private investment. In particular, by its direct
control of the Bank of England, it was able to co-ordinate management
of the public debt with control over the supply of money, short-
term credit and the level of interest rates. It was in these ways that the
Labour Government set out 'to combine a free democracy with a
planned economy . . . to create a Happy Country in which there is
equality of opportunity, and not too great a disparity of personal
income'.[9]

Behind this structure of public ownership and State planning of the
private sector the Labour Government created its system of welfare
provision. True to its promise of alleviating the individual insecurities
and destitution endemic to untrammelled private capitalism, it created
a system of universally available social insurance, which provided
guaranteed minimum incomes and provisions to those subject to unemployment, ill-health, industrial accidents, disablement, infirmity and
old age. It continued the new family allowances as a form of supplementary benefit to those with children of school age or under. It raised the
school leaving age to fifteen, and continued the guarantee of secondary
education for all embodied in the 1944 Education Act. It created a
national health service. It committed itself to a house-building

* 'The Ministry of Food, for example, bought directly 75% of all the imports of
food and animal feed, and the Board of Trade and the Ministry of Supply
purchased 25% of all raw materials.' (A. Rogow and P. Shore, *The Labour
Government and British Industry*, Oxford, Basil Blackwell, 1955, pp. 29-30).

programme which, though subject to economic retrenchment and resource-starvation later, still built 806,000 permanent houses and carried out 333,000 conversions in the first five years of office. Its taxation initiatives, especially in the early years, placed an even heavier burden on higher incomes than had the Coalition Government. Combined rates of surtax and income tax reached 19*s*. 6*d*. in the pound on incomes in excess of £20,000 a year, and taxation on inheritances, and on luxury and semi-luxury goods, was greatly increased. Distributed business profits were taxed at 50% by 1951, and the remaining 10*s*. in the pound was then subject to income tax at the standard rate.

Of all this, later Labour Party politicians were rightly to be proud. The Labour Government's welfare achievements were real and of lasting value, and a challenge to the inherited structure of social inequality. Evelyn Waugh was not alone amongst the privileged and the rich in thinking that 'the kingdom [under the 'Attlee-Cripps regime'] seemed to be under enemy occupation'.[10] And yet it was not. For the impact of the Labour Government of 1945-51, for all its promise and its vast body of legislation, was 'profoundly ambiguous'.[11] When the rhetoric of partisan debate had died, this became quickly apparent, and was almost taken for granted by academics and commentators of the mid 1960s. There had undoubtedly been important social reforms. But power had not shifted between classes. Qualitative social transformation had not come. Nor was it any nearer for the six years of office. In essence the Labour Government of 1945-51 had not created a socialist commonwealth, nor even taken a step in that direction. It had simply created a mixed economy in which the bulk of industry still lay in private hands, and the six years of its rule had only marginally altered the distribution of social power, privilege, wealth, income, opportunity and security.

2

There are lots of reasons for this. One is certainly the moderate nature of the Labour Government's programme of public ownership. As we saw in chapter 2, the Labour tradition had always been ambiguous on the purposes and social consequence of nationalisation. There had always been a radical strand within the movement for whom the taking of an industry into public ownership had been only part of a wider process of 'socialisation', in which elements of workers' control over the productive process could be introduced. It was this strand in the

47

Labour tradition which had been dominant in the early 1930s. But, as we saw, this view of public ownership as a mechanism for shifting class power *within* industry had always run counter to a view of nationalisation as a means of increasing the efficiency of total production *across* industries, a view which had gone along with a commitment to the retention in the new public corporations of traditional managerial hierarchies. When out of power, these mutually incompatible expectations of public ownership could be, and repeatedly were, married in suitably ambiguous phraseology and rhetoric; and significantly, in all the years of Opposition, the two views had publicly clashed *only* when Herbert Morrison was actually piloting his Bill on London Transport through the Commons. But though in that clash the advocates of workers' control won their paper victory, when the Labour Party took office in 1945 it was the defeated Morrison who was given responsibility for the Government's nationalisation programme, and public ownership under Labour thus involved no major concessions to the advocates of workers' control.

The Labour Government did not use its nationalisation measures to shift class power *within* industry. On the contrary, each of the new public corporations was run by a Board of Directors, with a managerial structure beneath, and though trade union personnel were included at Board and managerial levels, they were there not as workers' representatives but as managerial personnel. The Nationalisation Acts explicitly stated that 'expert' managers would be appointed by the responsible Minister, that these managers would be answerable not to the labour force within the industry but to the Minister and hence to Parliament, and that they would be expected to manage their nationalised industry in the spirit of business efficiency. These managerial cadres were to negotiate with trade unions representing their work force (and with trade unions whose procedural rights - it must be said - were much strengthened in the Nationalisation Acts) but the trade unions, and the work forces that they represented, were not to become involved in areas of traditional managerial prerogatives.

It is indicative of the Labour Government's retreat from the Party's radicalism of the 1930s that the men chosen to head these new public corporations were, with a few notable exceptions, members of the managerial and ownership class of the former private industries. Of the Bank of England, even the *Economist* (a journal hysterically opposed to the Party and its programme in this period) conceded that the Labour Government did 'not contemplate revolutionary changes in personnel'.[12]

Indeed, of all the top men appointed to the Bank of England, only one came from the Labour side, and there were no appointments from financially experienced Labour circles, such as the Co-operative movement.* Nor was this just an exception. The man appointed to head the National Coal Board, Lord Hyndley, was a leading figure in the largest colliery company in Britain, a man who held a number of private directorships, and one whose coal industry experience was entirely in the sales and finance sections of private colliery management. Most of the regional, district and even colliery directors and managers under the Coal Board represented also 'the same old faces'.[13] For though there were two trade union leaders on the N.C.B. itself, they were outnumbered even there by 'five people drawn from the upper classes, including one managing director of a colliery company. There was one part-time member, [and he] was a former director of colliery companies and a director of a bank, a railway company and an insurance company.'[14] All this set the pattern for the Nationalisation Acts that were to follow.

Of course, this pattern of appointment did not go without challenge. The Labour Party Conference of 1946 voted that the direction of nationalised industries should 'not be left with those who were previously in control'; and amazingly, the Minister of Fuel and Power (who had just appointed Lord Hyndley to head the nationalised coal industry) accepted this. He went on however to say that 'we must employ the best men for the job',[15] and those, as the appointments later to the British Transport Commission, the Electricity Authority and the Gas Council made clear, were invariably taken by the Labour Party leaders to be men drawn from the existing managerial hierarchies. By 1951 only 9 of the 47 full-time members and 7 of the 48 part-time members of the Boards of the nationalised industries were trade unionists, and five of the Boards had no trade unionist amongst their full-time members at all. The opinion of the Labour Party leadership was honestly if bluntly put by Sir Stafford Cripps in 1946.

There is not yet a very large number of workers in Britain capable of taking over large enterprises. I have on many occasions tried to get representatives of the workers on all sorts of bodies and working

---

* One left-wing critic at the 1932 Labour Party Conference had rejected Morrisonian-style nationalisation of the Bank of England, saying 'I suppose we shall call in Montague Norman to manage the Bank of England for us'. (Quoted in Hutt, *The Post-War History of the British Working Class*, p. 239). Horrific as this was to the conference that year, when nationalisation came the Labour Government did rely on just this type of ultra-conservative banker.

parties. It has always been extremely difficult to get enough people who are qualified to do that sort of job, and, until there has been more experience by the workers of the managerial side of industry, I think it would be almost impossible to have worker-controlled industry in Britain, even if it were on the whole desirable.[16]
- which clearly, for Cripps by the late 1940s at least, it was not. Nor did the Labour Government seriously attempt to transform the selection procedures and educational opportunities by which this situation of supposed worker-incapacity could be rectified. Least of all did they do it by allowing the workers to gain managerial experience by direct, regular, and systematic involvement in the full range of decision-making at the point of industrial production. That way of gaining managerial skills was to remain, as hitherto, the preserve of the tiny managerial strata.

All this was in keeping with the predominant Fabian tradition within the Labour Party, with its faith in the 'expert' and its commitment to Parliamentary democracy,* and was at one with the Labour Government's own need to attain a rapid rate of economic growth from a predominantly capitalist economy. But it nonetheless 'implied a far-reaching departure from basic assumptions of traditional socialist doctrine', and indicated how far class interests had always been seen and pursued by the Party leadership within the parameters of a wider, supposedly supra-class, national perspective. 'Instead of identifying all of society - as socialists had been wont to do - with the interests of the industrial working class, industrial workers were now viewed as one major interest group amongst many'.[17] The decision to take over industries without unduly disturbing the existing managerial hierarchies, whilst concentrating only on shifting the locus of accountability, made clear the Labour Party leadership's acceptance of the traditional capitalist distinction between managerial responsibilities and prerogatives on the one hand, and trade union functions and workers' tasks on the other.† That the debates of the 1930s on workers' control should

---

* 'Two features of the Fabian conception of state and government led inevitably to the rejection of workers' control. The first was the acceptance of parliamentary supremacy as an expression of the majority will . . . the other determining feature of the Fabian conception of government was an uncommon respect for the expert; turning a problem over to some expert body was the invariable Fabian solution for each new governmental difficulty'. (R. A. Dahl, 'Workers' control of industry and the British Labour Party', *American Political Science Review*, vol. XLI, 1947, pp. 877-8).
† It is worth noting here that the bulk of the official trade union leadership were equally adamant that this distinction must be maintained.

have culminated in the creation of Morrisonian-type corporations in the 1940s tells us an immense amount about the character of the Labour Party leadership even at its most radical. For it implied that the Labour Government accepted as permanent the need for discipline and sanctions over workers as part of the productive process. Whatever Labour Party public ownership appeared to offer in the 1945 pro-gramme, the end of 'labour alienation', and that increase in efficiency which accrues from genuine participation in industrial democracy, was never realistically on the agenda.

Given that the Labour Party leadership saw nationalisation as part of its overall programme of increased material production, and not as a vehicle for shifting class power within industry, it is not surprising that it restricted the boundaries of public ownership to those industries whose previous performance in private hands had retarded the growth rate of G.N.P. Because the goal was not workers' control, there was no need to take all industry into public hands. *Let Us Face The Future* was clear on this. The next Labour Government would only nationalise industries which were 'basic' or which were inefficient and falling down on the job; and it distinguished these, if not explicitly then certainly by implication, from 'many smaller businesses rendering good service which [could] be left to go on with their useful work' and from 'big industries not yet ripe for public ownership'. Even 'basic' industries like coal, to whose nationalisation the Labour Party had been com-mitted since 1913, were taken into public ownership in 1945 on the purely technical ground that 'amalgamation under public ownership [would] bring great economies in operation and make it possible to modernise production methods and to raise safety standards in every colliery in the country'.[18] Herbert Morrison made clear very early in the Labour Government's period of office that this was the restricted role of nationalisation in Government thinking. Nationalised industries, Morrison said, were 'not ends in themselves . . . the object [rather] is to make possible organisation of a more efficient industry, rendering more public service, and because of its efficiency and increased productivity enabled to do progressively better for its workers'.[19]

This had a number of quite specific consequences for the pattern and range of nationalisation. It meant that, in nationalising basic industries, the Labour Government after 1945 was almost invariably taking into public ownership industries whose absorption into the State had already been proposed by Inquiries dominated by and reporting to earlier Conservative Governments. It also meant that nationalisation

51

was too often restricted to industries that were in particularly bad internal condition, requiring vast investment programmes before they could be renovated, and ultimately needing to shed labour on a substantial scale. This both gave nationalisation a bad electoral image, as synonymous with industrial decay and poor performance, and more critically, left in private hands all the growth industries, the high profit industries, and the whole financial structure outside the Bank of England. The result was that, far from weakening private capitalism, Labour Party nationalisation after 1945 actually *strengthened* it as a system, and reinforced the economic and social position of its ruling groups. It did this by relieving them of the responsibility for derelict industries, by removing from them the economic consequences of their inter-war policies of low investment and inefficient management, and by providing them instead with an infrastructure of publicly owned basic industries whose pricing policies could be designed so as to subsidise the private sector on which economic growth and export earnings so critically depended.*

When this is realised, the Labour Government's decision to pay generous compensation can be seen to have lessened still further the impact of nationalisation on the redistribution of class power in post-war British society, and if anything to have strengthened the economic position and social prestige of the very groups which had prospered amid inter-war depression, and which *Let Us Face The Future* had attacked. For with their compensation, many companies re-invested in the private profitable sector. 'Typical examples,' J. W. Grove tells us, are

> Cable and Wireless (Holdings) Limited . . . which has invested its free moneys to build up an interest in about 850 different companies; and Thomas Tilling (Holdings) which continues [1962] to manage the interests of the old Tilling Group that were not acquired by the British Transport Commission, and has used its compensation to acquire holdings in some 25 companies in industries ranging from light engineering to glass and plastics and from insurance to book publishing.[20]

For in taking over a completely run-down coal industry, the Labour Government paid the princely sum of £164,000,000 to the former coal

---

* 'The role of the state was not to break down class privilege and wealth, but on the contrary to lubricate the awkward machinery of the market. Power and transport, for instance, could not be provided for the export industries if coal and the railways remained under private ownership and control.' (P. Foot, *The Politics of Harold Wilson*, Harmondsworth, Penguin, 1968, p. 65).

52

owners, and in doing so added a financial burden to the neck of the
new nationalised industry that it could not easily shake off. For the
Bank of England the Labour Government paid £58,000,000, and for
the railways and canal system 'in the end [it paid] £1,000,000,000
... in the form of 3% transport stock'.[21] As R. Brady concluded (and
he, as an observer addressing a conservative American audience, was
not prone to left-wing polemic) 'excepting the Bank of England, and
parts of the gas and electricity industries, most of these properties
were badly run down, or badly organised, or underdeveloped and in
need of new investment, or suffering from other difficulties and short-
comings. State ownership [had] not altered the general structure of
ownership of securities, or of income claims on the community's real
resources, except, possibly, somewhat to improve the status of the
rentier'![22]

It is hardly surprising then that Clement Attlee could report that
'there was not much real opposition to our nationalisation proposals,
only iron and steel roused much feeling'.[23] For the social peace which
accompanied the Labour Government of 1945-51 was a measure of its
limited impact, and of the sense of relief with which the inter-war
ruling groups experienced its moderation in office. For as the
Economist, voice of the Establishment throughout the Labour Government, said in 1945, the Labour Government could easily have done
more. 'The country', it reported, had

> very clearly expressed its preference for a Labour Government ...
> and the voters were not so naive as to imagine that they could get a
> Labour Government without a Socialist policy ... From this point
> of view Mr Morrison's list is most moderately short. An avowedly
> Socialist Government, with a clear Parliamentary majority, might
> well have been expected to go several stages further. There is nothing
> in the list about the land ... ocean-going shipping ... merchant
> shipping ... [or] petroleum, which, in its domestic aspects, might
> be thought the most obvious target of all. Nothing is said about any
> sections of the food distributing industry - such, for example, as
> milk distribution. Clearly Mr Morrison might have gone a great deal
> further ... The programme ... is almost the least it [the Labour
> Government] could do without violating its election pledges.[24]

But the Labour Party in power chose not to follow even the
Economist's list; and in the process failed to take its historic moment.
Its pattern of nationalisation, its administrative policy within the public
sector, and its payment of compensation strengthened the very classes

it had promised to reform. At the point of production, in the mines for example, little actually changed, as observant Conservative and Liberal critics were the first to point out. As the Liberal leader said in the House in 1946:

> On the date when the State takes over the mines what will be the effect [on the miner]. He will go to the same pit and get the same lamp from the same man; he will go into the same cage, will probably be lowered by the same man, and when he gets to the bottom he will, if he is in certain parts of the country, see the same expression on the face of the pony. He will see the same manager, the same deputy . . . and on the Friday he will probably be paid by the same man.[25]

The Labour Party could not but lose from this, for it raised greater expectations of nationalisation than in the event it chose to deliver. It had been tacitly supposed that 'the private sector would rapidly wither away once Labour was voted into power'.[26] Yet it did not. Employer-employee relationships in the public sector were supposed to be transformed by public ownership. But they were not. On the contrary, 'the workers in the industries had not been accorded a new status or responsibility',[27] and it became commonplace by the early 1950s to talk of mass working class 'disillusionment . . . with the results of nationalisation' and to concede that 'ideologically, as far as the great mass of trade union members is concerned, nationalisation has been a failure'.[28] For 'as the hopes held, frequently with deep emotion by many workers, prior to nationalisation [were] not fulfilled'[29] the end product was that rapid alienation from nationalisation amongst large sections of the Labour electorate that has bedevilled the Labour Party ever since. As Rogow said, 'by 1948 the popular enthusiasm and support which had attended the 1945 General Election had largely evaporated, and certainly by 1950 nationalisation in principle was an evocative slogan only in some circles in the Labour Party'. One of its three 'socialist' planks - nationalisation - had broken in the Labour Party's hand.

3

This would not have mattered so much if the Labour Party's much-vaunted second string to its 'socialist' bow - the democratic State planning of the 80% of the economy that it left in private hands - had lived up to the claims that Party leaders in the past had made for it.

For the inter-war critique of capitalism to which the Labour Party had subscribed had particularly stressed the chaotic nature of private enterprise; and *Let Us Face The Future* had specifically compared Labour Party planning to the social misery of untrammelled private enterprise. But in the event, Labour Party planning had only a limited and shortlived impact, and did not markedly transform either class relations or capitalist economic imperatives.

For the Labour Government hardly had an economic plan as such, if by that is understood a set of economic objectives that are integrated and consistent in their assumptions, and on the basis of which resource allocation is effectively directed. Rather 'scarce resources were distributed . . . among the many claimants according in the main to the skill and tenacity with which their points of view were pressed,' and though all important questions reached senior civil service or Cabinet level, where they were resolved by reference to broad policy objectives, even there decisions 'were often more the result of inter-departmental negotiation and amateur judgement than of consistent and scientific planning'.[30]

The controls which the Labour Party took were negative rather than positive, and consequently State control, where it came, was more effective in blocking certain patterns of resource distribution than in accurately placing scarce resources in the hands of producers and consumers as part of an overall socialist economic strategy. This was partly because the coverage of controls was limited, extending neither to manpower, nor to personal incomes, profits or exports. The Economic Survey of 1947, for example, the high spot of Labour Party 'planning' after 1945, set detailed manpower and output targets for particular industries, and laid out a comprehensive import programme, but it contained no mechanisms for the attainment of the targets that it had so carefully specified. And when these targets were not attained, later Labour Party 'surveys' did not respond by tightening controls but by toning down their aspirations and claims, to that point at which the 1950 survey could be described as 'a humble document, meek almost to the point of being meaningless'.[31] Indeed, but for the Korean War, it is likely that by 1951, 'planning' under the Attlee Government would have been 'confined to Budget policy and certain balance of payments controls',[32] and as such, to a mere shadow of Labour Party claims in 1945.

Moreover the Labour Government's planning was weak because controls, where they did apply, left large loopholes and permitted considerable degrees of evasion. So though investment controls applied to factory building, they did not apply to the plant, machinery, stocks and vehicles that the factories would use, house and produce. Though the 'dollar gap' prompted tight control of imports, the direction of the whole export drive was left in untrammelled private hands, and the Government did little to increase the economy's dollar earnings beyond exhortation and the giving of technical advice to private export companies. And though exchange control was tight for most of the Labour Government period, the Government still found itself subject to currency speculation, and to 'flights' of capital away from sterling through the weaker exchange controls of the sterling area countries. Balogh estimated that the illegal export of capital, mainly by under-valuing exports and overpayment for imports, reached almost £2,000,000,000 between 1946 and 1949.[33] To avoid controls, as many as '202 public companies with an issued capital of over £80 million had either migrated to the Dominions or radically extended their manu-facturing capacity there' by 1949.[34] As the Labour Government itself later reported 'of £645 million of private capital which left Britain between 1947 and 1949 only £300 million represented genuine invest-ments in new projects. Some £350 million was "hot" money quitting Britain because its owners disliked the Labour Government's policy . . . or were engaged in currency speculation.'[35]

For just as with nationalisation, the senior managerial strata of private industry and finance found quickly after 1945 that the radicalism of Labour Party rhetoric did not tap the reality of Labour Government policy. The Labour Government of 1945-51 did not use its planning machinery to curtail the economic power and social privileges of the class it had attacked in *Let Us Face The Future*. On the contrary, *it sought a close and co-operative working relationship with them*. As the P.E.P. survey in 1950 accurately observed 'Government Depart-ments and Ministers, believing that an ounce of willing co-operation was worth a ton of compulsion, set themselves out to establish friendly con-tacts and consultations and to use their compulsive powers as little as possible.'[36] To this end, the bulk of the machinery of planning was staffed by the managers, or embodied in the firms and trade associations, that planning was supposed to control. As Rogow has said,

> In the early years of the Labour Government, particularly, the personnel of planning and controls was extensively drawn from the ranks of private industry. Beginning at the top strategic level of policy, the Chief Planning Officer, 1947-51, was . . . a Director of

British Aluminium and two other companies. The Capital Issues
Committee . . . consisted of seven bankers, stockbrokers, and industrialists . . . The principal industrial adviser to the Board of Trade for
most of the period was the Chairman of the British Rayon
Federation. The majority of advisers and commodity directors of the
Ministry of Food were unpaid representatives of business, in most
cases of the leading firms in the controlled industries. Indeed the
employees of one firm, Unilever, filled ninety posts in the Ministry
of Food, twelve of them senior positions. The important Steel
Re-armament Panel of the Ministry of Supply was headed by a
Director of the Iron and Steel Federation, and the personnel of the
various metals controls were largely drawn from the Non-Ferrous
Metals Federation, itself a Federation of trade associations . . . [And]
in addition to encouraging the formation of trade associations . . .
the Labour Government often delegated to such associations the
administration of controls. Thus, for example, newsprint was
allocated by the Newsprint Rationing Committee, a trade body . . .
The cocoa and confectionary trade associations were largely responsible for a group of controls over the 'sweets' trade, and in 1950 they
were given power to classify and distribute the relevant raw materials
without further authority from the Ministry of Food. A number of
controls were administered by firms, or a group especially organised
for the purpose. For example, the Mond Nickel Company, on behalf
of the Government, imported all nickel and allocated it to users
through an unofficial allocation system working between the Mond
Nickel Company and the Ministry of Supply.[37]
Moreover, the Labour Government made it clear early on that it did
not envisage State planning as an alternative to the imperatives of
market forces. As the 1947 Economic Survey pointed out, 'controls
cannot by themselves bring very rapid changes or make fine adjustments
in the economic structure . . . under democracy the execution of the
economic plan must be much more a matter for *co-operation* between
the Government, industry and the people than of rigid application by
the State of controls and compulsions'.[38] But contrary to the
impression created by the Survey, 'the people' were not directly
involved in the planning process - not even that part of 'the people' (the
work force) who were employed in the industry concerned, and who
might have been reasonably thought to have an interest and an
expertise on which the Labour Government could draw. Rather, 'co-
operation' occurred on terms set by the senior managerial strata, and

hence by the needs of the corporate institutions that they headed.

Surveying all this in the mid-1950s, Rogow came to the conclusion that, but for the existence of post-war shortages, planning under the Labour Government 'would have been largely confined to the compilation of economic information and of forecasts . . . with the use of a small number of key controls to guide resources into the right places. In other words, the shape of the economy, the decisions as to the quantity and kind of industrial output required, would have been left substantially to market forces.'[39] This may be to underestimate slightly the early optimism of Labour Party leaders, that their planning opened a new way of economic management. Attlee at least had told the Commons in 1946 that Labour Party planning approached 'the economic situation in what is really a new way of attacking the problem. We attacked it from the point of view of manpower rather than finance - our human resources rather than our financial resources.'[40] There seems no reason to doubt his sincerity. This was after all how the Coalition Government of which he was a leading member had organised the war-effort. But in the end the Labour leaders learnt quickly that State planning of a complex economy in peace time is far more difficult than they had anticipated in the 1930s. The repeated inaccuracies of planning forecasts, the unanticipated crises of fuel and convertibility in 1947, and the growing evidence of bureaucratic incompetence and of administratively generated blockages - all shook the early optimism of Labour Party leaders in the potential of State planning. They learnt too - without much heart-searching it must be said, in spite of their 'socialism' - that State planning requires the co-operation of the very business personnel it is supposed to control, and that their position will accordingly have to be strengthened (and planning goals bent to their purposes) unless a Labour Government chooses instead to rely on the industrial power and competence of its own working class to man and implement its planning machine. But that, of course, would involve shifting class power within industry - which the Labour leadership had already rejected as impractical *and* undesirable. So the Labour Party in power found itself dependent on the business community, who proved as ungrateful as ever to a Party that had strengthened rather than weakened its position. For because the existence of physical controls was seen by the senior managerial strata as a threat to their class prerogatives and market freedom, they increasingly demanded of the Labour Government that they dismantle the complex edifice of wartime controls and return to the so-called 'free' play of market forces.* It was a demand to which the Labour Government was increasingly obliged to succumb.

So what of the reality of 'planning' under Labour? Whilst the Labour Government of 1945-51 kept their armoury of physical controls they did not use them for socialist purposes. Rather, as Schumpeter said, 'once more it is a question of administering capitalism'. As he saw in 1950, most of the planning 'that has actually been done or suggested has nothing specifically socialist about it unless we adopt a definition of socialism that is much too wide to be of any analytical use'.[41] And in the end, subject to daily pressure to be rid of controls, and finding the electorate responding to this ideological onslaught, the Labour Government divested itself of its own powers at a very rapid rate. Harold Wilson, at the Board of Trade, presided after 1948 over periodic 'bonfires' of licenses and quotas, that left the Attlee Government by the end almost entirely dependent for its economic management on the indirect structuring of the profit-aspirations of private companies through its use of vestigial fiscal and monetary techniques. The problem with this, as Balogh saw, was that it 'brought nearer the point where private financial power could reimpose a veto on economic policy'.[42] Yet the Labour Party was not to realise the truth of this until after 1964, and by then the machinery of direct physical planning had been totally dismantled and long forgotten. By fudging its 'planning' strategy after the war, the Attlee Government discredited direct physical planning for a generation, and left later Labour Governments that bit less well armed to control, let alone to transform, a remarkably resilient private capitalist economy. It also made its own contribution to that misconception that has since bedevilled the Labour Left, that because socialism involves State planning, any State planning by a Labour Government must involve socialism. Yet, as we have seen, this was hardly the case between 1945 and 1951.

---

* 'Pressure to de-control industry, put upon the Government by its advisers, was a factor of importance in the controls 'bonfire' of 1948-50. It was an unusual week . . . when the newspapers and periodicals did not feature a detailed criticism of the Government policy by a present or former administrator of that policy . . . Controls, it is fair to say, are not likely to be best administered by hostile or antipathetic controllers; but aside from this, the effect of published criticism was to weaken public confidence, on which the controls' ultimate success depended'. (Rogow, *The Labour Government and British Industry*, p. 66).

4

For if the Labour Party came into power in 1945 committed to the creation of a society in which, as Attlee had said before the war, incomes and life experiences were to be as nearly equal as possible, in the event it left in 1951 one in which the structured inequalities created by untrammelled capitalism had been ameliorated only at the margin. This was partly because of the way in which the Labour Government chose to pay compensation to the owners of industries nationalised. It was partly because, in its creation of welfare services, its use of flat-rate contributions introduced a new and substantial element of regressive taxation. It was partly because the Labour Government failed to introduce a capital gains tax. But it was also because in its pursuit of sustained industrial output the Labour Government of 1945-51 actually abandoned its search for the progressive reduction of income inequalities.

This is clear in the pattern of budgetary policy after 1948, a pattern which would be repeated with uncanny accuracy after 1964. For the Labour Government found itself in the late 1940s facing a substantial deficit on its balance of payments that reflected the inherited competitive weakness of the British economy, the wartime sale of foreign assets, the wartime dislocation of both domestic industry and foreign markets, and the heavy overseas military expenditure made necessary by the fight against Fascism and then by the supposed threat of communist aggression. Throughout the 1940s, the Labour Government sustained that imbalance on its foreign payments only by tight exchange controls and foreign lending. Obliged in 1947 to relax exchange controls as a condition of big American loans, it experienced heavy speculation against the pound, which both drove it to re-establish sterling inconvertibility and later, much against its wishes, to devalue the pound. The Labour Government under Attlee proved to be increasingly preoccupied in such a situation with strengthening British export industries, and with improving the investment record (and hence competitive, import-saving position) of private industry; and so pursued a policy route that the 1964-70 Government would also follow. Indeed, Harold Wilson first learnt the politics of subordinating social reform to export production in this period, as the young President of Attlee's Board of Trade.

That policy route was well signposted by the Marshall Aid Administrator in a speech to the United States Congress on the Labour

Government's 'austerity programme' which it initiated in 1948. 'The austerity programme', he said,

> is part of the broad policy which Britain has adopted to funnel as much of her total annual resources as possible into exports, especially to the dollar area, and into capital. She is trying to hold down her consumption, that is to say her personal ... and her governmental consumption, to the minimum possible so that as much as possible of what is left over will be available for capital formation and exports ... In other words ... her policy is to step up her gross national product by increasing her production to the maximum, to hold down governmental consumption by cutting back social programmes instituted when the Labour Government came into power, and then to divide up what is left between exports and capital formation.[43]

So domestic consumption was dampened to ease the pressure on imports and to free resources for export industries. Attempts were made to redirect factors of production into export-based industries, not least by cutbacks in the percentage of G.N.P. allocated to public sector social services: to health, housing, education and social insurance. There were substantial cuts in the housing programme in the wake of the sterling convertibility crisis in 1947, when most local authorities were forbidden to sign contracts for new houses or to give licenses for new houses to private builders. Later, on the receipt of Marshall Aid and in the wake of devaluation, there were cuts in both the health and education programmes. Progressive forms of taxation were no longer introduced lest they add fuel to domestic consumption, undermine private enterprise incentives, and discourage capital formation in the private sector.* And attempts were made to persuade organised labour to restrict its wage settlements and earnings levels to a rate no greater than the growth of the economy as a whole.

In Sir Stafford Cripps' budgets of 1948 and 1949, the Labour Party began its shift back to a reliance on indirect taxation, and actually cut rates of income tax. 'Redistribution of wealth', Cripps told the Commons 'could go no further until new wealth had been created - and in the meantime there must be a ceiling on the social services'. Indeed 'short of launching ... an assault on the social services', by significant

---

* This is one key to the Labour Government's decision to introduce flat-rate contributions for social insurance. As Brady said, 'this means that the Government has sacrificed the direct social objective of redistribution of income to the object of full employment through high and stable production'. (R. Brady, *Crisis in Britain*, Cambridge University Press, 1950, pp. 344-5).

cuts in benefits, 'it is hard to see how Cripps' fiscal policies could have been significantly less egalitarian than they were'.[44]

Given this, it is a measure of the strong loyalties of trade union leaders and officials to the Labour Government that Cripps was able to implement his incomes policy. For unlike Governments in the late 1960s and early 1970s, the Labour Government of 1945-51 was remarkably successful at incomes control, in that union leaders in 1948 accepted wage restraint in return for a promise of profit restraint, for a once and for all capital levy, and for a continuation of food subsidies at a level and to an amount that far exceeded the Attlee Government's initial intentions. That wage agreement lasted until the latter part of 1950, when growing rank and file opposition fuelled by rising prices forced even the T.U.C. leadership to oppose any further wage restraint, 'and the Labour Government was forced to prepare legislation, for largely "psychological" reasons, to limit dividend payments - in the hope that this measure would ease the mounting pressure for higher wages'.[45] With the Conservatives returned to office by 1951, this first Labour Incomes Policy provided yet another model to which a later Labour Government would return.

5

We shall discuss in chapter 6 the reasons for the failure of the Attlee Government to make any significant progress towards the creation of its promised 'socialist commonwealth'. But we must note here, in passing, several features of that Labour Government that contributed to its growing lack of purpose and socialist impact.

There is first the growing moderation and theoretical unpreparedness of its Parliamentary leadership. This was noted as early as 1945 by the young Woodrow Wyatt, who found on arrival at Westminster that, as he put it, 'at present the country is far to the Left of Labour Ministers'.[46] This was perhaps not surprising. For the Labour leaders found themselves facing problems which they had not anticipated with policy proposals whose impact had been muted by secular changes within private capitalism. They came to power prepared to fight the inter-war bogies of unemployment and underconsumption - and found instead new problems, of underproduction and excess demand, which would be exacerbated by precisely those policies of social reform with which Labour was electorally associated, and on which in the 1930s it had staked its claim to be a socialist party. In any case, the years of coalition government in the war had mellowed the radicalism of men like Attlee and Cripps, and intensified the moderation of men like Morrison, and had already removed from the agenda of the Party, as far as they were concerned, any attempt at workers' control or at the introduction of public ownership on the scale anticipated in 1934. The experience of Government office had left the Labour Party in 1945 with a leadership that was ever willing to temper its policies to the requirements of 'sound reason and the national interest' - entities which, as Morrison made clear to the Labour Party conference in 1946, had nothing in common with 'the Left' of the Party.

Instead, Labour leaders increasingly took their definitions of the limits of the possible from two other groups with whom they worked closely in office: from senior civil servants in their own Departments and from senior managerial personnel who manned their planning structures, sat on their advisory committees, and headed the private companies on which sustained economic growth depended. The memoirs of this generation of Labour leaders are full of praise for the civil servants with whom they established such a close relationship. Indeed, in promoting them, Labour Ministers always explicitly selected for 'competence and not for . . . loyalties',[47] as though a job could be competently done by men out of sympathy with it. Yet these senior civil servants *were* largely out of sympathy with the radical features of the Labour Government's programme. They had served and learnt their own political views in the Conservative-dominated social and political milieu of the 1930s. Even more than today, senior civil servants after the war came from a social class, and tended to hold political views, far removed from the Labour Party at its most radical, and they tended to have close personal, social, ideological and institutional connections with the world of private business and finance. This must have influenced the intellectual environment in which Labour Ministers came to make their critical policy decisions. As Brady observed, all the Labour Government's

plans, attempts, and hopes of technical modernisation must immediately come to grips with a vast, closely interwoven, politically conscious network of private monopoly and cartel-like controls, the policies of which are shaped by a mentality which is dominated by financial and trading interests . . . It is not only restrictionist but also it is unusually conservative in technical matters; it is shot through and through with nepotism, and it is firmly rooted in both Parliament and the British administrative system. When the [Labour]

Government acts in Britain it is the civil service which make top administrative policy decisions, (immediately below the Minister in question). The colonial, foreign and military services are manned largely by persons drawn from Opposition ranks; in many leading offices, perhaps most notably the Board of Trade, the situation is only slightly less true at home.[48]

It is hardly surprising that, in the face of this daily experience of men opposed to radical initiatives in a socialist direction, Labour Ministers who were in any case increasingly worn down by the sheer burden of office should have succumbed very rapidly to the potency of their advisers' arguments and recommendations.

These senior civil servants were not alone in arguing against radical initiatives by the Attlee Government. Their pressure for moderation was reinforced by the views of the senior managerial personnel with whom the Labour Ministers worked and whom they appointed to high administrative office. Critics from the left of the Party argued strongly against this heavy reliance on men so politically hostile to Labour's programme, men 'selected from circles which in the past Labour [had] sworn to liquidate'.[49] But the Labour leaders needed the co-operation of private industry to achieve sustained industrial output, and chose to ignore their own left wing. In any case, Labour leaders do appear to have subscribed fully to the Fabian belief in the politically neutral expert. Brady puts this well,[50]

Now this 'expert' is a sort of emotionally disembodied ideological eunuch whose formal training and professional outlook tend unwittingly to make of him at once the scientifically ideal organiser and guardian of the common welfare, and define for him a disinterested role which, elevated above and removed beyond the hurly-burly of politics, stands in the sharpest contrast to the tendentious and emotion-clouded outlook of the partisans of special interests and causes who go to make up the rank and file that treads the hurried streets. The latter, strange as it may seem, include the partisans of the particularistic interests of organised labour. Hence the rule in the nationalised industries is that any trade union member appointed to any position of responsibility in any of these industries must first sever his connection with the union. Only then is he able [on the Labour leadership's view] to act independently, and *on behalf of the larger public interest*.

This notion of something called 'expertise' that is based on, guided by, and embodies a national interest divorced from the class position

and aspirations of individual technocrats, taps a deep strand in
Labourism, as we shall see. Yet there is a certain naivety in this belief
of many Labour Ministers that on taking public office business men
shed their identity, and that business corporations, when carrying out
Government functions change psychologically and materially into civil
service departments with different principles and objectives. The
Labour Party in the 1930s had been quick enough to attack
Government-business interpenetration and certainly the businessmen on
whom the Labour Party depended were not of this kind. They had the
attitudes and interests of their class and of their managerial colleagues
to defend against a Government that had ostensibly radical, socially-
levelling purposes. The times were too dangerous for political
neutrality.

In the event the Labour Government did not seriously encroach
upon their class prerogatives and power. On the contrary, by
encouraging the cartelisation of industry as part of their planning
structure, and by using these men as the planning staff, the Labour
Government of 1945-51 *actually strengthened* the position of the
business community.* For the Government desperately needed sustained industrial growth to alleviate balance of payments crises and to
provide the real wealth on which extended social services could be
built. 'In Britain today', Morrison said in 1947, 'the battle for socialism
is the battle for production'.[51] But having declined any move to
workers' control and, because of the limited nature of its nationalisation
programme, having left the critical 80% of industrial production in
private hands, the Labour Government quickly found that it could
achieve growth only through the voluntary co-operation of senior
managerial personnel in private business and financial institutions.
Henceforward the Labour Government was limited by what the
business community would volunteer to do, and was obliged to respond
to the terms which this highly class-conscious sub-group specified as
the conditions of its continued co-operation. Not that this was a simple
case of business men deliberately obstructing a Government whose

---

* The Labour Government's dependence on trade associations for planning
  actually encouraged the cartelisation, amalgamation and centralisation of
  British business. In spite of all their 1930s criticism of monopoly, they
  worked after 1945 as though industrial self-government was compatible with
  Parliamentary sovereignty for an ostensibly socialist government. Yet is was
  not, as even the fate of the Development Councils showed. For here an
  initiative that would have established close relationships between the Government and individual industries was effectively blocked by the opposition of
  the very trade associations which the Labour Government's planning

'class' background they disliked. There are examples of that, especially on the nationalisation of steel, as we shall see. But capitalists operate under market constraints, and require certain social, political and economic conditions to be able to pursue their private enterprise profitably. The terms they specified (the abolition of controls, reduced taxation, wage restraint and high profit returns) were simply the necessary preconditions for the 'health' of a private economy, even a 'mixed economy' of the Labour Government type, that relies for its economic growth on the satisfaction of the profit motive.* The Labour Government grew more conservative because in meeting these conditions in its attempt to encourage private economic growth, it had to abandon aspects of its social reform programme that clashed with them. Moreover, to the extent that the Labour Government created this healthy environment for private enterprise,† it ended by strengthening the political and economic position of the very social groups that it had once promised to bring down.‡ Here was the dilemma at the heart of its politics.

For at the root of the business community's leverage over the Labour Government was that Government's need for a 'healthy' economy. The British economy after 1945 was far from that. As Morrison said in 1948, the 'capacity to produce efficiently an abundance of goods and services is the very foundation of all our plans; and that capacity, owing to past neglect, is still lagging and cannot be made good by Acts of Parliament or by votes. It can only be made good by an all-out drive to make our nation a modern scientifically-minded, vigorous industrial nation.'[52] But the Labour Government inherited in 1945 an economy that was traditionally dependent for many of its raw materials on imports from overseas, an economy that between the

---

machinery strengthened.
* Hugh Gaitskell, the Leader of the Party 1955-63, realised this. As he said in April 1951, 'there are some who disapprove of profits in principle. I do not share their view. In an economy three-quarters of which is run by private enterprise, it is foolish to ignore the function of profit as an incentive.' (Quoted in Rogow, *The Labour Government and British Industry*, p. 129).
† And it did. As Angus Maude said in 1951, 'since the war ended it has been easier to make high profits without being really efficient than probably at any period in my lifetime'. (Quoted in Foot, *The Politics of Harold Wilson*, p. 58).
‡ It did so too by the direct subsidy of private industry. Agriculture was clearly the main beneficiary of Labour Government subsidies; but the Labour Government also gave loans to the watch, film, aluminium and cotton industries - and, through the Bank of England's participation in the Finance Corporation for Industry, supplied one-third of the funds regularly lent to industry for large scale projects such as blast furnaces and petro-chemical plants.

wars had been in a seriously weakened condition, and an economy
which had now experienced the ravages of war itself. The war had taken
a heavy toll. The capital loss due to bombing and the inability to repair
or renew machinery and plant meant that, at pre-war rates, it would
take seven years to make good the damage suffered between 1939 and
1945.[53] In the course of the war, financial assets of over
£1,000,000,000 had been sold to finance the purchase of food and
armaments, and this had cut net income from foreign investments from
£175,000,000 a year in 1938 to less than £73,000,000 a year after
1940. In addition, forced borrowing by the British Government from a
number of Commonwealth countries - from India, Burma and Australia
in particular - had created £3,500,000,000 of sterling balances which
were destined to restrict the latitude in economic policy experienced
by later Governments. The war had also distorted the distribution of
the employed labour force. 'At the end of the war less than 2% of the
labour force was engaged on exports, compared with 9.5% before the
war'.[54] On the other hand, nearly one million men were still under
arms as late as 1948, presiding over the military occupation of the very
export markets whose animosity up to 1945 and destruction during the
war had cut the economy's export earnings to less than one-third of
their pre-war level. And even in the less disrupted trading conditions of
the 1930s, the economy which the Labour Government inherited had
shown deficits on its balance of payments because of its heavy
dependence on industries, coal and cotton in particular, whose
exhausted capital, low investment, poor productivity and low rate of
growth had left them even then internationally uncompetitive and
incapable of off-setting growing expenditure on imported goods. After
six years of war, and facing a revitalised American economy, the
situation was even worse. There was scarcely a major section of British
industry which could compete on open terms with the American
industrial combines that were poised to expand and to 'export the
American depression' abroad. Yet in this intensely competitive
situation, and with so many of the pre-war invisible earnings gone, the
Labour Government after 1945 had to create an export sector selling at
levels far above those of 1939 if the trade deficit was to be narrowed.
In these conditions it is little wonder that Labour Ministers grew
increasingly preoccupied, not with socialism, but with 'the export gap'.

   In other words the Labour Government inherited an economy that
was in need of structural renovation, that had a truly astronomic deficit
on its balance of trade, and that was as a result acutely short of

essential raw materials and foodstuffs. It was an economy that the Labour Government could sustain at all only by tight import and exchange controls, and only because of the substantial foreign (and particularly American) financial aid that it received. The Board of Trade estimated in 1948 that, but for Marshall Aid, 'rations of butter, sugar, cheese and bacon would have had to be cut by one-third, cotton goods would have disappeared virtually from the home market, timber shortages would have reduced the housing programme from about 200,000 new buildings a year to about 50,000, and shortages of other raw materials would have led to 1,500,000 unemployed, with the situation worsening'.[55] And with this aid came further constraints on the radicalism and freedom of manoeuvre of the Labour Government.

These foreign constraints were most visible in the field of foreign policy and hence military spending overseas. Marshall Aid was part of the United States' strategy to contain Russian communism, and the American Government looked to Britain to play its part in 'defending' the West against the supposed threat of Russian aggression. In this the Americans found a willing ally in the Labour Government's Foreign Secretary, Ernest Bevin, whose military expenditure abroad both kept labour out of productive manufacturing industry and played a substantial part in the continuing deficit on the economy's foreign payments. In 1947, for example, when the balance of payments deficit was £600,000,000, over £200,000,000 of that represented expenditure on military personnel and installations abroad.

But the dependence on foreign aid also limited the Labour Government's freedom of manoeuvre on domestic reform. The Marshall Aid programme went so far as to appoint an American overseer,* whose job it was to review in detail the internal policy of the Labour Government and to report back to an American Congress that was increasingly reluctant to maintain the aid programme. Aid continued only because the Chief of the Special Mission was able to reassure the Congressmen that the Labour Government - unlike parallel democratic governments in Czechoslovakia, Rumania and Hungary - was not on the slippery slope to communist take-over. On the contrary, as he told the Congress in an intriguing exchange in 1948, though in the early years of the Labour Government the situation had 'worsened' (by which *he* meant that social expenditure as a percentage of G.N.P. had risen!) that situation had been rectified by 1947 and was continuing to 'improve'.

* Technically, The Chief of the Special Mission of the European Co-operation Administration to the United Kingdom.

For, as he said reassuringly 'the housing programme has been quite seriously cut back. So has the health programme, and so has the programme for education'.[56] So that, in addition to the specific requirements in the Marshall Aid programme for military expenditure and trade liberalisation, the Labour Government of 1945-51 legislated on social questions only at the risk of this critical American aid.

The whole thrust of the American aid programme was to open up world markets to American exports, and the Americans' pressure for trade liberalisation and the easing of exchange controls ate away at the Labour Government's ability to control resource-use and to prevent domestic retrenchment. It was as a condition of the American Loan Agreement of 1945 that sterling convertibility was reintroduced in July 1947, when in one disastrous month the Labour Government lost gold and dollar reserves to the value of $150,000,000. Even the Americans then had to concede that sterling convertibility should be suspended - but that one month's crisis in payments had already forced the Labour Government to cut back food imports, to reduce the petrol ration by one-third, and in a special November Budget to restrain domestic consumption. And when in 1950 the countries in receipt of Marshall Aid were persuaded to liberalise trade between themselves by removing import licenses, the consequent upswing in imports drained $420,000,000 of gold from the Government's limited stock of foreign currency in nine months. Only electoral defeat in 1951 prevented the Labour Government from having to re-establish trade restrictions in the Spring of 1952.

6

The interplay of American pressure, business opposition, civil service inertia and leadership conservatism could be a powerful blockage on Labour radicalism, as the Labour Government's attempt to nationalise steel shows only too well. This was a critical issue for the Labour Government, since it marked its first major inroad into the profitable sector of private capitalism, and since it was 'broadly recognised by all sides that the monopoly, inefficiency and pre-war history arguments for nationalisation were less important (in this case) than the fact that ownership and control of the industry gave crucial power over the economy to the Government'.[57] As Dalton said in his memoirs, 'we weren't really beginning our socialist programme until we had gone past all the public utilities - such as transport and electricity - which were publicly owned in nearly every capitalist country in the world. Practical socialism in Britain', he said, 'only really began with coal and with iron and steel, two cases where there was a specially strong political argument for breaking the power of a most reactionary body of capitalists.'[58] Certainly 'the body of capitalists' agreed that this was the breaking point. They saw in steel nationalisation the move of State power into a profitable sector of private industry, from which a Labour Government could dominate shipbuilding, engineering and vehicle production. Under Conservative leadership they fought the legislation stage by stage.

The Labour Government and the wider labour movement were not solidly committed to the nationalisation of steel. Steel nationalisation, absent from Labour Party programmes in the late 1930s, had been re-introduced under pressure from the T.U.C. in 1944; but at least two of the leading trade unionists in the industry - Lincoln Evans and Harry Douglass - publicly admitted their opposition to it.[59] Within the Labour Cabinet, both Attlee and Morrison, who had worked in the Coalition Government with the industry's leading post-war spokesman as the Minister of Supply, were reluctant to see the industry nationalised, and responded easily to counter-arguments from, as Dalton put it caustically, 'some friends of ours in the City'.[60] Indeed Morrison went as far as to negotiate unofficially with the steel masters a hybrid scheme that stopped well short of nationalisation. But in the end he was defeated: in 1945 by Dalton's insistence that steel nationalisation be included in *Let Us Face The Future*, and in 1947 by Bevan's threat to resign if the 'Big Bill' did not go through.

The 'Big Bill' thereafter met sustained Conservative pressure. Its introduction was delayed by the time taken to prepare a detailed scheme by officials 'not all of whom were privately in favour of nationalising steel,'[61] as well as by Morrison's opposition. For a while the Labour Government was slowed by the Marshall Aid adminis-trator's warning that 'if the British Government asked for . . . shipments to modernise the steel industry and then announced that the industry would be nationalised, the shipments would probably be denied'.[62] In the Commons and in the Lords, the Conservatives led a stubborn resistance, and managed, in the Lords, to delay the vesting day by twelve months, and hence beyond the end of that particular Parliament. In the country the industry's massive public relations exercise against steel nationalisation became part of a much wider and even larger publicity campaign against the whole nationalisation programme - one that compared the advantages of 'free' (that is 'private') enterprise to the bureaucratic penny-pinching, resource-starved, inefficient and run-down nationalised industries. And when the Labour Government was returned in 1950 with a much reduced majority, the steel companies refused to submit 'names of experienced men who would be acceptable to their fellow industrialists for inclusion in the [Steel] Corporation'.[63] As the Minister in charge said, this was a 'political strike' - a gentlemen's agreement between firms not to co-operate with a Labour Government that had had the audacity to nationalise a profitable private sector industry.

To all this, the Labour Government responded doggedly, with compromise and repeated searches for conciliation. There was no effective Labour Government counter-propaganda to point out that the nationalised industries were run-down because they had been in private hands between the wars, and that rationing was an attempt to guarantee greater equality in the consumption of scarce resources than the free market system would allow. Rather the Labour Government went along with the industry's counter-arguments as far as was compatible with taking the industry into public ownership. Its compensation terms were generous. It did not break up the old structures of organisation. Instead the concerns taken over were allowed to keep their old identities and names. Their personnel and internal organisation were left intact. In a word, nationalisation was introduced in a manner conducive to de-nationalisation - which happened, of course, immediately on the Labour Government's defeat in 1951.

For the last years of the Labour Government were marked by increasing moderation in the policies of its leadership, and by a rapid move away from the optimism, confidence and radicalism that had marked the Party in 1945. Its leaders had been in office for ten years, and they were exhausted. They had lived through repeated financial crises, fuel shortages, long Parliamentary struggles, and growing Conservative, business and press opposition. Bevin and Cripps were soon to die. Morrison and Attlee were both sick men at critical periods. And by 1948, the legislative programme of *Let Us Face The Future* had been implemented. Faced with a critical choice of future direction, the leadership chose to 'consolidate'.

This consolidation took a number of forms. It did not prevent the Labour Party from going again to the electorate rejecting capitalism (where 'Big Businessmen, aristocratic landowners, bankers and merchants directed the life of the nation'[64]) or from talking of

71

socialism. It did not prevent the Party from committing itself, in 1950 at least, to further encroachments into profitable private industry (via the nationalisation of insurance, cement, sugar, the wholesale meat trade, the water supply and 'suitable minerals') nor from threatening a 'careful examination' of the case for the public ownership of the chemical industry. Rather, consolidation could be seen in the lack of enthusiasm of men like Morrison for this residual radicalism, and in the leadership's growing belief that the listing of further industries for nationalisation would be electorally unpopular. As one commentator reported at the time,

> even during the February 1950 campaign . . . nationalisation was almost entirely absent from Labour's electoral programme . . . The Party's 1950 election manifesto *Let Us Win Through Together* is a good case in point. Its reference to the major industries already nationalised . . . was neither substantial nor prominent. Nor was much said about the iron and steel industry, for which nationalising legislation had been enacted but not put into effect. Most of what the Party suggested for further nationalisation was buried under the heading of 'Encouragement for Enterprise' . . . What was emphasised instead of nationalisation was the Labour Party's full employment and social security policies . . . This was also the tenor of Labour's radio broadcasts during the February campaign . . . Morrison pointedly avoided drawing the line between Conservative and Labour on the issue of public ownership. 'We believe in quite different economic systems,' he said. 'We believe in full employment and the planning necessary for it. The Conservatives do not.'[65]

When Labour was returned to office in 1950 with its much reduced majority, it made no attempt to implement even the limited amount of new nationalisation that its manifesto had promised. The King's Speech mentioned only the possibility of legislation affecting water supplies, 'but for the rest, victory was implicitly conceded to the anti-nationalisers'.[66] Instead, as the Korean War began, the Labour Chancellor (Hugh Gaitskell) expanded military expenditure by the traditional Conservative method of cutting back on social services,* and in doing so drove Nye Bevan, Harold Wilson and John Freeman to resign. And in

---

* Here was history repeating itself. 'Like Philip Snowden before him, the Chancellor found it much easier to place the major share of the burden on the poor than on the rich. Snowden's economies on unemployment benefits had no relevance to the economic problem he faced; nor had Hugh Gaitskell's economies . . . on the National Health Service'. (Miliband, *Parliamentary Socialism*, p. 313).

1951, going back to the electorate with the policy statement *Labour and the New Society*, the Labour Government dropped all its specific nationalisation proposals in favour of a commitment to take into public ownership industries or firms 'which fail the nation' or which, in public hands, would better 'serve' it: firms or industries, that is, which were basic, inefficient or monopolistic. Though in principle this could have extended the public sector into virtually every industry in post-war Britain, in fact it meant that the radicalism of 1945 was gone, and the emphasis in the Party manifesto was clearly towards the use of other methods of economic control than public ownership. The Labour Government left office in 1951 exhausted, convinced that it had fundamentally transformed British capitalism, and reluctant to extend public ownership on grounds other than those of economic efficiency and supra-class, national needs.

Yet worse, the Labour Government left office in increasing difficulties with its own trade union movement. Though elected in 1945 with trade union support and massive working class backing, the Labour Government's relationship with the trade union movement had become strained over the six years. The trade union leadership had not seriously opposed the pattern of appointments to the Boards and managerial structures of the nationalised industries (they too had no interest in workers' control,[67] but they had resisted any substantial retention of wartime labour direction by the post-war Attlee administration). The Labour Government, for their part, had not hesitated to use troops in strikes that affected national production and exports; and had gone to the trade unions in 1948, as we have seen, to request wage restraint amid continuing income inequality. The trade union leadership had gone this far with a Labour Government to which they were inordinately attached. But as prices and profits boomed after devaluation and in the early stages of the Korean war, they had been no longer able to contain growing rank and file opposition. Only electoral defeat in 1951 prevented the Labour Government coming face to face with this tension within its own movement - a tension that was overshadowed between 1949 and 1951 only by the Government's growing difficulties with organised business. For by then it was clear that policy initiatives on nationalisation would meet even greater business and Conservative resistance than had occurred over steel; and for this fight the Labour Party leadership showed no stomach at all.

In the event, the Labour Party was saved the fight by defeat at the polls. In a turn-out of 84% in 1950, the Party increased its vote to nearly 13 million, but as the Conservatives did considerably better than they had in 1945, the Labour share of the poll dropped from 48.3% to 46.1% to cut the Government's majority to a bare six seats. Finding this majority unworkable, and under heavy Conservative pressure, the Labour Party went to the polls again in 1951 and was defeated. Yet paradoxically the Party lost power only because of the vagaries of the British electoral system to which it was so attached. For it received its biggest ever popular vote in that election. Nearly 14 million people gave it their support, slightly more indeed than voted for its Conservative opponent. But the Conservative vote was sufficient to win back crucial marginal seats, and the Labour Party found itself out of power for the first time in ten years. Yet with so much achieved, the Labour leadership were grateful for a breathing space, and they left office expecting to be back at the next election, after the Conservatives had demonstrated their inability to maintain full employment and the welfare state.

In fact, as one of their later leaders observed at the time, the Labour Government had merely created a system of 'welfare capitalism'[68] in which the concentration of capital and economic privilege remained, and in which the old power structure was undeniably intact. This was a system which the Conservative Party proved capable of running with ease; and in consequence the breathing space was to be far longer than any of the Labour Ministers had anticipated.

4. The Labour Party in Opposition 1951~64

Between 1951 and 1964 the Labour Party was in Opposition, denied access to that Parliamentary power which alone could give it any direct influence on the changing character of the post-war society whose foundations it had laid in its period of government. The years in Opposition were ones of bitter internal dispute within the Party, as the expectations with which its leaders had left office gave way to the trauma of prolonged Opposition. The Party leaders in 1951 expected to be returned to office on the next swing of the electoral pendulum. In fact they were defeated in three general elections in succession, and saw the Labour vote fall absolutely, and as a proportion of the total, on each occasion.* They expected the benefits of public ownership to become apparent (and hence their own period in office to be vindicated) as the years passed, only to find nationalisation increasingly unpopular even amongst sections of their own working class electorate.†
And they had expected Tory retrenchment, unemployment, and the dismantling of the welfare state to follow the Conservative victory of 1951, but instead were forced to respond to that sustained if slow economic growth, full employment and growing material affluence over which successive Conservative administrations presided.

It was against this background that power passed within the Labour Party from the generation which had led it since the 1930s to a generation of men who entered Parliament in 1945, and who had learned their socialism not under and in reaction to MacDonald but under Attlee. The internal politics of Labour in the years of Opposition are dominated by their struggle for the succession, by their prolonged

---

* In 1955 the Labour vote was 1.5 million less than in 1951, at 12,404,970; and it fell again in 1959 to 12,215,538. The percentage vote for the Party was 48.8% in 1951, 46.4% in 1955, and 43.7% in 1959.
† 'The real shift in opinion (on nationalisation) has taken place within the ranks of Labour supporters. In 1949, 60% were in favour of extending public ownership; in 1960, 58% are opposed'. (M. Abrams and R. Rose, *Must Labour Lose?* Harmondsworth, Penguin, 1960, p. 37).

dispute on the causes of Labour failure, and by their attempt to shape
the policies to which the new Labour leadership would be committed
and on which it might return to power. Because the old leadership was
standing down the disputes were complicated by the interplay of
personal ambition. Because the Party was in Opposition the issues on
which they fought were invariably not of their making, and come down
to us now as a bewildering array of unconnected battles. And because
the Party was not in power the disputes were invariably resolved in
paper compromises whose ambiguities made them acceptable to all
sections of the Party only at the cost of obscuring the long-term drift of
policy that they collectively constituted. Yet there was a drift and it
was a fundamental one. For between 1951 and 1964, amid all the
struggles for power, the faction fighting, the personal abuse and the
temporary compromises, the Labour Party moved away from the class
perspectives and socialist rhetoric which had buttressed the aspirations
of the inter-war generation, and downgraded in importance the policy
initiatives through which in 1945 the Labour Party had attempted to
realise its inter-war potential and promise. This retreat from the Party's
inter-war desire to create the 'Socialist Commonwealth' had already
been evident before the Labour Party lost office in 1951, and it neared
completion as the Party again took office in 1964.

The internal policy disputes of the 1950s moved through a number
of quite distinct stages. Between 1951 and the Labour Party's first
electoral defeat in 1955, those who favoured a return to the radical
platform of 1945 were systematically defeated in their attempt to
break the Party's foreign policy commitment to N.A.T.O. and the
American alliance, but on questions of domestic reform they were able
to force concessions from a Party leadership which, in the main,
favoured a continuation of the policy of consolidation on which the
Labour Government had latterly settled.* So both Morrison and Dalton,
leading advocates of consolidation, lost their seats on the National
Executive at the Morecambe conference in 1952, as the party activists
in the constituencies gave their support instead to the Bevanites Wilson

---

* That battle had gone on from 1949 onwards, and consumed vast amounts of
time and energy. Bevan's biographer, Michael Foot, reports a tired Bevan
saying, after an afternoon's long struggle with Morrison at the N.E.C.; 'It is a
form of torture unknown to the ancients . . . to be compelled on the last
Wednesday of every month to convert the leaders of the Labour Party afresh
to the most elementary principles of the Party; to be compelled to fight every
inch of the way to recapture territory occupied by Beveridge'. (M. Foot,
Aneurin Bevan, Volume 2 1945-1960, London, Davis-Poynter, 1973, p. 262).

and Crossman.* This same Party conference also rejected Morrison's 1951 strategy, of replacing specific commitments on nationalisation by general criteria for public ownership. Instead, it called upon the National Executive 'to draw up a list of the key and major industries to be taken into public ownership during the five year programme', inspite of speeches against such a move by Shinwell, Morrison, Gaitskell and George Brown. The resulting N.E.C. document, *Challenge to Britain*, reflected both this resurgence of rank and file militancy and the unease of the bulk of the Party's Parliamentary leadership. For though it still proposed to leave the vast majority of industry in private hands, it at least committed the Labour Party to the renationalisation of iron and steel, and of road haulage (both of which had been largely returned to private ownership by the Conservatives), to the nationalisation of water and sugar, and, for the first time, to taking particular sections of the engineering industry into public ownership. The definition of the engineering industry used in *Challenge to Britain* was a wide one, taking in vehicles, machine tools, aircraft, shipbuilding, farm tractors and agricultural machinery. Referring to the machine tool section of the industry in particular, the Labour Party document promised that the next Labour Government would 'acquire in the public interest a number of the key . . . firms'; and in the aircraft industry, would nationalise any firm 'which falls down on its job'.† Nor was this quite the high spot of left-wing influence. A year later, at the Party conference in 1954, the Labour Party leadership only narrowly avoided defeat on the question of German rearmament, which they supported within the general context of their support for N.A.T.O., but which the Labour Left opposed as part of their search (which had begun as long ago as 1947) for a 'third way' between their leadership's pro-American foreign policy and the Communist Party's slavish loyalty to the current Moscow line.

But thereafter the tide turned against the Left. The Party's election manifesto of 1955, *Forward with Labour*, carried the Party forward only to the renationalisation of steel and road haulage, and to the

---

* The 'left wing' of the Labour Party in the early 1950s were led by Nye Bevan. For the policy and defects of the Bevanites, see chapter 7, pp. 190-7.
† Even here, of course, the ambiguities remained; for the same Labour Party conference rejected - by substantial majorities - amendments which would have committed the next Labour Government to the outright nationalisation of machine tools, mining machinery, aircraft, electrical equipment, shipbuilding, radio manufacture, textile machinery, motor vehicles and armaments. So the 'shopping list' of industries was back, but the *hard, specific* and *definite* commitments were still missing.

nationalisation of 'sections of the chemical and machine tool industry'. Machine tools apart, no other section of the engineering industry was threatened with nationalisation, and 'a whole series of proposals that had been included in official Party programmes since the war had been dropped . . . of land nationalisation (that had been in the programme in 1945), of sugar (1949), of meat wholesaling and fruit wholesaling (1949), of cement (1949) and of industrial insurance (1949). By 1955 the Party was yet again committed to a moderate programme and the flood-gates that 1953 could have opened remained firmly closed.'[1]

Moreover in the wake of the general election in 1955 Hugh Gaitskell defeated both the left-wing Bevan and the 'consolidationist' Morrison for the Party leadership, and soon made clear his own affinity for a body of theory and a set of policies (known collectively as 'revisionism') which marked a sharp break with the preceding generation's commitment to capitalist transformation via nationalisation, democratic state planning and welfare provision. In the 'rethink' which the new leadership initiated after 1955, and which produced a series of major policy documents on which the Labour Party fought the next election, the new ideas (and the young, middle class Parliamentarians around Gaitskell who formulated them) predominated; and the Party went to the country in 1959 on a domestic platform heavily influenced by revisionist ideas. This included an almost total break with public ownership as a policy-tool of the next Labour Government, so that by 1959 the Labour Party leadership, beyond its long-standing commitment to renationalise steel and road haulage, promised to use public ownership only 'where an industry is shown, after thorough inquiry, to be failing the nation'.[2] In its election manifesto that year, the Party leadership mentioned socialism just three times - in each case in the fourth paragraph from the end of a document otherwise notable for its reluctance to indulge in even the rhetoric, let alone the policies, of the Party's 'socialist' past. The word 'capitalism' was not mentioned at all, having vanished from Labour Party documents in the early 1950s; and this departure from the practice of the Party till as late as 1953 was significant and fundamental.

Yet for all its moderation, the Labour Party lost the 1959 election heavily, and faced with its third electoral defeat in a row, turned again to internal dissension. Within two months of the defeat, Gaitskell made his famous attack on Clause 4 of the 1918 constitution.* The thrust

---

* Clause 4 of the 1918 constitution committed the Party 'to secure for the workers by hand or by brain the full fruits of their industry and the most

of his attack was fully in accord with revisionist thinking; that Clause 4 as it stood was incompatible with the Labour Party's preference for a mixed economy, and was a barrier to power, being electorally unpopular with the 'new social groups' to which the Party leadership was attempting to appeal. In this frontal assault on Labour's past however, Gaitskell was defeated by the residual loyalty of trade union and constituency activists to the rhetoric of Labourism; and when also defeated in 1960 by the advocates of unilateral disarmament, the tempo of the revisionist onslaught eased. *Signposts for the Sixties*, which the Labour Party issued in 1961, though still reflecting revisionist preoccupations, was more critical of private industry than had been *Industry and Society*, the revisionist-dominated Party document of four years before. Yet revisionist ideas were everywhere dominant in the Parliamentary Party by 1962; and though Gaitskell's death brought to power a leader with a more radical reputation and a leadership team drawn from both sides of the disputes of the early 1950s, even so the Party went to the 1964 election behind a leadership which had effectively abandoned the search for the 'Socialist Commonwealth' that had inspired its predecessors in the generation before. This retreat from the Party's radical and 'socialist' past would come fully into the open after 1964, but the 'victory of revisionism' in the years of Opposition was a critical stage along the way.

2

For the 1950s saw the rise to power and influence within the Labour Party of ideas and men that were anathema to the Party's own left wing. Left wing hostility initially focused on leading members of the Attlee administration - on Shinwell, Morrison and Gaitskell in particular - who systematically opposed the pressure after 1951 for a list of industries to be taken into public ownership. Out of their experience of office, these ex-Ministers were reluctant to embark again on the major confrontation with organised business and finance that the left wing 'list' of nationalisation candidates would inevitably involve, and demanded instead time to strengthen the existing public sector. Attitudes among 'consolidationists' and 'revisionists' to public

---

equitable distribution thereof that may be possible, upon the basis of the common ownership of the means of production, distribution, and exchange, and the best obtainable system of popular administration and control of each industry or service'.

ownership clearly differed. Revisionists like Gaitskell were increasingly convinced that the size of the public sector need not be (and for electoral reasons should not be) much expanded. Morrison's attitude, on the other hand, reflected the views of an earlier generation, that socialism and public ownership were inherently intertwined, and that the Party would therefore continue with it 'until we have got the nationalisation of all the means of production, distribution and exchange'. But that for the moment, as Shinwell told the 1952 conference, 'in view of our achievements in the sphere of nationalisation ... it is desirable that we should bring these schemes to full fruition before we proceed to embark on a great many others'.[3]

Yet such a strategy made sense so long - and only so long - as its parallel assumptions held: that the Conservatives in office would dismantle the achievements of the Attlee years, would return the country to the unemployment of the 1930s, and, amid increasing material deprivation, would return the Labour Party to power to repeat the performance of 1945. These expectations were widespread on all sides of the Party immediately after 1951. Nye Bevan and Bessie Braddock both told the 1952 conference that 'there will be mass unemployment while a Tory Government is in power, since that is part of the capitalist system that the Tory Party stands for'.[4] But the electoral defeat of 1955 totally discredited this whole strategy; and in reaction the Labour Party, as James Griffiths put it that year, 'went back to the classroom' to assess their policies, their image and their electoral performance. It was here, in the policy documents taken back to conference by the N.E.C. between 1956 and 1958, that the revisionist presence began to make itself felt.

Revisionism as a body of theory was most closely associated with the writings of Crosland and Strachey, and those of Jay, Jenkins, and Gaitskell himself.[5] The thrust of their thesis was that we no longer lived in a capitalist society, and that in consequence policies designed to transform capitalism were no longer appropriate for a Party of the Left. Rather, the ideas of 1918 had been rendered redundant by their successful implementation after 1945, and by the post-war prosperity of Keynesian Britain. Instead, revisionists drew attention to the apparent ability of democratically elected Governments, using Keynesian techniques of budgetary policy, to avoid the social and economic consequences of what in the 1930s had appeared as the inherent and unavoidable instabilities of capitalism. The worse excesses of an unregulated market economy could, it seemed, be removed without a total transformation of the property rights of society. The revisionists pointed also to structural changes within the private sector, and in particular to the 'managerial revolution' that had separated industrial ownership from industrial control, and given private industrial power to a new group of professional business managers, whose salaries and life-styles were not directly connected to the level of profit-return, and for whom, in consequence, the pursuit of corporate profits was now tempered by the more socially responsible corporate goals of company growth and stability, prestige and public reputation.[6] And in the wake of the 1959 election - with its evidence of continuing Labour Party unpopularity - the revisionists drew attention to the changing social structure and rising material affluence of the labour force of this post-capitalist society of abundance; whose industrial power left them less dependent on political parties for the provision of basic material requirements, and whose political sympathies could no longer be cemented by appeals, programmes and policies geared to a pre-war, deprived, class-polarised society that was no longer in evidence.

The consequences of this theorising for the role of the Labour Party - for its policies and for its electoral appeal - were enormous. The revisionists called into question the relevance of public ownership as a mechanism (and certainly as *the* mechanism) of socialist change in a world of professional managers of proven social responsibility, by clearly asserting that nationalisation was at best a *means*, and normally an inappropriate means, of achieving a socialist society that was defined by reference to social changes and *ends* other than public ownership itself. Crosland in particular suggested that further nationalisation should come only where large amounts of risk capital were at stake, or where private and social costs diverged, and should take the form less of State monopolies and more of public corporations competing with private ones, less of taking over existing firms and more of creating new ones. Indeed, precisely because of the separation of ownership and control in the private sector, the revisionists tended to see the taking of companies into public ownership as important - not as a central mechanism of economic control, as had their predecessors in the Party - but as a mechanism for ending the *social privilege* that property-ownership transmitted between generations of private share-holding *rentiers*; and as such, less immediately important or effective than other policies to end social privilege, like taxes on capital gains and on inherited wealth.

Instead the revisionists argued for alternative forms of State *control* over business activity: controls, moreover, which would avoid the bureaucratic inertia of the Attlee Government's direct physical controls by harnessing the private incentives of the socially responsible managerial cadres to a State 'Plan'. That is, the revisionists, in arguing for a planned but mixed economy, were suggesting (in contradiction to the fundamental beliefs of the 'socialist generation' within the Party) that it was safe, necessary and indeed inevitable that a future Labour Government should rely on 'the price mechanism . . . [as] a reasonably satisfactory method of distributing the great bulk of consumer goods and industrial capital-goods, given the total amount of resources available for consumption and industrial investment'.[7] The role of the State, in such a situation, was indeed to plan, but to do so by using budgetary controls, investment incentives, and industrial location policy in order to stimulate expansion in the economy and to help the balance of payments.* Planning of this kind was thought crucial both to alleviate possible discrepancies between private and social costs, and to generate that increased Gross National Product which alone could provide the surplus for heavy social expenditure.† The message that the revisionists pressed upon the Party's economic policy was that *it needed to come to terms with, and to operate within, the imperatives of the very market economy which in the 1930s the Party had promised to abolish*. Since for Crosland, what the Labour Party had proposed in the 1930s would now - in the changed conditions of the 1950s - be an unacceptable form of paternalism in a situation in which capitalist irrationality in production and consumption had been solved by the growth of working class industrial power. As he put it,

> Production for use and production for profit may be taken as broadly coinciding now that working class purchasing power is so high. What is profitable is what the consumer finds useful, and the firm and the consumer desire broadly the same allocation of

---

* Not that all physical controls were necessarily to be abandoned. High investment 'might well require special incentives to industrialists to invest, and the use of controls - for example, on building, on imports, on credits, and possibly on international capital transactions - to ensure that expansion did not precipitate inflation or a balance of payments crisis'. M. Shanks 'Labour Philosophy and the current position' *Political Quarterly*, vol. 31(3) July-Sept. 1960, p. 252.

† As Shanks put it, 'the easing of poverty, the expansion of welfare services (including housing, education, and superannuation) and the general raising of living standards can only be achieved on the basis of a steady expansion in the rate of industrial production'. *Ibid.*

resources. And while paternalists may dislike this allocation, wishing that less were spent on drink and pools and television sets, they must swallow their dislike in the interests of personal freedom.[8]

In consequence, the revisionists shifted the emphasis of Labour Party reforms away from the problems of production and ownership, which had apparently solved themselves, towards those of consumption and distribution, where inequalities transmitted down the generations still awaited socialist change.* In the process they offered a definition of socialism that no longer turned on the common ownership of the means of production, distribution and exchange, and no longer operated on a class or collective level, but which was embodied in a series of *individual* goals, values and end-states, in which 'equality', 'fellowship' and 'personal freedom' figured prominently. It was on reform in these areas that the revisionists urged the Labour Party to act: 'the attack was to be on privilege in a social rather than an economic sense',[9] to end inherited privilege within an inadequate education system, to end the residual material deprivation of the old, to tax the returns to share-holders and property owners on their inherited wealth, and to create a richer and more equal physical and cultural environment. That is, the revisionists replaced public ownership as the first priority of a Labour Government with the achievement of material affluence and equality, by 'the bolstering all along the course, of those who may fall behind'[10] in a programme of heavy social expenditure on education, housing, health, social security and leisure within the context of a rapidly growing, high-investment economy. Or, as it would be put after J. K. Galbraith published his influential study *The Affluent Society*, the role of the Labour Party was to right the balance between private

---

* So Crosland could write a chapter headed 'How much do economics matter?', and say: 'The programme for economic growth . . . should increasingly be overshadowed by the social policies . . . and we should not now judge a Labour Government's performance primarily by its record in the economic field. This may require a mental adjustment in many quarters on the Left. Traditionally, or at least since Marx, socialist thought has been dominated by the economic problems posed by capitalism . . . But . . . capitalism has been reformed almost out of recognition. Despite occasional minor recessions and balance of pay-ments crises, full employment and at least a tolerable degree of stability are likely to be maintained. Automation can be expected steadily to solve any remaining problems of under-production. Looking ahead, our present rate of growth will give us a national output three times as high as now in fifty years . . . The pre-war reasons for a largely economic orientation are therefore steadily losing their relevance; and we can increasingly divert our energies into more fruitful and idealistic channels and to fulfilling earlier and more fundamental socialist aspirations.' (A. Crosland, *The Future of Socialism*, London, Cape, 1956, p. 517).

affluence and public squalor. The issue for socialists in the 1960s, on the revisionists' arguments, was not one of ownership and control so much as the balance between public and private spending.*

Given their later political record, it is worth stressing that no one in the 1950s could deny the sensitivity of the revisionist theorists to the continuing problems of poverty and social deprivation; and in this they were fully in the Labour tradition. Where they differed from their predecessors of the 1930s was in their faith that poverty and deprivation were no longer endemic to the system. Rather, 'the existence of widespread poverty, the deterioration in standards of medical care, regional and social class inequalities in educational provision, the spread of the slums, racial and class inequalities in the administration of the legal system - all these and more came to be defined as "isolated" social problems, unconnected with the whole structure of society'[11] and, as such, open to amelioration and resolution by discrete acts of social legislation. According to revisionist theory, it was no longer necessary to totally transform society. Rather, the Labour Party had a more limited task, of completing the social transformation that was already well under way as capitalism *replaced itself* with a post-capitalist society.

Moreover, in the wake of the 1959 electoral debacle, the revisionists urged the Labour Party to alter its image to fit the changing social and material reality which economic growth and affluence were supposedly bringing, and to connect the Party's aspiration for political power with the private ambitions of an increasingly affluent and 'middle class' electorate. They relied on the studies of voting behaviour and political sociology to show that the old manual working class was a dwindling section of the labour force, that affluence was in any case mellowing the class dimensions of political and social attitudes, and that the electoral fortunes of the Labour Party turned on its ability to woo the new and rapidly growing white collar, scientific and technical classes who were the key workers in this post-capitalist, scientifically based industrial system.† And so they urged the Labour Party leadership to

---

* 'Much the most important priority is for social expenditure as a whole - capital expenditure even more than current. A Labour Government should commit itself to a definite increase in the proportion of national resources devoted to social welfare'. (*Ibid*, p. 519).

† The most immediately influential study appears to have been Abrams and Rose, *Must Labour Lose?*, which was a write-up of a *Socialist Commentary* opinion survey. Its findings were succintly put: 'Why is the tide of opinion set against Labour at the present time? The survey suggests three main reasons. The first is that Labour is thought of predominantly as a class party, and that

appeal to these groups directly, particularly by using the new mechanisms of mass communication; and to reduce the influence of the heavily
bureaucratised extra-Parliamentary power centres within the Labour
movement (the trades unions in the Party conference, and the constituency parties) whose vestigial loyalty to the rhetoric and aspirations
of an earlier generation of Labour Party activists was making this
'modernisation' of the Labour Party programme and image so much
more difficult. In the process, revisionist theory challenged the rhetoric
and the policies of the Attlee generation within the Party, by re-
defining socialist policies as a set of discrete liberal social reforms
that involved no systematic attempt to transform the structure in total,
and by turning the Labour Party from a party of the working class into
a *people's party* with non-class appeal and responsibilities. The consequence of revisionism within the Labour Party in the 1950s was a
'flight from class'.*

Yet even so it is not surprising that revisionist ideas and personnel
had such an impact on the Party in the 1950s, for there was much in
Labour's previous theory and practice to lend support to the revisionists' claim that they were merely restating old Labour ideals in a new
context. By arguing for a mixed economy, and for a close and co-
operative relationship with sets of socially responsible business
managers, they were echoing the old Labour view of the politically
neutral expert and stressing as a desirable end-state what had long been
the practice of Labour in power. By stressing that 'the cake must grow
larger before it can be shared' they reflected the Labour Government's
own desperate search in 1929 and after 1945 for the conditions in
which private economic growth could be achieved, and Labour's

the class which it represents is - objectively and subjectively - on the wane . . .
The second reason for Labour's unpopularity is its identification with
nationalisation . . . The third factor telling against Labour is the impression of
weak, divided leadership' (p. 100). Earlier in the same study, Mark Abrams
wrote, 'the finding which is perhaps the most striking [is] the almost complete
failure of the Labour Party to attract the interest and sympathy of young
middle-class people' (p. 48).
* 'The old image of cloth cap socialism was held to be incompatible with the
requirements of winning power in an affluent society. The old working class
base of socialism was seen increasingly as an electoral encumbrance, unless it
could be supplemented by successful incursions into the middle class. Thus
Anthony Crosland, in 1960 . . . spoke of changes in the labour force that took
the form of "a continuing move away from a proletariat, towards a salariat",
and went on to warn that, even amongst those still in working class occupations, many had already acquired "a middle class income . . . and sometimes
a middle class psychology".' (J. Gyford & S. Haseler, *Social Democracy:
Beyond Revisionism*, Fabian Research Series 292, March 1971, pp. 15–16).

repeated experience of the need to subordinate social policy to private economic imperatives. By downgrading public ownership and the use of direct physical controls, the revisionists were only drawing the lesson of the last years of the Attlee administration. And in their social radicalism - on welfare, taxation and education - they were again tapping the pre-war view of capitalism as a system of structurally induced income inequalities which a reforming government could alleviate. Moreover, their specific proposals here, on comprehensive education and capital gains tax in particular, had long been regarded 'as the mark of the Left'.[12]

For these reasons, revisionist arguments were more easily accepted than might otherwise have been expected by a Parliamentary leadership whose early expectations of Opposition had not materialised, and whose experience of junior office under Attlee had accustomed them both to the limits of Labour Party radicalism and to the possibilities that co-operation with private industrial and financial hierarchies opened up to a 'modernising', growth-oriented Government. The 'victory' of revisionist ideas in the Labour Party of the 1950s reflected not just the inadequacies of the Labour Left's alternatives (to which we will come in chapter 7). It also was a product of the extent to which such revisionist arguments tapped the lessons that the new Party leadership, and particularly Gaitskell himself, had learned from six years in power and, by 1959, from a further eight in frustrating Opposition. The limits of the possible when in power, and the fear of the electorate when in Opposition, combined to open the Parliamentary leadership of the Party to the arguments of the revisionists in the years that followed the first electoral defeat in 1951.

3

This adoption of revisionist ideas was accompanied by a changing relationship within the Labour Party, between the Parliamentary Party and its leadership on the one side, and the Party conference on the other. As we saw, the generation of Party leaders that followed MacDonald had seen conference formally restate its predominance on questions of policy in the early 1930s; and they had been expected to consult with the extra-Parliamentary party before taking office. In the event, both in 1940 and in 1945, the question of entering and leaving the wartime coalition coincided, by chance, with Labour Party conferences, and so Attlee was able to fulfill the letter of the 1932 resolution by seeking N.E.C. approval for the course of action he proposed. Yet thereafter, the Parliamentary leader, when in office, appointed and dismissed Ministers, determined legislation, and dissolved Parliament with as much autonomy as had MacDonald before him. The possible tension between Parliamentary autonomy and conference control which this again suggested was masked, for the Attlee generation, only by the basic consensus on policy which both the Parliamentary and extra-Parliamentary sections of the Party shared, and by the care and preparation which the Attlee Government took in office to avoid defeat at the annual conference. It was masked too by the genuine commitment of that generation of Labour Party leaders to conference sovereignty; and they took conference seriously precisely because - as Attlee said of a particular vote in 1954 - to be defeated there 'would tie the Parliamentary Party's hands'. Even in Opposition in the early 1950s, conference and the Parliamentary leadership were in accord, because conference was still dominated by the bloc votes of three unions still solidly under the control of right-wing, pro-Attlee trade union leaders. Only as these men were replaced after 1956, and as the Labour Party went into its third consecutive electoral defeat in 1959, did the leadership of the Parliamentary Party and the votes of conference begin to diverge.

The two first clashed on Gaitskell's proposal, announced to the Party conference in December 1959, to seek an amendment to Clause 4 of the 1918 constitution. It was clear by early 1960 that the votes of the big trade unions could not be delivered, even by pro-Gaitskell trade union leaders, on such a direct challenge to the rhetoric and symbols of Labour orthodoxy, and in consequence Gaitskell was forced to settle for an N.E.C. statement which incorporated his proposed amendments 'as a valuable expression of the aims of the Labour Party in the second half of the twentieth century'. And later in the same year Gaitskell was defeated again, on the question of unilateral disarmament, by a set of trade union votes that reflected the impact of the C.N.D. campaign on the trade union conferences held in the spring and the summer of 1960. Only a dedicated and well-organised pro-Gaitskell counter-offensive by loyal trade union leaders and young right-wing Parliamentarians and constituency activists (the Campaign for Democratic Socialism) managed to reverse that vote at the Party conference in 1961, as Gaitskell lived up to his promise 'to fight and fight and fight again for the Party' he loved.[13]

These clashes between conference and the Parliamentary leadership foreshadowed the breakdown of extra-Parliamentary control under the 1964-70 Government, and marked the end of the long honeymoon between conference and the Party leadership which stretched back to 1932. It was in their wake that the revisionists began to argue strongly against both the legitimacy and desirability of extra-Parliamentary control, especially by a conference dominated by the votes of a bureaucratised trade union movement whose political views did not reflect the wider electoral trends with which the Parliamentary Party had to come to terms. In this way, the revisionists, and Gaitskell in particular, challenged the principle of conference domination which they had been happy to accept in the hey-day of right-wing control in the early 1950s, and which had been a fundamental principle of the preceding generation's politics; and here, as in the wider area of actual policy, the revisionists in Opposition began the retreat from the inter-war 'socialist' consensus in the Party which the 1964-70 Wilson Government would complete.

Paradoxically, the clashes at conference in 1960 and 1961 emphasised the dominance of the Parliamentary leadership in the Labour Party of the early 1960s. Clearly the defeats on Clause 4 and on unilateralism indicated that in Opposition at least, limits still existed on the freedom of manoeuvre of the Parliamentary Party. They also made clear, as the left-wing revival of the late 1960s was also to indicate, that the 'victory of revisionism' was a victory without deep roots within the Party, a victory achieved at elite level rather than a victory over the hearts and minds of the Party.[14] But the aftermath of those conference defeats made clear that the limits on the leadership were verbal and rhetorical only, obliging the Parliamentarians to indulge in paper compromises and verbal ambiguities, but requiring no return to a set of policies that might give Clause 4 (or unilateralism) any real significance in the Labour Party programme.

On the contrary, the revisionist leadership of Gaitskell was stronger after 1960 than before as, in the immediate wake of defeat at conference, Gaitskell received the overwhelming support of the Parliamentary Party when he was challenged, first by Wilson and then by Greenwood. Increasingly after 1956, the issues on which the Labour Party fought internally were revisionist issues. Unilateralism is the exception, not the rule, in a period in which Labour Party debates were shaped by Gaitskell's initiatives and revisionist arguments. Because the Labour Party conference did not reflect wider electoral trends, because

Gaitskell himself possessed the potential patronage of future office, and because the 'left' alternatives to revisionism made only a limited impact within the Parliamentary Labour Party, Gaitskell found after 1960 that his position at Westminster was stronger for his assault on conference domination. Because the Parliamentary Party played so large a role in shaping *actual* Party policy even in Opposition, and because the Parliamentarians alone would implement that policy if in office, he who controlled the Parliamentary Labour Party was in a position to have a predominant influence on what that policy would be. Gaitskell himself did not live to benefit from the fruits of his policy of confrontation; but he left behind a leadership of his former supporters and ex-Bevanites, men who had learnt their politics not in the Depression but under Attlee, and men whose roots in their working class electorate were either non-existent or long weakened by university education and political careers, who were able to go to the country in 1964 with a perspective and a programme far removed from that with which the Labour Party had left office in 1951.

4

The 'victory of revisionism' did not occur overnight. Rather the shift away from the theory, class categories, and specific policies of the Attlee generation was a gradual one, proceeding step by step through successive policy documents and election manifestos. Because the Party was internally divided, the process was not a uniform one. Because the Party was in Opposition - and hence nothing *real* was at stake beyond agreement on a form of words - the documents that emerged were invariably ambiguous and open to as many interpretations as there were factions. Yet with the revisionists and their ex-Bevanite allies doing most of the document drafting and occupying most of the new leadership positions, the drift away from the inter-war view of what the Labour Party had to do to create the 'socialist commonwealth' was unmistakable, and it began early.

The downgrading of public ownership as the major policy instrument of a Party seeking socialism began even before the Labour Government lost office in 1951. The 1949 policy document, *Labour Believes in Britain*, conceded that 'unless there is economic necessity, there is no reason for always socialising whole industries. For private and public enterprise to compete fairly with each other can be good for both';[15] and by 1950 the notion of nationalising *firms* within a private industry was well established. It was proposed for the chemical industry in 1949, and for machine tools and aircraft in *Challenge to Britain* in 1953. That document also proposed that a Labour Government might restrict itself merely to taking 'a controlling interest' (by which presumably it meant buying shares) in existing enterprises. *Labour and the New Society* in 1950 had already presented nationalisation in the context of a wider set of *controls* which a Labour Government would use over industries it would leave in private hands: controls on investment decisions, on the location of industry, on foreign exchange, and against monopolies and restrictive practices.

These concessions to a 'mixed economy', and to a dependence on the private incentives of what in the 1930s the Party would have called the 'capitalist sector' but which was now increasingly known as 'private enterprise', 'business' or simply 'industry', was carried to far greater lengths in the Labour Party's policy document of 1957, *Industry and Society*. In the main, this was a revisionist document, whose drafting was dominated by men sympathetic to, or part of, the new Gaitskellite leadership. The document had a number of intriguing features. The first was the absence of the hitherto standard Labour Party attack on the iniquities of private enterprise. *Industry and Society*, on the contrary, subscribed explicitly to the revisionist thesis of the socially responsible managerial strata, and argued that 'under increasingly professional managements, large firms are as a whole serving the nation well. Moreover [it] recognise[d] that no organisation, public or private, can operate effectively if it is subjected to persistent and detailed interventions from above'. The Labour Party 'have therefore no intention,' the document insisted 'of intervening in the management of any firm which is doing a good job'.[16]

From this a number of crucial policy consequences followed. The first was the restriction of the role of the State to that of planning and controlling a predominantly private economy, in co-operation with these new managerial personnel, in order to affect patterns and levels of investment, to regulate large scale industrial building and to achieve a balance between exports and home consumption. This went along with a reduction in the role, and a change in the character of nationalisation. For in its initial draft, *Industry and Society* is reported to have contained, as one possible strategy for the Labour Party in the 1960s, the nationalisation of the big companies to whose economic domination its analysis drew attention; but this was blocked by the revisionist leadership. Instead, no specific nominees for nationalisation were proposed beyond the left-over business of 1945, steel and road haulage, on the quaint ground that the Labour Party suddenly did not have enough information to say which industries were in need of public ownership.[17] Perhaps surprisingly, the document was opposed by the old Labour leadership - Morrison and Shinwell - precisely because in abandoning nationalisation, it was leaving behind what Shinwell called 'the vital principle on which this Party was founded'.[18] For it even restricted the general criteria for nationalisation to that in which public ownership was proposed only for firms or industries that were 'seriously failing the nation', and made no mention of nationalisation of basic industries, monopolies, or of industries with high investment needs. In all this, it was a retreat even from Morrisonian 'consolidation'. Instead, in the very document in which the Labour Party recognised that 'shareholders no longer exercise even indirect control over company managements',[19] *Industry and Society* proposed that socialism under the next Labour Government would be enhanced by the State joining this band of redundant *rentiers*. It suggested that a gradual extension of public ownership could occur by the creation of a public corporation (which would be in effect a large investment trust, 'not so different in . . . operation from the insurance companies or some other financial institutions')[20] that would buy shares for the State in existing private companies; and that death duties should also be paid in shares and land rather than in cash. Yet the document was explicit that, in this latter case at least, this share-buying was *not* to be accompanied by any extension of State *control* into firms so purchased.[21] Its purpose was rather to enable the State to benefit from the surplus generated by this private economic activity, and to reduce the impact of shareholding on the long term inequality of income distribution. In all these ways, *Industry and Society* marked a sharp break with the inter-war generation's commitment to social transformation via public ownership, and a critical stage in the Labour Party leadership's accommodation to the requirements and class structure of a private capitalist economy.* And this at least, Shinwell, speaking for that inter-war generation, recognised. As he told the 1957 conference that adopted *Industry and Society*,

---

* Haseler, in his pro-revisionist account of the Party in the 1950s, saw this as a major revisionist success. As he put it, 'a further success was the acceptance by an erstwhile suspicious Party of the need to work within the capitalist system and thereby accept the permanence of the mixed economy. Share-buying and profit-making by the state had previously been alien to many socialists and its acceptance in 1957 was a measure of the influence of revisionist thinkers on official policy.' (S. Haseler, *The Gaitskellites*, London, Macmillan, 1969, p. 106).

We either take it this way, the capitalist way - for, after all, it is the capitalist way, not likely to be seriously objected to by the Tories - after all, to invest in private undertakings, bolstering up shares, becoming shareholders and investors, all the capitalist bag of tricks will not alarm them unduly. I say it is either that way or to stand firmly by our fundamental principles.[22]

That the 'fundamental principles' were no longer so firm is even clearer in *Industry and Society*'s companion policy document of 1958, *Plan for Progress*. This N.E.C. policy document, which emerged from a study group chaired by Harold Wilson, did not even make the verbal concessions to socialism which had characterised *Industry and Society*. It was a plan for a non-socialist future in line with the 'modernisation vision' on which Wilson led the Labour Party into power in 1964. The problem of British industry was located, not in the system of private ownership and control, but in stagnation, low growth and the dissi-pation of the enormous potential for investment that lay in the 'new industries' of science and technology - 'automation, electronics, atomic energy and plastics'. The cause lay in Conservative policies themselves, of retrenchment followed by short boom without rhythm or plan. 'The British economy under a Tory Government', *Plan for Progress* said, in terms Wilson was later to make famous, 'is like a car driven only on the accelerator and the brake - but without a steering wheel'. The solution was planned expansion, on the basis of higher investment: to strengthen our international position, to provide full employment, and to provide the surplus on which social services could expand. And that solution could come only under a Labour Government, using broad planning controls, in 'a partnership between the State and both sides of industry'.

So by 1958 the Labour Party was committed to a conscious search for a collaborative alliance between the trade unions and business, to create the conditions under which sustained economic growth could permit expanded social services and higher living standards. Here, even *before* the fight over Clause 4, the Labour Party's pre-war aspiration to radically transform a system of private ownership had given way to a conscious commitment by the Party leadership to an alliance between the State and a private sector to create a high-investment, high-output economy in which social expenditure could then also expand. And the priorities were clear: 'the first task of the next Labour Government,' *Plan for Progress* said, 'is to raise and then maintain the level of invest-ment in industry'. So too was the role of the Labour Government: to lay down broad investment criteria, and in close co-operation with 'the few hundred dominant firms . . . in the private sector' to draw up a National Plan within which future investment priorities could be publicly determined and implemented. So too was the relationship of the next Labour Government to the world of international finance. 'The strength of the pound', it was made clear in the document, 'will be the first priority of our external economic policy'. To bolster this shibboleth the Labour Party insisted that building up exports was the prerequisite of continuing home expansion, and industrial efficiency the condition of export competitiveness.[23] Only within these priorities of investment, sterling and exports were social services to expand. By 1958 the scenario for 1964 was already established.

It was for this reason that the defeat of Hugh Gaitskell's attempt to amend Clause 4 of the 1918 Constitution - which committed the Labour Party to strive for the common ownership of the means of production, distribution and exchange - was a shadow fight without any real significance for the pattern of economic and social policy to which the Labour Party leadership were by then committed. Even in defeat, Gaitskell's *Amplification of Labour Party Aims* entailed the acceptance as permanent of the mixed economy, in that Aim 'j' (which recognised 'that both public and private enterprise have a place in the economy'[24]) ran directly counter to Clause 4's commitment to the eventual abolition of private enterprise in total. The Labour Left, in defeating Gaitskell on this, won the form of victory without its substance, and the limits of their success were clear in *Signposts for the Sixties*, the policy document on which the Labour Party went towards the 1964 election. Here all the revisionist arguments were consolidated, in a rhetoric only made slightly more critical of private enterprise by the repeated stagnation of the economy under Macmillan and by Galbraith's newly introduced liberal attack on private affluence and public squalor.

Signposts was a compromise document like all before it, and in its reference to 'a small and compact oligarchy' at the top of private industry, and to 'the capitalist begging bowl', it made the statutory verbal genuflections to the Labour Left. But in the detailed analysis it offered, and the strategy it rejected, it marked no fundamental change from *Industry and Society* and *Plan for Progress*. As in those documents, the Labour Party recognised that industrial power was increasingly concentrated; and as before, declined to make what might have appeared the logical policy recommendation - of public ownership -

that the Labour Left, and the whole Labour tradition, offered as the appropriate socialist response. Instead, it promised that the next Labour Government would 'control the commanding heights' of this private economy, a phrase which, as Peter Sedgwick later observed, 'typifies, in its pregnant vacuity, its slippery indefiniteness, and its trance-like Utopian quality, the entire bent of Labour policy-language in the present epoch'.[25]

For little had changed between 1958 and 1961. The critique of British industry that *Signposts* offered was that of *Plan for Progress*, namely that the British economy was falling behind, as it consistently failed to invest a sufficient percentage of its surplus in new plant and machinery. The explanation remained unchanged with but one amendment. British investment was low because of Conservative policies of unplanned expansion and retrenchment - as in 1958; but now, also because of the existence of social privilege at the top of private managerial hierarchies. Here, the Labour Party by 1961 was blending its critique of Tory policy with the revisionist call to seek the new middle class vote; as in a famous paragraph, the document observed that

> with certain honourable exceptions, our finance and industry need a major shake up at the top. Too many directors owe their position to family, school or political connections. If the dead wood were cut out of Britain's boardrooms and replaced by the keen young executives, production engineers and scientists who are at present denied their legitimate prospects of promotion, our production and export problem would be much more managable.[26]

Beyond this, the answers Labour offered by 1961 were again those of 1958. The need was for a high-investment, export-competitive, and rapidly growing economy, and the Labour Party alone could achieve this through detailed indicative planning in a co-operative relationship with both sides of industry. The State was to enter the field of industrial investment directly, though now grants and loans to private firms were to be accompanied by State participation in management. Public ownership would still be used: for vast monopolies, like steel, or in situations of market chaos, as with transport. Though in form, in true revisionist style, public ownership was to vary enormously: from the nationalisation of a whole industry to partnership in individual private firms, and to the creation of wholly new State concerns in the 'new industries based on science'. Through these mechanisms, the Party leadership was confident that the State could again guarantee a growing

94

economy from whose surplus output the revisionist social aspirations of public affluence could be fulfilled. So within this high-growth economy, the Labour Party in 1961 promised a radical collection of revisionist social and fiscal measures: educational expansion, a capital gains tax, graduated National Insurance contributions, half-pay pensions and wage-related sickness benefits. This was the state of the Party programme on Gaitskell's death - a redefinition of Labourism as 'a national plan for which the people feel actively responsible and a taxation policy which ensures that burdens are fairly shared'.[27]

In this process, the ambiguous legacy of the Labour Party's past had been resolved in a way which removed from the next Labour Government the aspirations and world views of its predecessor. As far as can be deduced from the policy documents and public statements of Wilson, the new leader, the Parliamentary leadership in the early 1960s no longer saw society as their predecessors in the 1930s had done. Society was no longer seen as a set of potentially antagonistic classes within a social environment that was in need of qualitative change. Rather, Labour leaders of the early 1960s appear to have seen society as made up of a collection of functionally differentiated social categories (managers, technicians, scientists and workers) who shared a set of common interests in material prosperity and economic growth. Shorn of any vestigial class perspective by their response to the 1959 election defeat, in which 'class' had been defined as an anachronism by a range of revisionist theories and political scientists, the Labour leadership were left with a commitment to this 'national interest' of investment, growth and exports as the central dynamic of their policy. This gave them a view of the role of the State on which they could both criticise their political opponents and offer a Labour alternative: of a Labour Government, in the pursuit of this national interest, creating institutions of indicative planning and intervening directly in the growth sectors of industry to achieve high rates of output and a strong, export-based economy. The old radicalism still found vestigial expression, in the leadership's continuing commitment to the revisionists' attack on *social* privilege; but by the early 1960s the social expenditure which that attack would require was clearly a subsidiary priority to the achievement of economic growth itself.

The 'socialism' of the Labour Party leadership under Gaitskell and Wilson was thus largely devoid of class content, and was even lacking that strong organisational and personal connection with trade union and working class aspirations and interests which had characterised the

Attlee generation. Rather socialism had become synonymous with the achievement of a high-growth capitalist economy and with the State encouragement of private industry. It no longer involved major programmes for the redistribution of wealth and income beyond the taxing of capital gains, but placed its faith instead in the creation of even greater material abundance from which all could benefit. And it involved little criticism of, and even fewer policy proposals for changing, the existing distribution of social and economic power, but stressed rather the potential of a partnership between both sides of industry under a Labour Government to create the material abundance through which Labour's social policy could find realisation. Because it was in Opposition, the Party was free from the daily necessity of indicating where its priorities lay if economic growth and welfare, exports and social reform, should prove incompatible. But the signs were clear that Labour's *New Britain* would grow before it would redistribute, and export before it would reform. The long retreat from the inter-war generation's search for the 'socialist commonwealth' was approaching its conclusion.

5. The Labour Governments of 1964-70

The Labour Party returned to power in 1964 on the promise of a 'New Britain' and, after so long in Opposition, returned with a renewed faith in their own ability to create it. In the campaign which preceded the election, and in their manifesto, the Labour leaders' reading of the situation that they faced reflected closely the developments within the Party during the years of Opposition. In their manifesto, *The New Britain*, in contrast to earlier Party electoral appeals, the Labour leadership did not attack the Conservatives directly for their private-enterprise philosophy or for the business interests that supported them. 'but rather for their fustiness, incompetence and out of date attitudes'.[1] The 'problem' which the Party placed before the electorate was not that of capitalism against socialism, but one of 'a sluggish and fitful economy' which had fallen behind its international competitors, which was inefficient, whose management was drawn from too socially restricted a background, and which had failed to invest with sufficient vigour in the new scientific and technological industries. The 'cause' of this unhappy situation, according to the Wilson leadership, was Conservative mis-management: a series of Tory Governments whose unplanned expansions and retrenchments of the economy had 'slowed up Britain's rate of economic growth', had 'resulted in intermittent bouts of high unemployment', had led to stagnation in all regions north and west of Birmingham, and 'had led to a pervasive atmosphere of irresponsibility, to a selfish, get-rich-quick mood in which the public interest is always subordinated to private advantage'.[2] And the 'solution' which they offered, inevitably, was the election of a Labour Government 'to energise and modernise our industries'[3] and 'to make Britain up-to-date, vigorous, and capable of playing her full part in world affairs'.[4]

For the Labour Party went to the country in 1964 behind a rhetoric of 'science' and 'modernisation' that served both to unite the Party in

the wake of Gaitskell's death, and to express in a highly ambiguous
fashion the Wilson leadership's overriding priorities of economic
growth, a strong currency, and an interventionist State. Harold Wilson
himself had said as early as 1960 that 'we must harness socialism to
science, and science to socialism' - whatever that meant - and at the
1963 Labour Party conference had associated the Party directly with
the widespread application of scientific innovations and technological
change to industrial and social life. No longer was the motor of a
private economy seen by Labour leaders as a class one, in which the
pursuit of private advantage by a capitalist elite distorted social production to such an extent that it required their total replacement.
Instead the Labour leadership went to the electorate in 1964 offering a
technocratic vision of reality: of a world in which the structures of
ownership and control need not prevent the exploitation of man's
technological and scientific potential for the common good, and which
had done so hitherto only because of the absence of purposive and
persistent intervention and planning by a democratically responsive
State. In such a society, the 'New Britain', there would no longer be
that incompatibility of interests between conflicting social classes to
which Labour leaders in the 1930s had alluded in their analysis of
capitalism, but rather a common pursuit of a 'national interest' of ever
greater material production by functionally differentiated but socially
harmonious groups of scientists, technicians, managers and workers
under a 'dynamic and purposeful' Labour Government that would
control 'the commanding heights of the economy' in such a way as to
stimulate investment, efficiency and growth. This was the vision that
Harold Wilson himself had created in his speech to the Labour Party
conference in 1963, when he said: .

> If there is one theme running through this Conference this week
> . . . it is the theme of change, the over-due need for this country to
> adapt itself to different conditions . . . We are living perhaps in a
> more rapid revolution than some of us realise. The period of 15 years
> from . . . 1960 to the middle of the 1970s will embrace a period of
> technical change, particularly in industrial methods, greater than in
> the whole industrial revolution of the last 250 years . . . The
> problem is this . . . It is the choice between the blind imposition of
> technological advance, with all that means in terms of unemploy-
> ment, and the conscious, planned, purposive use of scientific
> progress to provide undreamed of living standards and the
> possibility of leisure ultimately on an unbelievable scale . . . First,

98

we must produce more scientists. Secondly, having produced them we must be a great deal more successful in keeping them in this country. Thirdly, having trained them and kept them here, we must make more intelligent use of them when they are trained than we do with those we have got. Fourthly, we must organise British industry so that it applies the results of scientific research more purposively to our national production effort . . . Let us be clear, unless we can harness science to our economic planning, we are not going to get the expansion that we need . . . we are re-stating our Socialism in terms of the scientific revolution . . . The Britain that is going to be forged in the white heat of this revolution will be no place for restrictive practices or for out-dated methods on either side of industry.[5]

To create this 'meritocracy with a social conscience' the Labour Party went to the country in 1964 offering a particular set of 'solutions' to the 'problems' its leaders had so defined. The key to Labour's own policy was economic expansion. Harold Wilson had said this time and time again, that Labour '*begins* from the need to strengthen Britain's economy, to secure a clear and purposive expansion in industrial production'.[6] 'Our vision for a New Britain', Wilson said in Swansea at the start of the 1964 campaign, 'depends on what we turn out from our factories, mines and farms; our laboratories and our drawing offices'.[7] 'There is *no solution* to our problems except on the basis of expanding output, expanding investment and rising productivity.'[8] This was accompanied by, and was seen as perfectly compatible with, the main-tenance of a strong currency. Labour leaders had made clear many times before that, as far as the Labour Party was concerned, 'the strength of sterling [was their] first and primary consideration', taking 'priority over all other considerations'.[9] And the Labour leadership believed that they could achieve both the growth and the strong pound sterling which successive Conservative administrations had failed to secure because they allotted to themselves in Government a new and significant role.

On this, their election manifesto was explicit: 'full employment, a faster rate of industrial expansion, a sensible distribution of industry throughout the country, an end to the present chaos in traffic and transport, a brake on rising prices and a solution to our balance of payments problems' could be achieved only 'by a deliberate and massive effort to modernise the economy, to change its structure and to develop with all possible speed the advanced technology and the new

99

science-based industries with which our future lies. In short, they will only be achieved by Socialist planning.' Planning, and active State intervention in the economy, were thus offered as the key to economic growth and social justice. In 1964 Labour had a plan for everything: a National Plan for the economy and economic growth, a plan for the regions, a plan for transport, a plan for tax reform, and a plan for the controlled growth, in a socially just fashion, of profits, dividends, rents, wages and salaries. It was these plans, and particularly the National Plan, which were 'to frame the broad strategy for increasing investment, expanding exports and replacing in essential imports'.[10] This was to go along with direct State intervention and incentives to specific industries to encourage extra exports, to inject modern technology, to establish new industries, to forecast future manpower needs, and to secure higher rates of labour mobility.

What was missing of course in this new Labour panacea for British capitalism was any mention of public ownership (beyond steel). 'Control' and 'guidance', under new Ministries of Technology, Economic Affairs and Overseas Development had replaced Labour's old faith in the nationalisation of specific industries or firms that 'were failing the nation'. Labour no longer faced the business community as socialists against capitalists, but as the new technocrats ('players' rather than 'gentlemen' on Wilson's favourite cricketing analogy) against the old amateurs of a fusty, Tory Britain. Socialism had been redefined as the application of technological and scientific skills in a classless reality.

So the Labour leadership could claim in 1964 that only in this way, 'by the mobilisation of resources . . . within a national plan' and 'the maintenance of a wise balance between community and individual expenditure' could the Party's social programme be achieved, of 'the ending of economic privilege, the abolition of poverty in the midst of plenty, and the creation of real equality of opportunity'.[11] For by 1964, the Labour Party's programme had shifted its emphasis slightly from the revisionist hey-day of 1959. In that election year, Labour had gone to the country preoccupied with the revisionists' attack on social privilege and with their tendency to treat as secondary the problems of growth and investment. The election manifesto that year had begun with sections on houses, jobs, schools, hospitals and old-age pensions. But the intervening years of economic recession, and of Gaitskell's replacement by Wilson, were reflected in the 1964 preoccupation with the problems of low economic growth and industrial stagnation. The accent had switched from reform to efficiency; or, as Callaghan put it to that same 1963 Party conference, 'innovate, modernise, plan, produce - that is our motto; that is what we intend to put to the people of this country'.[12]

Yet in their optimism, Labour leaders promised in *The New Britain* the social reforms that the revisionists had sought: a capital gains tax, the reorganisation of secondary education on comprehensive lines, the raising of the school leaving age, an increase in national insurance benefits, a guaranteed income for the retired and for widows, wage-related retirement, sickness and unemployment benefits, the abolition of charges within the National Health Service, and the repeal of the Rent Act. As the Manifesto put it, 'The country needs fresh and virile leadership, Labour is ready. Poised to swing its plans into instant operation. Impatient to apply the New Thinking that will end the chaos and sterility . . . restless with positive remedies for the problems the Tories have criminally neglected'.[13] It was all heady stuff!

2

In the event, the optimism of 1964 was misplaced and things did not transpire as the Labour leaders had anticipated and hoped. Indeed they entered office largely unprepared even to implement the promises they had made. The very policy ambiguities which had united a divided Party had precluded the detailed policy study that had preceded earlier Labour elections, so that whilst there were plans on 'social security, land, higher education and regional planning . . . on the central problem of the balance of payments and the modernisation of the economy only sketch plans were available'.[14] For in the 1950s, as in the 1930s, the Labour Party had spent its period in Opposition discussing the 'wrong problems, [that is] not discussing the problems which an incoming Labour Government would face'.[15] They entered office equipped to run a high-growth economy, anticipating that the barriers to growth would be technological and scientific. They in fact inherited a low-growth economy, where the barrier to growth was primarily a financial and a competitive one. Just as between the wars Labour Party thinking on underconsumption and overproduction had left them ill-equipped to handle the reverse problems that they met after 1945, so the revisionist preoccupation with social equality in a high-investment economy left the Labour Party after 1964 ill-equipped to deal with the persistent imbalance on the economy's international payments that repeatedly constrained their own freedom of manoeuvre in Government.

The Labour Governments of 1964-70

There were moments in the 1950s when Labour leaders had publicly recognised that, as Harold Wilson put it to the 1957 conference, a Labour Government would inherit 'some sort of a mess to clear up'. Significantly however, he was not sure at that point 'whether it will be a slump or a problem of inflation'.[16] For the debates within the Party in Opposition had not recognised the full significance for a Labour Government's freedom of manoeuvre of the weakening balance of payments (and the lack of competitiveness of British capitalism that it reflected) that dogged the last years of the Macmillan Government. Indeed, both of the Labour Chancellors between 1964 and 1970 (Callaghan and Jenkins) had castigated the Tories in the early 1960s for following the very policies that they themselves would later adopt. Jenkins was certain in 1961 that the next Labour Government 'should be prepared to go through a period of weak balance of payments . . . a period of losing reserves if necessary, in order to get over the hump of stepping up our rate of growth'; and Callaghan had asked 'which do the [Conservative] Government want most? Do they want stagnation here and a firm balance of payments, or do they want growth and to handle the difficulties that would arise in the balance of payments as they occur? I would choose the second'.[17] But in office he did not. He chose the first. For the Labour Party in the 1950s under-estimated the tenacity of the deep structural economic weakness that the balance of payments reflected. Those payments were just kept in surplus in the 1950s by the accident of an 'exceptionally rapid downward drift in world commodity prices',[18] and they were in persistent and growing deficit thereafter. On each expansion of the economy the deficit had grown larger in the 1950s, on each retrenchment of the economy the surplus had grown smaller; and it was the repercussions of this that the Labour Party had to face and which conditioned their politics in office. Far from 'purposive' and 'virile' leadership, the Labour Government of 1964-70 lived in perpetual crisis, swinging from policy panacea to policy panacea in a desperate search for economic growth and balance of payments surplus, and in the process both failing to fulfill the bulk of its major electoral promises and losing sufficient of its electoral support to be ejected from office in 1970.

The sequence of events will be relatively well known. The Labour Government found on its arrival in office that it faced an immediate balance of payments deficit of £800,000,000, and widespread uncertainty in the international money markets as to Labour's intentions, particularly on the question of devaluation. Labour Ministers were

offered by their civil servants a relatively restricted and almost equally
unpalatable set of policy alternatives: to devalue, and to internally
deflate; to borrow abroad on terms yet to be defined; or to impose
temporary controls on the international movement of money and goods
whilst attacking the underlying problems which had created the deficit.
The Wilson Government chose not to devalue - largely, it appears, for
reasons connected with their statements in Opposition and with their
own narrow Parliamentary majority. But clearly they were also acting
in line with sustained and heavy pressure against devaluation from the
Bank of England and from an American Government concerned with
the repercussions on an already weakened dollar of a reduction in the
international exchange rate for sterling. From this point on, the Labour
Government had therefore the added problem of convincing foreign
and domestic holders of sterling that that initial decision would continue to be maintained.[*]

In the event, the Labour Government imposed a temporary sur-
charge of 15% on imported goods, in breach of the G.A.T.T. agreement
signed by its Conservative predecessors.[†] Then, when this and the
November Budget (which promised increased pensions and the introduction of corporation tax and capital gains tax inspired a massive
movement of foreign and domestic investors out of sterling, Labour
Ministers were forced to increase the bank rate by 2%, to arrange a
substantial stand-by credit of $3,000,000,000 with the central banks,
and early in December to go to the International Monetary Fund for a
further $1,000,000,000. To stem this flow of funds, the Labour
Government had even eventually to impose a slight squeeze on bank
credits on 8 December. Within a hundred days of taking power, the
search for economic growth had run into the need for domestic
deflation to stem the outflow of funds and to correct the deficit on the
balance of international payments.

From that moment on, the possibility of a repetition of such a
'savage sterling crisis' hung over the Labour Government, and increasingly preoccupied its leading figures. As one who watched them at close
quarters, Marcia Williams, recorded, 'they moved from crisis to crisis

[*] 'Until we were in surplus it meant that every action we took had to be
considered against a background of the confidence factor, particularly
against our assessment of what the speculators might do.' (Harold Wilson, *The
Labour Government: a Personal Record*, London, Weidenfeld and Nicolson
and Michael Joseph, 1971, pp. 32-3).
[†] Import quotas, which were allowed under G.A.T.T., were rejected apparently
because of problems experienced with them in the 1940s (see *ibid*., p. 7).

and spent so much time solving the crises as they went along that their minds were totally dominated by this'.[19] As the 1965 Budget approached, the flow of funds away from sterling began again, and was only temporarily abated by the mildly deflationary nature of the Chancellor's proposals. Bank credit was restricted further in May, and more loans were arranged with the I.M.F. and with Swiss bankers. Yet wage increases continued to rise at more than the incomes policy norm, and this, with the bad trade figures of June and July, again inspired movements of funds away from sterling; and led the Labour Government to cut back on public spending (by delaying certain capital projects for six months) and to tighten hire purchase restrictions still further. By July 1965 the promise of economic growth (and of the *National Plan*) had already been surrendered to a policy of domestic deflation, two months before the Plan itself was published. As the currency crisis continued through the summer of 1965, the Labour Government 'added teeth' to its prices and incomes policy in order to ease currency speculation and to appease a major creditor, the United States Government. With this done, the Labour Government enjoyed nine months relatively free of currency movements, in which short-term debts were repaid and the gold and dollar reserves strengthened. It was not however to last.

Thereafter crisis followed crisis. In the wake of a six-and-a-half week seamen's strike in May and June 1966 and a heavy run against the pound, the Labour Government introduced a massive deflationary package which cut public expenditure, tightened building licenses, increased purchase tax, forced up unemployment, and imposed a prices and wage freeze in an attempt to reduce the pressure of demand in the home market and to strengthen the cost-position of the export industries. Yet even this - 'though it was Mr Wilson's finest hour in the upper reaches of the City'[20] - did no more than delay until the spring of 1967 further balance of payments deficits and further sterling crises. In November 1967 the Labour Government devalued from an exchange rate of \$2.80 to \$2.40. To ensure that a payments surplus would be achieved at this new parity, the Labour Government introduced a series of deflationary budgets, and immediately cut its own social expenditure heavily: taking £300,000,000 off expenditure in health, education and housing in the first financial year, and £400,000,000 in the second. This included postponing the raising of the school leaving age, the reintroduction of prescription charges, the ending of free school milk in secondary schools, and a prohibitively tight control on local government spending on educational provision for the rest of the Labour Government's period of office. And at the end, the Labour Government produced its balance of payments surplus, which it left as a useful legacy to a Tory Government voted into office on the alienation of the electorate with a Labour Party that had promised so much and yet deflated so often.

3

Now the debate goes on, and will doubtless continue to do so, about whether the Labour Government could and should have done otherwise. There is a strong body of opinion within the labour movement that suggests that the Labour Party should have devalued earlier (in October 1964 perhaps, in July 1966 certainly[21]) but it is by no means clear that this would have made any considerable difference to the Labour Government's freedom of manoeuvre. Certainly to be effective devaluation at any time required the very deflation and cut-back in social spending that we saw in January 1968, which destroyed what remained of Labour's social programme. And we have seen under the Conservative Government that followed, that the cost of devaluation at any point is a level of domestic inflation that, through its impact on trade union wage claims and industrial costs, makes its own contribution to undermining the competitiveness of the export sectors on which the whole strategy depends for success. It is possible that direct physical controls could have been used more on both the movement of goods and money, but official Whitehall opinion was solidly opposed to these, because they broke international trade agreements, invited retaliation in our export markets, made it more difficult to raise foreign bridging loans from both central banks and the international monetary agencies, and fed the uncertainty about sterling that caused so many of the money movements to begin.*

It is abundantly clear from the Labour Government's experience between 1964 and 1970 that Labour politicians had seriously overestimated the freedom of manoeuvre that they would enjoy as Ministers; and that their ability to initiate changes in domestic and foreign policy was tightly restricted by the international payments situation that they persistently faced. For because the Labour

---

* The Labour Government did use some direct controls, but these were limited and relatively insignificant. On this see S. Brittan, *Steering The Economy* (London, Secker and Warburg, 1969) pp. 197-8 and 228.

Government was so dependent on foreign loans, the institutions which linked Ministers with international financiers occupied a strategic position from which to influence policy, and possessed immediate sanctions against recalcitrant Parliamentarians. Harold Wilson has described the daily reality of these repeated financial crises in his memoirs,

> The Governor of the Bank of England became a frequent visitor . . . It was his duty . . . to represent to the Chancellor and the Prime Minister the things that were being said abroad or in the City; to indicate to the Government the issues on which, in the City's view, it was necessary to win confidence if a disastrous haemorrhage were to be averted.
>
> That is why we had to listen night after night to demands that there should be immediate cuts in Government expenditure, and particularly in those parts of Government expenditure which related to the social services. It was not long before we were being asked, almost at pistol point, to cut-back on expenditure, even to the point of stopping the road building programme, or schools which were only half constructed . . . Indeed . . . I challenged him specifically on this point . . . Was it his view, I asked him, that we should cut them off half-finished - roads left as an eyesore on the countryside, schools left without a roof, in order to satisfy foreign financial fetishism? The question was difficult for him, but he answered 'Yes' . . . And this discussion took place not against the background of a critical run on sterling, but in the period of calm, following his successful swap operations.

In fact, the leader of the Labour Party went on to record,

> Not for the first time, I said that we had now reached the situation where a newly-elected Government with a mandate from the people were being told, not so much by the Governor of the Bank of England but by international speculators, that the policies on which we had fought the election could not be implemented . . . The Governor confirmed that this was, in fact, the case.[22]

The situation was so acute at one point that the Governor of the Bank of England had only to cut short his holiday to start a run on the pound, and only to publicly criticise Government policy (as in February 1965) to create a currency crisis.[23] Few industrialists have that kind of leverage on Governments, and certainly trade unions do not. Because the Labour Government depended on these foreign loans to maintain the flow of essential imports, it had to fit its domestic policy to the terms on which the loans were granted. And even where these terms were not formally specified, the Labour Government soon learned that its every policy initiative was assessed by holders of sterling; and that, in consequence, policies that were at variance with their expectations of 'realistic' measures to correct the trade deficit would start yet another currency movement. The law of anticipated reactions is everywhere visible in Government policy in this period. And because so many of these foreign and domestic holders of sterling were big multi-national corporations, the Labour Government found both that it was necessary repeatedly to raise domestic rates of interest to attract in their cash flows, and also vital that Government policy on prices and incomes, on industrial relations and on the free movement of trade and money was congruent with the requirements of the multi-nationals themselves.

The examples of these foreign controls and pressure are numerous. The sterling crisis of November-December 1964 was sparked by foreign reaction to a budget which attempted to implement Labour Party promises on pensions, prescription charges and taxation - when, as Brittan said, foreign 'hostility reflected a more generalised resentment that, having shouted from the rooftops about the mess they inherited, the new Ministers were showing that they still put welfare benefits above economic recovery. In this syndrome free prescriptions played a role out of all proportion to their very trivial Budgetary importance. They became a symbol to financial opinion at home and abroad of Labour's alleged tendency to put Party doctrine before urgent economic needs'.[24] The Labour Government put 'teeth' into its income policy in 1965 because of heavy American pressure, at a time when American support was essential if a fresh bridging loan was to be achieved. George Brown reportedly bullied the T.U.C. into co-operation precisely on this threat of American hostility, by disclosing that 'Britain had to get new international support for the pound, that in fact negotiations with the United States were already under way and had reached a critical stage; [and that] he must be able to reassure Washington that he had the support of both sides of industry for a stronger incomes policy'. Reportedly 'the factor which swung the unions behind him was his warning that a firm . . . pledge was necessary for the Government to win the support of European bankers at a meeting to be held in Basle in a few days' time'.[25] Again, the Labour Government cut their capital building programme in higher education in July 1965, as part of a deflationary package to strengthen the pound.

It abandoned its 'planned growth of wages' for a simple wage freeze in July 1966 to the same end. And it consciously created unemployment to ease labour pressure on export costs in the same deflationary package.

These foreign constraints were particularly visible around the time of devaluation itself. In its *Letter of Intent* to the I.M.F. in November 1967, the Labour Government made clear that after its devaluation of the pound it was willing to cut back on its entire social welfare, health and education programmes to create the conditions in which growth could be achieved and I.M.F. requirements of a limit on Government borrowing be met.* The key sentences of that *Letter* ran,

> Before making purchases under this requested standby arrangement with the International Monetary Fund, the Government of the United Kingdom will consult with the Managing Director on the particular currencies to be purchased from the Fund.
>
> The Government believe that the policies here outlined are adequate to achieve the economic goals described in this letter. If, however, present policies should turn out to be inadequate, the Government is firmly determined to take such further measures as may be necessary to achieve these goals. If, in the opinion of the Government of the United Kingdom *or the Managing Director of the Fund*, the policies are not producing the desired improvement in the balance of payments, the Government . . . will consult with the Fund, during the period of the standby arrangement and as long thereafter as Fund holdings of sterling exceed 125 per cent of quota, to find appropriate solutions.[26]

There 'can be little doubt that the views of the Treasury's frequent visitors from the I.M.F. carried great weight, both with the Chancellor and with Treasury officials' and that 'the Chancellor became increasingly dominant within the Cabinet as the country's indebtedness became more severe'.[27] So when Barbara Castle told the Labour Party conference in 1969 that she would reactivate the Second Part of the Prices and Incomes Act regardless of how conference voted, the *Times* was probably quite correct to report that this was 'the price that had to

* The power of the I.M.F. is clear in Harold Wilson's memoirs. He records that, approached before devaluation, the I.M.F. Secretary General (Schweitzer) made clear that I.M.F. assistance would come only in return for 'the imposition of rigid restrictions. M. Schweitzer instanced strict credit control, a tightening of prices and incomes policy - presumably statutory - a limitation on growth, and an agreement that, while we might during the currency of the loan decide to devalue, we must pledge ourselves never to float.' (Wilson, *The Labour Government: A Personal Record*, p. 453).

be paid to help out Mr Jenkins in the negotiations which he was
currently conducting in New York with the representatives of the
I.M.F.'.[28] Equally I.M.F. pressure was one factor that apparently lay
behind the Labour Government's decision to introduce industrial
relations legislation in the face of trade union opposition;* and the
Americans reportedly suggested it as early as 1965.[29]

In fact history repeated itself closely. For just as the Attlee Government in its last years was answerable to a Marshall Aid Controller
appointed by the U.S. Congress and Administration, so the Wilson
Government had to live under the shadow of an I.M.F. mission fulfilling exactly the same function. The Labour Party in power, that is,
repeatedly discovered the truth between 1964 and 1970 of Harold
Wilson's insight when in Opposition: that 'you can get into pawn, but
don't then talk about an independent foreign policy or an independent
defence policy . . . If you borrow from some of the world's bankers
you will quickly find that you lose another kind of independence
because of the deflationary policies and the cuts in social services that
will be imposed on a Government that has got itself into that
position.'[30] And that, sadly, is exactly what happened between 1964
and 1970.

4

It became customary at various points during the Labour Government
to treat this external financial pressure as a crude class conspiracy
against Labour, as an attempt by politically motivated 'speculators'
and 'gnomes of Zurich' to bring a democratically elected Labour
Government to heel. There are shades of this conspiracy theory in
Harold Wilson's own memoirs, when currency movements in December
1968 are described as 'lunacy' and the men responsible for them as 'not
. . . rational people', 'fit only to be sent, with their gambling instincts,
for training in a betting shop'.[31] And to a degree this is probably true.
Certainly the international financial community and the national press
later proved infinitely more tolerant of payments deficits and currency
floating under a Conservative Government than they ever did under

---

* As P. Jenkins reported, 'The Chancellor's reason [for announcing the
legislation] was that he wanted to put something in the hole left by the
incomes policy. The representatives of the International Monetary Fund were
in London at the time and making difficulties about the terms on which
Britain should receive further credits'. (P. Jenkins, *The Battle of Downing
Street*, London, Charles Knight, 1970, pp. 93-4).

Labour. Yet even so this view, of tightly knit groups of money speculators dictating policy to Labour Ministers, does not locate the true
character of the international financial power structure faced by any
Labour Government. Nor does it adequately explain the basis of the
leverage that the financial community can exercise over governments of
any political persuasion, nor the motivations of the financiers who
watched the Labour Government of 1964-70 so carefully. Indeed, by
suggesting or implying that if only such men would be 'reasonable' the
'problem' would go away, this tendency to paranoia in Harold Wilson's
memoirs actually underestimates the true nature of the constraints that
any Labour Government must inevitably face.

For it is now clear that the largest single set of institutions responsible for money movements and 'speculation' are not individual
financiers but multi-national corporations moving their financial
holdings between strong and weak currencies in order to bolster their
own profit levels and to finance their own internal transactions.[32] It
was these companies, many of which are British based, which were
responsible in the words of one Labour Minister, for 'around 650 to
700 million pounds of extra foreign exchange commitments . . . in
1964 over 1963,' of which 'not much more than £100 million . . . can
be attributed to the growth of trade'.[33] It is these companies who are
the main private buyers and sellers of foreign currencies and who carry a
heavy responsibility for the movement of short-term funds that so
critically affected balance of payments surpluses and deficits throughout
the 1960s.* Their 'speculation' was and is in no sense 'irrational', given
an economy and a social order that requires the continued accumulation of private corporate profit.[34] It is in the interests of these
companies to hold their cash reserves in currencies not likely to be
devalued, and to move those holdings to money markets in which
rates of interest are high. The very weakness of sterling throughout
the 1960s just made it *too dangerous* for multi-national
corporations to long remain holders of it; and it is hard to see how they

---

* As Christopher Tugendhat reported, after surveying the multi-national
corporations, 'the companies' role in international currency crises has played
a large part in bringing them to the attention of governments and the general
public. The companies did not cause these crises . . . But the ability of
corporate treasurers to move vast sums of money across frontiers and from one
currency to another within a matter of days has enormously exacerbated the
basic difficulties.' (C. Tugendhat, *The Multinationals*, Harmondsworth, Penguin,
1973, p. 13).

could reasonably have been expected to do otherwise. Unprofitable firms do not long survive in the international capitalist jungle.*

Yet further, it would be a mistake to dismiss *all* the terms laid down by foreign banks and by international financial agencies as the ideological machinations of anti-socialist bankers. It is probably true that most if not all bankers are anti-socialist, and that leading financiers in the 1960s had little sympathy with the social reforms planned by the Labour Government. But bankers are not stupid men. The loan terms they specified were not sheer class prejudice. The terms which they laid down were precisely those which conventional economic opinion believed necessary to strengthen British capitalism, and hence to remove its long-term indebtedness. And international confidence in sterling was missing precisely because those terms embodied nothing less than a strengthening of corporate profits, a redistribution of resources out of domestic consumption and social expenditure, and an attack on the industrial power of the working class itself: terms, that is, which the radical pretensions of the Labour Party and the nature of the Party's electoral base suggested that the Labour Government would be reluctant to meet. The sensitivity of the international money markets was thus partly at least a response to the Labour Party's own rhetoric, and to the reluctance of the Wilson Government to publicly admit that it could achieve economic growth in a weak capitalist economy only by abandoning its programme of social reforms. 'Speculators' feared that the Labour Government would not be willing to create the conditions for private capitalist growth that would remove the need for devaluation. It was this weakness of British capitalism that gave the financial agencies their leverage on the Labour Government, and

---

* As Tugendhat put it, 'in financial matters, the principal fear of companies in international business is that they will lose their money owing to factors outside their control . . . they are permanently worried about changes in the value of currencies . . . Hoover estimates its losses from the devaluation of the British, Finnish and Danish currencies in 1967 at over £68m., while Firestone Tire and Rubber Company lost $6.5m. in 1967 and $4.2m. in 1966 owing to devaluations. Other companies have made profits in these and similar circumstances, but this does not diminish their fears of being caught short . . . There is nothing particularly new about any of the activities conducted by multinational companies to avoid foreign exchange losses. International traders have always tried to hedge their foreign exchange positions . . . Despite the abuse hurled at "speculators" by politicians and central bankers it is not immoral to do this. Quite the reverse; a company or individual would be foolish not to take such precautions. If by some means they were prevented from doing so the volume of international trade would be much reduced.' (Tugendhat, *The Multinationals*, pp. 164, and 167-8).

dictated the terms on which they would lend. And for a Labour Party committed to growth as a basis for its social programme, it was this economic weakness that was the Government's ultimate constraint.

For the Labour Government inherited a particularly weak economy, which had grown more slowly than its competitors even in the 1950s, and which between 1964 and 1970 was subject to trends in the wider international capitalist system from which the economy under the Conservative Governments of the 1950s had been mercifully free. These weaknesses were deep and structural ones, which no easy Parliamentary rhetoric could readily solve. In the public sector, the coal and railway industries were in a process of internal restructuring, shedding labour and cutting back on capacity in an attempt to meet fierce internal competition from other sources of fuel and transport. Parallel processes of restructuring were affecting agriculture, textiles and shipbuilding in the private sector. At the same time, in the profitable areas of the manufacturing industries, the easy market conditions of the 1950s had enabled well-organised groups of workers to establish a considerable degree of job control over items such as the level and flexibility of manning, the speed of throughput of work, overtime, piece-rates and even occasionally work discipline itself; with resulting wage drift and higher production costs.[35] The level of domestic industrial investment was lower than in the economies of foreign competitors, and indeed the low rate of manufacturing investment through the 1950s had made its own contribution to the poor balance of payments which the Labour Government would inherit. To this low investment record, Government retrenchments prompted by balance of payments crises then added - to leave the economy cumulatively weaker. It was such an economy, relatively cost-inefficient, with low rates of domestic investment and a strongly entrenched working class, that was exposed in the 1960s to a marked increase in the intensity of international competition, and which as a result saw its share of world trade dwindle rapidly and its home markets consume ever greater volumes of imported manufactured goods.* It was these trends which, by the late 1960s, had combined to produce a quite cataclysmic fall in the rate of profit return across large sections of British manufacturing industry.[36]

* Britain's share of world trade fell from 19.3% in 1953 to 16.3% in 1960 to 13.7% in 1965 and to 10.5% by 1970. Between 1958 and 1968 the volume of imported manufactured goods increased almost fourfold, so that whereas only 8% of all manufactured goods consumed were imported in 1956, by 1970 that figure was 15%.

For this economy to produce the economic growth which the Labour Party had promised, its profit margins *had* to be restored, its investment levels raised, its productivity increased, its resources concentrated in its export sector, and its working class pressure on costs eased. If it took repeated balance of payments crises to underline this fact, and foreign financiers to drive it home, even so the problem was not the creation of those financiers themselves. Certainly the difficulties of British manufacturing industry were exacerbated by the particular requirements and political leverage of the City.[37] But if the Labour Party was to run a capitalist economy better than the Tories, and this was the promise that it had made in 1964, then these were the minimum conditions that it had to fulfill. But fulfilling them had a quite traumatic effect on the implementation of other policy promises made in the halcyon days of Opposition up to 1964. Fulfilling them cost the Labour Government its social programme. It transformed the promise of national planning and control into a simple drive to strengthen the national capitalism. And it forced a Party elected on working class votes to spend the bulk of its period in office attempting to undermine the industrial power, job security and living standards of its own electorate.

5

The revisionist aspirations of the mid 1950s, that the next Labour Government should complete the transformation begun in 1945 by an attack on the bastions of *social* privilege, did not find expression in the policies of the Wilson Government, even though the leading revisionists occupied senior posts in that Government throughout. It is true that the period of office did see innovations in the fields of taxation and social welfare that had long been demanded by sections of the Party: attacks on capital gains and distributed profits, higher family allowances, increased pensions, official support for comprehensive education, the beginnings of a system of wage-related social security contributions and benefits, and increased expenditure on health care, educational provision and social security payments. But even so the distribution of wealth, income and social privilege remained firmly intact under Labour. It was left undisturbed by the appalling inertia of the responsible Labour Ministers, who proved impotent before civil servants, inland revenue staffs and private pension trusts alike. It was reinforced by the periodic cutbacks in Government expenditure which followed balance of payments crises; and it was intensified by Government-induced unemployment and domestic inflation. The promise of a new social contract that came with the Labour Government's initial moves to increase pensions and prescription charges, and raise supplementary benefits was lost in the deflationary packages of July 1965, July 1966 and January 1968; and the early hopes of egalitarian tax reform were overshadowed by the succession of ever-more deflationary budgets after 1965.

For the growth in expenditure on health, education and social security did no more than keep pace, if that, with the growing demand for social provision and the growing cost of providing even basic services. Labour Ministers used global expenditure figures to defend their policies and to create the illusion that a substantial shift was occurring in the allocation of resources between private affluence and public squalor. The reality was different.* Insufficient resources were directed into school buildings to make a reality of the Labour Government's promise of comprehensive schooling. The private sector in education was left intact. The rate of growth in educational spending, which had to increase if only to maintain even existing standards per child, was cut in the post-devaluation economies to a low level not seen since 1955. The housing target of 500,000 houses a year was abandoned in 1968, and in 1969 and in 1970 the number of houses completed actually fell. The promise of a new national minimum income guarantee was simply not fulfilled. The 'wage stop' was continued, and its coverage actually extended by the 1966 Act. Selectivity in a whole range of social services was expanded and means testing increased. The starting point of income tax was lowered, so making the tax 'a major cause of poverty'[38] for the first time. Indeed 'by the time the . . . Labour Government lost office in 1970 the income level at which earners began to pay income tax was actually below the equivalent poverty line operated by the Supplementary Benefits Commission'.[39] Yet with the exception of capital gains tax, the Labour Government made no sustained attack on those holding wealth, or on their ability to transmit that wealth between generations.

The Labour Government's promised pension reform, on which so much energy had been lavished and in which so much hope had been placed in the late 1950s, never reached the Statute Book, and the

* Most of the increase in expenditure on social provision reflected changes in population, growing unemployment, the trend for children to stay longer at school, and rising prices and salaries. On this see P. Townsend (editor), *Labour and Inequality* (London, Fabian Society, 1972) p. 145.

proposals that did emerge in 1969 made no substantial contribution to reducing social inequality in this area of traditionally large middle class privilege. The state pension increases that were awarded were more than eroded by inflation, and the increases in family allowances were undermined by the higher charges for school meals and by the reduction in free school milk. A substantial section of the Labour Government's much-vaunted increase in expenditure on social security went as unemployment benefit to men made redundant by the Government's deflationary policies - by 'shake out' as it was euphemistically known. A sizeable percentage of those officially in poverty who were poor because of low pay continued to receive that low pay from the Labour Government as their employer, and saw the Labour Party's promise of social justice through incomes policy turn into a series of wage freezes, incomes norms and N.B.P.I. judgements that discriminated against public sector employees and failed to give differential and advantageous treatment to the low paid.

For overall, the Labour Government's record in the field of social reform was appalling, and did not stand comparison with the much greater if still marginal achievements of the Attlee Government. The aspirations of the 1950s, to use State power to redress the uneven distribution of social privileges and rights, had been abandoned; and the search for the conditions under which sustained economic growth could be achieved had been allowed to drown completely any vestigial interest in social reform. As the *National Plan* said, a guaranteed minimum income 'would not contribute towards faster economic growth',[40] and thus was to be abandoned. So though the debate still continues on whether poverty actually increased under Labour or was marginally alleviated, no one is disputing the absence of any radical reduction of social privilege. As one of its more reluctant critics put it, 'the Government strayed from moral authority over race and withdrew from the obstinate pursuit of socialist objectives. Its social achievements were much smaller than claimed or believed at the time by Labour Ministers'[41]; and here at least the bankruptcy of 'socialism as science' could not but be recognised.*

* The new-found radicalism of the Labour Party in Opposition again after 1970 was itself evidence of the Party's failure in government in the 1960s. So too were the speeches and writings of former Labour Ministers. Roy Jenkins, for example, made the alleviation of poverty by a Labour Government in the 1970s a major theme of his specification of *What Matters Now*. He estimated that in the late 1960s 2 million people were still living below the official poverty line (as defined by the levels of supplementary benefits), that an extra 4.6 million people were receiving benefits, and that a further 4 million

Yet this retreat from socialist purpose in the Wilson Government's
policy towards the deprived was no accident. It was part of its overriding commitment to the creation of those conditions under which a
predominantly private economy could achieve economic growth. In the
pursuit of that commitment the Labour Government of 1964-70
rapidly dropped any pretence at 'controlling the commanding heights
of the economy' that it had once promised so athletically to scale. Its
much-vaunted *National Plan*, which George Brown in 1965 was calling
'Labour's blueprint for action', contained no teeth at all. It turned out
to be merely a compilation of industry-by-industry targets for output,
investment, manpower and exports *suggested by industry itself* in a
survey conducted by the Department of Economic Affairs in 1965 -
targets which were then modified slightly in hurried consultations
between the Labour Government and senior industrialists prior to the
Plan's publication in September 1965. Because the central growth rate
of the Plan was assumed before the survey, leading industrialists were
sceptical of its relevance from the beginning. Yet they had no cause to
worry about Government intentions, since the Plan contained no
provision for State direction of resources to achieve targets (beyond the
use of building licenses and, later, the incentive of investment grants).
Nor did it contain any sanctions that a Labour Government would
apply - least of all public ownership - to any industry that failed to
achieve the Plan's objectives. *The National Plan* was really an exercise in
creating economic growth by exhortation, and it failed. The Labour
Government hoped that by making public the overall situation faced by
the economy, private industrialists would be in a better position to
distribute their resources of machinery, plant and labour to maximise
efficiency, output and exports. But they did not. Nor, given the inter-

people had incomes only just above the poverty line. So on his calculations,
and after six years of a Labour Government of which he had been a leading
member, over 10 million people had incomes on or around the poverty line.
And as he said, 'poverty is not simply a question of having little money to
spend. The poor are deprived in terms of health care, housing, education, and
jobs. Not every poor person will suffer each and every one of these dis-
advantages. But most will experience one or more.' (R. Jenkins, *What Matters
Now*, London, Fontana, 1972, p. 44). Jenkins then called again for the
increased public expenditure which alone, on his view, could alleviate these
major social ills. But he did not explain why his similar calls before the 1964
election should have been disregarded when Labour was in office. Yet this
surely is the crucial question that must be handled before Labour promises in
the 1970s can be taken seriously.

national market conditions which they faced and the Government's budgetary policies that they had to endure, could they realistically have been expected to do so. For the Plan's targets were casualties of the Labour leadership's higher commitment to the foreign payments balance. And as under Attlee, so after 1964, when the Labour Government found that the promise of its planning was not being achieved, it retreated, and its later planning document, *The Task Ahead*, was published in 1969 only as a discussion paper, without pretensions or impact.

In fact, far from scaling the commanding heights of the economy, the Wilson Government became ever more enmeshed in servicing its every need. To this end, it created a series of little N.E.D.C.s (Stafford Cripps' old development councils) that linked individual industries to a sponsoring Department as a channel through which Ministers could be kept closely briefed on industrial problems and potentials as seen by senior managerial strata in the industries concerned. At national level, they continued to use the Conservatives' National Economic Development Council, and gave its chairmanship to a former director of British Aluminium. Indeed, all the Labour Government's interventionist agencies were headed by businessmen. For like the Attlee Government before them, the Labour Administration after 1964 continued to rely heavily on the co-operation and advice of men trained in and drawn from the senior managerial strata of British capitalism.[*]

The parallels with the experience of the Attlee Government are striking. For after 1964, as then, the Government's deflation policies added to the profit and investment problems of the private manufacturing sector; and in consequence and in compensation, the Labour leaders' 'purposive intervention' became more and more an exercise in using State funds, without any real controls, to bolster unstable private concerns and to assist in the creation of vast private monopolies through the merger of smaller private firms. So the Labour Government gave financial aid to the Fairfield shipyard in 1965, and to the Upper Clyde shipbuilding group that it later called into being. It set up a sponsoring relationship between its new Ministry of Technology and a number of crucial industries: electronics, computers, machine tools and manufacturing machinery, vehicles and mechanical engineering, shipbuilding, electrical and process plant, and, via its

[*]   The N.B.P.I. was chaired by a former Conservative Minister; the I.R.C. by a merchant banker; the Land Commission by a prominant chartered surveyor; and the nationalised Steel industry by a Conservative merchant banker, assisted by directors drawn from the boards of the private steel industry.

117

Aviation Group, it sponsored the aircraft industry. To each of these industries, MinTech directed money and the results of Government-sponsored research. And in 1965 the Labour Government introduced a system of investment grants, giving 'priority to those sectors which can make the greatest contribution to the balance of payments',[42] by which manufacturing investment could be offset by a 20% State payment, or by a 40% payment in the much expanded Development Areas.*

Most important of all, the Labour Government also created the Industrial Reorganization Corporation as a Government agency staffed by merchant bankers and by leading industrialists on secondment from major private firms.† The I.R.C. was initially given £150 million of State money to buy holdings in private companies, to assist mergers, and generally 'to help promote rationalisation, and restructuring of industries and firms where this was needed to help exports or to pool resources for new technological advance'.[43] It was the I.R.C. which bought 15% of the shares in Rootes Motor Company in 1967, and which later bought the ball-bearing firm of Brown-Bayley. It was the I.R.C. which gave financial assistance to the merger of Leyland Motors and British Motor Holdings Limited, and which supported the merging of English Electric with Elliott Automation, of G.E.C. with English Electric and later of G.E.C. with A.E.I.[44] And under its later Industrial Expansion Act, the Labour Government initiated a merger between the computer businesses of I.C.T., English Electric and Plessey; and helped to finance the building of aluminium smelters. As Brittan observed it was remarkable to see 'the way in which Labour Ministers actively encouraged the "take-over kings", whom they had denounced in Opposition, even when the expressed object of bids was to cut out unnecessary labour'.[45] ‡

---

* The system of investment grants was clearly open to abuse, by firms using State funds to re-tool their productive process and then moving the machinery out of the Development Areas. The events at Plessey Alexandria were a case in point.

† Described by Harold Wilson as 'the highest-powered group of industrialists and financiers ever to sit round one table as co-directors'. (Wilson, *The Labour Government: a Personal Record*, p. 202).

‡ As Edmund Dell, who was Minister of State first at the Board of Trade and then at the Department of Employment and Productivity between 1964 and 1970, later put it, 'the trouble was that the government went overboard for its new principle of industrial restructuring. "Structure" became the answer to all industrial problems. Competition became old hat' and in consequence the Labour Government ended up in pursuit of policies 'whose principal effect was to increase the power of a few large private companies'. (E. Dell, *Political Responsibility and Industry*, London, Allen and Unwin, 1973, p. 84).

118

The parallels with the experience of the Attlee Government were close, for once more a Labour Government ended its period of office desperately attempting to bolster a weak national capitalism and its managerial class by policies that were designed to protect the domestic economy from the worst vicissitudes of competition from stronger foreign rivals, and to make it 'capable of fighting the European giants on equal terms' as Harold Wilson put it.[46] Yet Labour's interventionist policy was not very successful even here. The application of the 'white heat of the technological revolution' to British industry proved more difficult, and altogether a slower process, than the rhetoric of 1963-4 had led the electorate to believe; and when applied seemed to make precious little difference to the growth rate of an economy bedevilled with deeper and more structural problems that could not be solved by the talk of politicians and the signing of paper plans. Nor was the Labour Party's policy consistent between its Departments; and the Ministry of Technology's push for economic growth was more than offset by Treasury policies of deflation that systematically ate away at profit returns and investment rates. Indeed, profit rates and investment in manufacturing industry hit an all-time low in 1969 and 1970, after six years of 'purposive intervention'. The Labour Government's panacea of economic growth continued to escape it, and in its increasingly desperate search for the conditions in which that growth could occur, the Labour Government of 1964-70 eventually turned its State power against the working class itself. This was so critical a threat to the continued existence of the labour movement as we have known it that its genesis and development is worth looking at in detail.

7

When the Labour Party took office in 1964, the working class sections of its electorate had already known twenty years of full employment, and in the critical engineering industry at least, had achieved by work-place bargaining a degree of job control that ate away at the cost-effectiveness and managerial prerogatives of the growth sections of British capitalism. The strength of this industrial power of work groups and their shop stewards was reflected in the wage drift which character-ised these sectors,* in the pattern of small, short, unofficial strikes seen

---

* There was in this period a very close correlation between the degree of wage drift in the engineering industry and the degree of shop floor organisation. On this see S.W. Lerner and J. Marquand, 'Workshop bargaining, wage drift and productivity in the British engineering industry', *Manchester School*, vol. 30,

there in the 1950s and 1960s,* and in the widespread recognition by
Government inquiries, Royal Commissions and management writings
that though the situation varied between plants, overall a large percentage of the immediate rules and agreements covering the use, size,
work-pace and job security of manual workers in engineering, in
chemicals and in printing lay now in the hands of the work force itself,
or at least were negotiated at plant level between line managers and
strongly placed shop stewards.

This shift in class power within industry had never extended to
questions of investments or sales, but in the engineering sectors of
British capitalism had been considerable even so; and had occurred
only in the situation of intense labour shortage and low foreign competition in the 1950s. Then, the very absence of an industrial reserve
army of the unemployed had reduced the potency of managerial
sanctions and strengthened the bargaining position of workers, at a
time when managements' ability to transmit wage increases on to their
consumers in the form of higher prices had removed any market
pressure on them to initiate a confrontation with their stewards. But by
the mid 1960s, as the Labour Party took office, these easy product-
market conditions had already gone as international competition
intensified; and the growing pressure on profit margins throughout
large sections of British industry was beginning to prompt a sensitivity
to the component elements of costs and to the loss of managerial
control, and to stimulate a major managerial counter-assault on the
industrial power of organised work groups.

In the early 1960s, and against the background of low but sustained
economic growth, the representative institutions of industrial capital
(and especially the Federation of British Industry at this time) urged
the State to play a more positive role in planning future levels of costs
and demand in order to facilitate profitable long-term investment and
to control wages. Under the Labour Government these demands became more insistent, and blending with the Labour Party's own

---

p. 26; and T. Cliff, *The Employers' Offensive* (London, Pluto Press, 1970)
p. 40.
* The great majority of stoppages in the late 1950s and early 1960s were
concentrated in those industries in which shop stewards were active: in motor
vehicles, in the docks and in shipbuilding. 60% of all days 'lost' between 1960
and 1965 were 'lost' in the engineering industry. 95% of all these strikes were
unofficial - that is, they were locally initiated and locally led. The vast
majority were very short (averaging 2½ days in the early 1960s) and involved
very few people (on average, about 600). It was by militant action of this kind
that organised sections of the working class established their industrial power.

interventionist propensities, produced a full blown attempt to make a slight but significant shift in the distribution of G.N.P. back towards profits.

In one sense, the Labour Government had no choice but to do this. The Wilson Government faced a distribution of economic power dominated on the one side by the resources of finance capital, and on the other by multi-national corporations that were themselves under intense market pressure, were tightening their own labour policies,[47] and were demanding assistance in this from the State. Ultimately, the Labour Government had to accommodate these demands. For to do otherwise would at best leave the British economy internationally uncompetitive, and at worst, would drive investment, plant and employment abroad. Even so, it would be a mistake to see the Government's involvement in industrial relations in the 1960s as the smooth working out of a coherent plan. Certainly some consequences of Government policy were anticipated. The higher level of unemployment after the July measures of 1966 is one example. But more normally, the Labour Government was 'pulled' into a more active and anti-working class role through a series of crises. It was pushed and prodded by a series of institutions (by the Washington Government, the I.M.F., the C.B.I., the City . . .) into discovering or facing certain 'problems' and seeking certain 'solutions'. In that sense, the very definition of *'the problem'* as one of 'wage drift' or of 'strikes' appears to have sealed the Labour Party from the recognition that class conflict is endemic to capitalism itself. Indeed, the Wilson Government appears to have persuaded itself by the late 1960s that the only way to help the poor and the unemployed amongst the working class was to attack working class shop floor power, and that the only way to reduce inequality was to prop up a system of industrial ownership to which massive inequalities of wealth and power are and always have been central.

Yet in retrospect there is a coherence in the historical sequence of 'problems perceived', 'solutions considered' and 'policies initiated', a logic that connects incomes policy, productivity bargaining and industrial relations legislation. For together they constituted a Labour Government-led attack on working class living standards, job security and industrial power in an attempt to shift class power back towards capital as a means of resolving the growing difficulties of British capitalism. The first moves in that attack came with the Labour Government's incomes policy in the months after its election in 1964.

121

The Labour Governments of 1964-70

By 1964 incomes policy was a central feature of the Labour Party programme, offered to the working class electorate as a means of achieving higher economic growth, increased industrial productivity, increased real earnings, and social justice for the lower paid.* Amid much publicity, the policy was launched in December 1964 with the *Declaration of Intent* to restrict prices, dividends, rents, salaries, and wages to agreed norms. With the creation of the National Board for Prices and Incomes (N.B.P.I.) in April 1965, a norm of 3½% was announced, and the conditions specified under which it could be exceeded. The payments crisis of July 1966 brought a 'wage freeze' for six months, and 'a period of severe restraint' with a nil norm from January to July 1967, and wages norms of 3½% and later 4½% between July 1967 and the Labour Party's electoral defeat in 1970. By then what had begun as a central mechanism of social democratic reform had turned rapidly (and with very little heart-searching by the Labour leadership) into a means of holding back wages, to strengthen profit margins by reducing labour costs† and to strengthen the balance of payments by making exports more price-competitive.

In the event, even as a mechanism for restricting the growth rate of wages, the policy was unimpressive in the long run. Before July 1966, it hardly affected levels of earnings outside the public sector at all, and its success between July 1966 and June 1967 (in reducing the increase

* As Harold Wilson put it to the T.U.C. in September 1964, 'we have the right to ask for an incomes policy because we are prepared to contribute the three necessary conditions. First, an assurance of rising production and rising incomes, so that the sacrifice, the restraint for which we ask is matched by an assurance that it will result in increased production and increased rewards. Second, an assurance of equity and social justice, in that our policies will be directed to the benefit of the nation as a whole and not to the advantage of a sectional interest. Third, an assurance that what we ask for in wages and salaries will apply equally to profits and dividends and rent. We shall not create a free-for-all for the speculator, and land profiteer and the landlord - and then ask wage and salary earners alone to show a concern for the national interest that others are not required to show.' (Quoted in Miliband, *Parliamentary Socialism*, pp. 365).

† As Stan Newens has observed, 'basically the objective of a prices and incomes policy is to restrain the rate of increase of incomes to assist enterprises to compete with their international rivals. Despite protestations that the objective is to assist the lower paid worker and provide for a planned growth of incomes, the attitude to both profits and prices is determined by considerations other than those of equality. The White Paper *Productivity, Prices and Incomes Policy after 1969* . . . makes this clear . . . "*The Government does not believe that any general reduction in the level of return on capital invested in British industry, whether privately or publicly owned, would be helpful in the context of the essential modernisation of the economy*".' (*Trade Union Register 1970*, p. 34-5).

in the total wage bill to 2%[48]) was bought at the price of a growing wages explosion thereafter. Seasonally adjusted earnings rose by 8.8% between July 1967 and March 1968, by 7.6% in the next nine month period, by 8.3% in 1969, and by 13.6% between January and June 1970.[49] In fact the impact of the policy was uneven. It was applied most rigorously to government employees, and it was their ten year experience of the differential implementation of income norms that helped to spread militancy into the public sector by the late 1960s, and to drive these sections of the working class into strike action for the first time. As such, incomes policy made its own unique contribution to the disillusionment of increasing numbers of workers with the Labour Party in power, and the policy was effectively broken in the public sector by the militancy of local government manual workers, firemen and teachers late in 1969.

In essence, the Labour Government's incomes policy in the 1960s failed. Through the decade, earnings (and the consequent pressure on profits) continued to rise in the engineering, shipbuilding and dock industries. The policy was effective only over the industrially weak, and failed to stop wage drift in those industries in which drift was most concentrated and where it was most damaging to the international trade position and profit margins of British capitalism. Incomes policy failed here (in engineering, for example) because it focused on nationally negotiated wage rates and left unaffected local negotiations and the shop floor power of organised work groups. It failed, that is, because it involved no structural attack on the industrial power of workers. This weakness was clear in the repeated attempt in the mid-1960s to 'give the policy teeth', and in the very rapid shift in the Labour Government's emphasis towards productivity bargaining within the context of incomes policy. The productivity component of incomes policy had always been there. As early as February 1962, under the Conservative Government, the White Paper *Incomes Policy: the Next Step* talked of exceptions above the wages norm as part of collective agreements 'under which those concerned made a direct contribution, by accepting more exacting work or more onerous conditions, or by a renunciation of restrictive practices, to an increase of productivity and a reduction of costs'.[50] But it was little more than exhortation at this stage, and it was only after the 'freeze' of July 1966 that, under heavy Labour Government pressure, productivity bargaining began to spread rapidly across British industry. The very failure of incomes policy to bolster the profit margins of British capitalism drove the Labour Government on to face the organised power of sections of the working class at the point of production, in productivity bargaining.

After July 1966 the only wage settlements that the Labour Government formally allowed through its vetting system were those below the specified income norm or those with genuine productivity clauses within them. Indeed by the late 1960s productivity concessions had to be made to justify even a settlement at or below the specified income norm itself.[51] Yet when the N.B.P.I. looked for productivity bargains to analyse in 1966 it could only find seven major ones. Only under State pressure did productivity bargaining spread through British industry, and then with great rapidity. By the end of 1969 6,000,000 workers were operating under some kind of productivity deal in industries that included general engineering, motor vehicles, ship-building, aircraft, food drink and tobacco, paint, chemicals, oil, clay, electrical engineering, textiles and distribution.[52]

These productivity bargains involved the buying out of control of aspects of the job by management from stewards and organised work groups. The struggle for control over production lay behind all the rhetoric of productivity bargaining, as any survey of the small print of Government White Papers will show. In Report 23 of the N.B.P.I., and in the White Papers after July 1966, exceptional pay awards were allowed only if it could be shown that the workers were making a direct contribution towards increasing productivity by accepting 'more exacting work or a major change in working practices'.[53] Report 23 made clear the substance of this - that a genuine productivity deal involved a 'reduction in overtime, freer interchange of tasks between different groups of workers, the removal of restrictions on output, manpower reductions, and changes in patterns of work'.[54] By the end of 1969, the 6,000,000 workers covered by productivity deals had signed agreements covering precisely these issues: the flexibility and mobility of labour, the rationalisation of wage structures and job evaluation, work study, interchangeability, shift working, changes in working practices, tea-breaks, overtime etc.[55]

The Labour Government's preoccupation with the reduction of the power of organised work groups is clear in the way that managerial aims were adopted and publicised by Ministers responsible for industrial relations policy and by the N.B.P.I. itself. The Board put its weight behind the buying out or modification of piece-rate systems, and their replacement by tighter managerial specification of job contents and

124

times.[56] Report 123 listed managerial aims in productivity bargaining, and gave them Board support: the increased flexibility in the use of manpower, the reduction of manpower, changes in working practices, the introduction of job evaluation schemes and changes in wage structures, and the establishment of managerial control of overtime.[57] In fact, the very way in which the D.E.P. vetting system and the N.B.P.I. worked - in close contact with local management but only loosely connected to even national trade union bureaucracies - allowed managerial perspectives, definitions and problems to dominate policy. This was no accident, but reflected the growing empathy of personnel and class interests between organised business and the Labour Government, as the latter struggled to achieve a high growth rate from a capitalist economy.

To all this, the Labour leadership gave its active support, even though it constituted an attack on the degree of job control established by certain sections of its working class electorate in the 1950s and early 1960s. Behind the rhetoric of 'reform' and the 'end of anarchy', the N.B.P.I. measured the degree of success in its policies 'very much in terms of the restoration or enhancement of managerial authority'.[58] It was precisely those issues over which shop stewards had established control (piece-rates, levels and flexibility of manning, overtime, and the rate and organisation of work) that, as if by chance, suddenly became the very changes that had to be conceded in order to win a wage settlement above the norm. Productivity bargaining was nothing more or less than a State-led attempt to shift class power back to management across key sections of British industry, to facilitate the restructuring of capitalism and to ease the pressure of labour costs on profit margins.

As with incomes policy, however, its impact varied with the degree of organisation and militancy of the working class. It undoubtedly hit the industrially weak, for to exploit productivity bargaining required a strong shop floor organisation, itself already a virtual monopoly of the higher paid sections of the class. In its early stages (in 1967 and 1968) the policy of productivity bargaining was generally effective in holding down the movement in the real wages of the working class to probably only 1% per annum.[59] But thereafter its impact fell away. For many productivity deals turned out to be bogus, connived at by managements and shop stewards in situations of local labour scarcity.[60] Many (especially amongst white collar workers) actually strengthened shop floor organisation by stimulating restrictive practices which could be

125

sold and stewards to sell them.[61] And in any case, hostility to productivity bargaining grew on the shop floor as the intensification of effort and the tightening of managerial controls were experienced and as the growth of unemployment undermined job security.

For the Labour Government did not hesitate to create unemployment amongst the working class in its search for growth and a payments surplus. The level of unemployment doubled between 1966 and 1969, partly as a result of deliberate Government policies of deflation, partly because of its continued run-down of the coal and railway industries,* and partly because of productivity bargaining itself. For even where 'no redundancy' clauses were included in productivity agreements, and (even rarer) where those clauses were honoured, one consequence of productivity bargaining was to reduce the total number of job opportunities in the local labour market. As Jack Jones said, 'the same output has been shared out among fewer men and the dole queues have lengthened. The Government got the productivity and the workers got the sack.'[62]

This attack by the Labour Government on its working class electorate culminated in its attempt in 1969 to introduce industrial relations legislation to buttress its flagging policies on incomes and productivity bargaining. The legislation was an attempt to mobilise the coercive and ideological forces of the State against the tactics which stewards had characteristically used to maintain their power base, and then to incorporate those stewards into trade union bureaucracies which were themselves to be used as policing agents of their own collective agreements.† In the event, that legislative initiative was blocked by T.U.C. opposition and backbench revolt,[63] but the damage to the relationship between the Labour Government and its working class electorate had already been done.

* In the mining industry, for example, pits were closing at an average of one a week between 1965 and 1970. Almost half a million jobs were 'lost' in this industry in the 1960s, the loss of four jobs in every seven.
† As Eric Heffer wrote, 'the offending proposals' of *In Place of Strife*, the Labour Government's White Paper that preceded its legislation, came 'under three headings: 1. Compulsory Strike Ballots for some official strikes. 2. The so-called "conciliation pause" for unofficial strikes, called by most people the "cooling off period", and 3. Fines for trade unionists that can be paid on the basis of attachment to wages.' In Heffer's view at the time, 'These proposals add up to a new type of interference by Government in industrial relations. They signify a departure from previous cherished methods. In a sense, it is an extension of the state intervention begun in the Prices and Incomes Act, and is in line with the new concept of state control.' (E. Heffer, *The Class Struggle in Parliament*, London, Gollancz, 1973, p. 113).

The Labour Governments of 1964-70

For the Party that long ago had been created to represent 'the labour interest in Parliament' had spent six years in office haranguing working class militants as industrial wreckers,[64] and misrepresenting the problem of British capitalism as 'the fault' of the working class, with its 'strikes', 'weak trade union leadership', 'restrictive practices' and 'industrial anarchy'. It had spent six years using 'the national interest' to justify every twist and turn of its policy, and to justify a job loss and social dislocation for large groups of workers that had been caused by the crisis in profits within capitalist institutions. In all this, the Labour Government of 1964-70 laid the foundations on which the Conservatives would build, and in the process demonstrated the bankruptcy of its own appeal to be the embodiment of the political interests of its predominantly working class electorate.

8

The parallels between the Labour Government of 1945-51 and that of 1964-70 were striking. Both Governments began with great optimism, confident in their ability to introduce major social reforms. Each overestimated the power of the State, 'that a few hundred intelligent chaps in Whitehall, backed by a few hundred million pounds of Government money and a Parliamentary majority passing the right legislation could somehow achieve the transformation of British industry which had eluded the previous generation of industrialists and politicians'.[65] Each learned quickly that the reality of State power was different; and instead of quiet, purposive planning, governed through a repeated series of monetary crises and policy shifts. Each was subject to policy constraints from foreign finance that gained its leverage from the economy's weak competitive position; and from private business that gained its influence from the Labour Government's own overriding commitment to economic growth. Each used State money to fund private capitalism and gave what protection international pressure would allow to shelter a weak industrial structure. Each strengthened the managerial and financial strata that it had criticised in Opposition, by drawing representatives of that strata into key Governmental positions, by taking over deficient industries, by articulating managerial goals in policy speeches, and by making public funds available for investment. Each renegued on social policy commitments, depressed the rate of increase of domestic consumption, and tried to tie working class wage rises to the growth rate of the economy as a whole. And each left office with the inherited structure of social privilege largely unaffected by its period in power.

Yet the two Governments were not the same. The Attlee Government's socialist rhetoric and class perspectives found no parallels in the 1960s. By 1964, the aspirations of social transformation had given way to those of technological excellence, and the internationalism of socialist faith had given way to the jingoism of the drive for national 'modernisation'. The post-war extension of the public sector was not repeated in the 1960s, beyond the nationalisation of steel. Major innovations in welfare provision that had come after 1945 were not repeated after 1964, and even the promised pension reform failed in the face of opposition from the private pension trusts. There was no redistribution of income and wealth under the Wilson Government to match the taxation policies of the Attlee Government's early years. The close relations between the industrial and the political wings of the labour movement under Attlee were lost after 1964 in a sustained attack by the Wilson Government on the living standards and industrial power of its own working class electorate, and in the growing hostility of Labour leaders to industrial militancy and working class activism. As far as can be seen, Attlee presided over a genuine labour movement; Wilson over a hollow electoral shell from which most genuine socialists had withdrawn in disgust or dismay by 1970. And the Attlee Government lost office on an electoral technicality, with its working class support intact and its popular vote increased. But the Wilson Government lost office in 1970 on a reduced popular vote and on a wave of working class abstentions.

In other words, by 1970 the radical potential of the Attlee generation within the Party had been lost. The search for the Socialist Commonwealth had been abandoned. Socialism had 'been quietly written off, allowed to lapse',[66] and we were, it seemed, at 'the end of labourism'.* And yet, within three years, the very men who had led the Labour Party to this debacle were claiming again that the way to socialism lay through the return of a Labour Government, and were

---

*   A stage at which, as Peter Sedgwick said, 'a crucial . . . change [had] overcome the mental structure of British Social Democracy, which [had] converted it into a technocratic or State-capitalist structure, capable at its best of isolated liberal modifications to the system and at its worst [which is much more common] of an anti-liberal efficiency drive which attacks British trade unionists and Vietnamese or Biafran peasants with an impartiality stemming from its single-minded concern with the balance of commercial payments'. (P. Sedgwick, 'The End of Labourism', *New Politics*, vol. 8(3) 1970, p. 83).

promising that there would be no repeat of the betrayals of the Wilson years. Ex-Ministers defended their record in office against heavy criticism from within the Labour Party, by explaining away their failures as the results of mistakes that need not be repeated, or - more candidly - as the result of the lack of socialist purpose which in Opposition the Labour leaders had miraculously rediscovered.

So we need to know whether this degeneration of socialist purpose is endemic to Labour politics, or whether it is something that the present generation of Labour leaders can and will avoid. There is no more important question facing the Left today, and to answer it we must probe the origins and logic of the pattern of policy that until now we have been content simply to lay out.

6. The failure of the socialist promise

In the record of the Labour Party over its first seventy years, two trends stand out as overridingly in need of explanation. There is first the Party's post-war retreat from its earlier promise of total social transformation, its abandonment up to 1970 of any pretence to seek a socialist commonwealth, and its subordination of its policies when in office to the unbridled pursuit of increased production from an economic system which Party leaders and activists in the 1930s would have rejected as in need of total overhaul. And there is secondly the related tendency of the Labour Party in power to renegue even on its promise of major social reforms (in income distribution, industrial conditions, housing, education and health), reforms which by 1964 had come to represent the basis of the Party's claim to be the embodiment of the political interests of its predominantly working class electorate. What has to be explained is the failure of the Labour Party's socialist promise amid its increasingly unhappy experience in government.

There are at least five major bodies of explanation already available in the literature on the Labour Party that are capable of coping to some degree with the Party's development since 1900. There is first that set of arguments, initially formulated in the 1950s and associated with the revisionist wing of the Labour Party, that explains the Party's development as a response to changes in the basic structure of an advanced industrial society that have removed the need for radical politics by resolving the fundamental economic and political injustices associated with early capitalist industrialisation. On this argument, the abandonment of old policies reflects the fact that the Party now faces a post-capitalist world, in which there is a role for a party of discrete social reforms but not for a party bent on the total transformation of the social order, even by constitutional and gradual means. And in this social transformation, which has rendered 'old style socialism' irrelevant, the success of earlier Labour Governments has played - we are told - a crucial role. Indeed, the very success of the Attlee administration is

130

supposed to have created for the Labour Party of the 1950s this problem of finding a new definition of socialist goals and of political practice. So at least the revisionists argued. But this will not do as an explanation of Labour politics. For as we have seen the record of even the Attlee Government was very moderate and left intact a society which, twenty years later, still exhibited that set of material, social and political *inequalities* which once stirred the Labour Party to seek a radical social transformation. Certainly the absolute standard of material provision in this society is higher now than ever before, and this did indeed create problems for Labour Party politicians in the 1950s. But the recent and growing instability of Western capitalism with its heightened class tensions, and the 'rediscovery' of substantial areas of poverty, degradation and despair within the so-called 'affluence', have combined to make clear that the arguments of the revisionists will no longer suffice as a total explanation of Labour Party politics.[1]

The same people often made a second and related argument, that explained the Labour Party's dwindling radicalism as a response to the political conservatism of an increasingly affluent and 'déclassé' electorate.[2] As we shall see later, it is certainly the case that electoral pressures have been one force moderating Labour Party performance, though we shall also argue that such electoral considerations have not been the major factor causing the Party leadership to abandon its search for a socialist commonwealth and to fail to sustain its programme of major social reforms. For as a total explanation of Labour Party politics, this 'fear of an affluent electorate' thesis will not suffice, particularly when it is realised that until the 1970 General Election at least there was little evidence of any disproportionately large defections from Labour by affluent workers.[3] In any case, there is some evidence that certain sections of the electorate tend to take their political cues from the parties they support, and for them at least it is not legitimate to explain the development of party policy in purely electoral terms.[4] But more important, the retreat of the Labour Party from the radical promise of the 1930s predates the growth of general affluence, and the fear of the electorate predates them both, being as old as the Party itself. Indeed, as an explanation of Labour Party politics, such characterisations of the relationship between the Party and its electorate are ultimately weak because they leave unexplored and unexplained the central paradox that underpins that relationship. Namely that in a society which is still intensely class-ridden and class-conscious, the

131

Labour Party has not only failed to sustain its own class image and perspective, but has also succumbed to the argument of its political opponents that any attempt to mobilise an electorate on class lines is both illegitimate and doomed to failure. This paradox has itself to be explained.

Moreover it is noticeable that the experience of Labour in office invariably prompts a further set of arguments which focus on the social groups or institutions that have apparently prevented the recent Labour administration from implementing at least the 'distinctly Labour' parts of its programme, and which have in consequence made their own unique contribution to the Labour Party's subsequent rejection by the electorate. Which group is singled out turns in part on the events of the Government period, but clearly depends more on the political per- spective and experience that the writer brings to the whole analysis. The list stretches from political agitators[5] to unofficial or official trade unionism,[6] to the civil service,[7] and to international financiers[8] - each being offered as the group which just 'blew the Labour Party off course'.

Now as we have already seen, the Labour Party in power has repeatedly experienced constraints from some or all of these groups, and to this extent this third explanation of Labour performance taps an important dimension of Labour politics. But it is insufficient to leave the analysis at the level of group conspiracy; and so we must consider in detail what most of the other arguments have not: namely why the Labour Party should find itself so constrained, how precisely those constraints operate, and with what impact on the future politics of the Party. And in particular here, we shall want to consider why the Labour Party in office has repeatedly been more willing to turn the power of the State machine against groups and institutions within its own electorate (and in particular against trade union and unofficial industrial militancy) than to confront the bankers, industrialists and higher civil servants whose political sympathies characteristically lie with the Labour Party's political opponents.

One such answer to that question, as indeed to the whole Labour Party record, has come from the Labour Left, as a fourth body of argument that seeks to explain Labour Party politics. This time, it is as a story of a movement dogged, especially at critical moments, by con- servative leaders and right-wing programmes, such that with different leaders things might well have been different, and could be again.[9] This too we will consider in the chapters that follow. For it is certainly the

The failure of the socialist promise

case that the Labour Party has been so dogged. The issue at stake between the Labour Left and socialist groups outside the Labour Party is whether that history of conservative leadership is accidental, or whether political organisations like the Labour Party invariably (and of necessity) throw up men of that calibre and programmes of that type. For if Ramsay MacDonald, Clement Attlee and Harold Wilson are just bad accidents, this is a particularly accident-prone Party. Whether they can be avoided in the 1970s should determine whether socialist militants rejoin the Labour Party or abandon it to its fate. For that reason, this is the argument to which we will return again and again in the remaining chapters.

The fifth and final body of argument on the politics of the Labour Party is particularly pessimistic on this last point. It explains the growing conservatism of the Labour Party over time as the inevitable consequence of the predominance within its governmental structures of a middle class leadership with interests at variance with those of its working class rank and file, and with the organisational ability to circumvent any working class pressure (at conference and the like). Such a Michelian thesis, of the inevitable predominance of a conservative oligarchy within any mass working class political movement, is an analysis that is more or less shared by men basically sympathetic to the process (like Robert McKenzie)[10] and by those hostile to it (like Barry Hindess).[11] These arguments at least have the strength of pulling the explanation of Labour Party politics back into the Labour Party itself, and of asserting that there are processes at work within the Party which mediate the impact on its politics of a changing social context, a conservative electorate and a well organised power structure. But in granting the Labour Party an active role in its own de-radicalisation, the arguments used are often question-begging and simplistic. It is not clear from Hindess' argument why 'middle classness' necessarily equates with conservatism. Certainly the middle class have no monopoly on that political philosophy, nor are all revolutionaries necessarily working class or peasant in their social origins and life-styles. Both Marx and Lenin were bourgeois to the core. Rather we need to know why the undoubtedly middle class leaders of the Labour Party end up so conservative, and this is never explained. Nor is the appearance that is perhaps implied by these arguments, of a party divided between leaders and led, true to the reality of a party in which the majority of each of its constituent sections have been united as often as not in a common set of political definitions and policies.

133

The failure of the socialist promise

For it is undoubtedly true, as Ralph Miliband has argued,[12] that this unity of definition and policy within the Labour Party has been built on an overriding commitment at all levels of the Party to Parliamentary politics, and that it is this commitment which holds the key to the growing conservatism of the Party's leadership. But even here, in the most profound essay on the politics of Labour yet produced, we are not told by Miliband why Parliamentarianism and socialism are incompatible.[13] Nor are we informed of precisely how and why the logic of de-radicalisation flows out of the particular tradition of working class politics that the Labour Party represents. To lay out that logic will occupy the rest of this chapter.

2

In looking at the Labour Party over the last seven decades we are looking at the emergence and development of a particular tradition of working class politics with its own place in the universe of socialist movements and with its own logic - its own internal motor of change - over time. For as continental Europe and North America industrialised after 1870, a series of distinct political orientations came to make their appeal for loyalty and support to the emerging working classes, and in the process offered to those classes a definition of how their own political interests should be defined and sought.[14] Existing conservative political forces appealed to the class with a philosophy of national unity and common effort that denied the existence of fundamental social divisions or of distinct working class interests. Craft unions, particularly in the United States, offered industrial self-help and a general distrust of separate political organisations of the working class. Parliamentary parties attempted to mobilise the newly enfranchised workers in Western Europe behind political representatives from their own class. Revolutionary socialists sought to capture the fledgling proletariats for the seizure of State power behind disciplined political leadership. Syndicalists offered that same objective but rejected the need for political action, and anarchists offered a libertarian route to that same socialist revolution. In each case, each political movement offered the working class different answers to the basic questions of its politics. Namely what were working class interests? By which route could they be most economically achieved? And by implication, how should the working class characterise the social order under which it worked, and how should it assess the likely response of the ruling class that it faced to its increasingly vocal call for radical change?

134

The failure of the socialist promise

In the period between 1870 and 1940 these prescriptions for working class politics competed for the loyalty of each of their national proletariats, and as one came to predominate, it laid down patterns of political thought and behaviour that were inherited by successive generations of the class as 'the tradition' within which they learned their politics and their socialism - indeed, within which they learned what 'politics' and 'socialism' actually involved. Across Western Europe and the United States the post-war generations of the working class have been watching the logic of their nationally predominant tradition playing itself out, have been watching the growing conservatism of Communism in France and Italy, of the Democratic Party in the United States, and of Social Democracy in Sweden and in Germany. And in Britain, the post-war generations of the working class have witnessed the growing bankruptcy of the Labour tradition that established its political hegemony in the inter-war period.

Because for specific historical reasons, the tradition that came to predominate in Britain was neither Conservative nor Revolutionary, neither Syndicalist nor Anarchist, but a particular variant of a Parliamentary tradition for the working class that was known elsewhere in Europe as Social Democracy. This was a tradition which after the split in the European labour movement after the First World War explicitly rejected the revolutionary and violent road to socialism in favour of the pursuit of working class interests through constitutionally sanctioned institutions (in particular, through the ballot box and the trade union). And once established, British Social Democracy - in the guise of the Labour Party - educated successive generations of workers, party activists and Parliamentarians in a particular analysis of British society, in a particular definition of 'politics', and in a particular set of working class political interests. Clearly each generation of Labour Party members modified and built on what had gone before, and there were moments of crisis when the Party initiated what were, for it, radical departures. But these changes did not occur in a random and unstructured fashion. On the contrary, the overall development of the Labour Party occured within, and remained remarkably faithful to, terms of reference laid down (as the core of the Party's theory and practice) in that period before 1931 in which the Party was struggling to establish itself as the predominant voice of the British working class. It is precisely because it is impossible adequately to understand the patterns of political thought and behaviour adopted by the modern Labour Party without some reference to the characteristic patterns of

analysis and performance that have come to be associated with the
Party over the whole of its 70 years that the tradition established by
the first generation of Labour activists can be said to hold the key to all
that was to follow.

We have seen already that the Labour Party in its creation was the
culmination of a long nineteenth-century tradition of working class
politics that had hitherto found its expression in the left wing of the
Liberal Party, and that the initial character of the Party was determined
by a small group of Parliamentarians schooled in and committed to
Liberal-Radicalism. It was this generation of Parliamentary leaders who
laid down the abiding features of the Labour tradition, by weaving a
series of ideological positions, organisational structures and modes of
political activity into an interconnected body of theory and practice
that we referred to as 'Labourism'. What later generations of Labour
Party politicians, activists and electors were more prone to take for
granted was in this initial generation the subject of conscious and
explicit choices by men who were often locked in dialogue with those
alternative specifications for working class politics (syndicalist, and
later communist) which rejected the central assumptions of their
Labour politics. That debate turned around the four issues at the heart
of Labourism.

(a) The interplay of nation and class
Labour Party politics from the beginning were marked by the absence
of any coherent and rigorous class analysis of British politics, and by
the rejection of any perspective (invariably Marxist) which asserted the
incompatibility of interests between the bourgeoisie and the proletariat.
At the very foundation of the Party it was this that divided the
Independent Labour Party from the Marxist Social Democratic
Federation. As Miliband has noted,

> As for the socialists of the I.L.P., their opposition to the inscription
> of the doctrine of the class war on the banner of the new organisa-
> tion was not simply a reluctant surrender to the tactical requirements
> of the moment. It was also an expression of the conviction, however
> various its grounds, that there were no irreconcilable differences in
> society, that politics was not civil war carried on by other means,
> that there was room for manoeuvre with opponents who were not
> necessarily enemies, and that compromise was not only necessary
> but desirable.[15]

This preference for social unity over class conflict is clear in all the writings of Ramsay MacDonald, who was undoubtedly the major intellectual and political figure in the Labour Party in its first three critical decades.

MacDonald associated the Party in his writings with a rejection of Marxism. 'Neither Marx nor Engels', he wrote, 'saw deep enough to discover the possibilities of peaceful advance which lay hidden beneath the surface . . . any idea which assumes that the interests of the proletariat are so simply opposed to those of the bourgeoisie as to make the proletariat feel a oneness of economic interest is purely formal and artificial'.[16] Instead he offered a definition of socialism that drained it of its class content in favour of a higher 'organic' social unity. 'Socialism marks the growth of society, not the uprising of a class. The consciousness which it seeks to quicken is not one of economic class solidarity, but one of social unity and growth towards organic wholeness'. 'Socialism is no class movement . . . It is not the rule of the working class; it is the organisation of the community'.[17]

And if the Labour Party later rejected MacDonald, it did not in the end reject his philosophy. Throughout its history, its pursuit of class interests has been conditioned, as we have seen, by the need to observe a wider national interest, no matter how nebulous and problematic such an entity is in a class-ridden society. Indeed the recognition of a national interest was a logical corollary of the Labour Party's view that there were grounds for compromise and concession between competing social classes in an industrial society - grounds rooted in interests common to all classes, and therefore, in some sense, above class. As the Labour Party Chairman put it in 1926, 'we transcend the conflict of classes . . . [because] we ask for the co-operation of all classes'.[18]

The precise interplay of 'nation' and 'class' in the rhetoric, programme and performance of the Labour Party has varied over time, with 'class' predominating only for a brief period after the First World War and in the early 1930s and mid 1940s. But from the beginning the pursuit of class interests was mediated through a sensitivity to national ones. This was clear in the bulk of the Party's jingoistic response to the First World War. It was clear in the amazing spectacle of a Labour Government using a revenue surplus in its very first budget (1924) to repay part of the National Debt rather than to alleviate immense working class poverty.* It was clear in the Party's repeated willingness

---

* The Chancellor of the Exchequer in 1924, Philip Snowden, claimed that his budget was 'vindictive against no class and against no interests'. In its very first year in office, the Labour Party reached the bizarre point of having a

The failure of the socialist promise

when in power to use the Emergency Powers Act (and even on occasions, troops) against industrial disputes that were deemed subversive of a wider national interest.[*] And of late it has been clear in the Party's conscious retreat from a class image under Gaitskell and Wilson, and its replacement by a preoccupation with England's national interests and sovereignty - a preoccupation as evident in the 'export or die' rhetoric of Wilson as in the 'little England' thrust of Labour's recent rejection of E.E.C. membership. This surrender of class before nation reached its peak in the election manifesto of the Labour Party in 1970, when the Party went to the electorate behind a rhetoric of national unity and growth that was once the monopoly of its political opponents. The search for compromise between classes has ended in the compromise of class itself.

(b) The possibilities of gradual change

Such a persistent belief in the ultimate empathy of nation and class had considerable consequences for the manner and the institutions through which, according to the early Labour Party leadership, the political interests of the working class could be realised. For the existence of areas of common interest between social classes opened the way to substantial social change by persuasion and the building of consensus, and rendered not just unnecessary but actually counter-productive those routes to socialism that were predicated on the violence of class to class. Instead, the Labour Party committed its working class electorate

---

Chancellor of whom his biographer could write, 'That he should seek a change in the law and use the £48 million for improving the social services or for public works to help the unemployed would not have occurred to him as a serious possibility. One of a Chancellor's prime duties, in his view, was to reduce the National Debt'. (C. Cross, *Philip Snowden*, London, Barrie and Rockliff, 1966, p. 203). He did the same thing in the midst of the Depression in 1929.

[*] As V.L. Allen has observed 'The [Labour] Government was drawn to intervene frequently, and in 1948, 1949 [and] 1951 ... it invoked the Emergency Powers Act; on some occasions it employed troops to move food supplies. The Government's primary concern was to maintain essential services. Its interventions, however, were not markedly dissimilar from interventions before 1926. Troops who moved food supplies were employed in the interests of the community, but in fact they were blacklegs who reduced the effectiveness of the strikes. Strikers did not openly resist as in earlier years; instead they resisted indirectly by extending the duration of the strikes, and making it difficult for a compromise settlement to be reached. Whatever the motives of the Government, troops invariably appeared as strike-breakers and as protectors of the interests of employers.' (V.L. Allen, *Trade Unions and the Government*, London, Longmans, 1960, pp. 127-8).

138

to a road to socialism that would take it slowly through the gradual change of institutions and processes in a piecemeal fashion and at a pace commensurate with the views of all the groups involved. And it committed itself, as the party of the working class, to a twin role of educator in socialist propaganda *and* faithful reflector of the degree of socialist support thus far achieved. One can see in the speeches of the Party's leading figures from the beginning this strange mixture of roles - the one optimistic, the other extremely cautious. Optimism, in the inevitability of socialism. So Sidney Webb described it as 'the inevitable outcome' against which all its enemies were 'ultimately powerless'.[19] But also extreme caution, on the speed with which the inevitable would come. Thus Snowden in 1922 was expecting 'a Labour Government to err rather on the side of conservatism than of extremism . . . hesitat[ing] to go too fast' but rather directing 'its legislation and administration . . . to the gradual supercession of the capitalist system'.[20] And in preparation for such a day, the role of the Labour Party was to educate its electorate ('educational propaganda from the outside and hard constructive thinking within our own ranks' as MacDonald put it)[21] to create a revolution 'of opinion and not of class'.[22] Since, according to MacDonald, 'under democratic government we can never have more Socialism at any given time than human nature will stand', it followed that 'Nothing will ever relieve the Socialist of the burden of making Socialists, or of persuading the community that his views of affairs are right'.[23]

This view of gradual movement towards a new society ('the inevitability of gradualism'[24] as Webb put it) went hand-in-hand with a definition of socialism that was effectively drained of its class content. Certainly there were militants in the Labour Party for whom the socialist commonwealth was the working class come into its own, but with the brief exception of Attlee's writings in the late 1930s, the leadership's projection of the socialist process was devoid of any substantial class content. For MacDonald, the route to socialism was dependent not upon class struggle but 'upon efficiency, planning, organisation, science; upon the understanding of economic change and the conscious pursuit of greater wealth'.[25] It was in essence a technocratic route, just as later, for Wilson, socialism 'meant applying a sense of purpose . . . Purpose means technical skill . . . if there was one word I would use to identify modern socialism it was "science" '.[26] Gone from such visions of socialism, if the term vision can be applied to such banalities, was any notion that the creation of a socialist society

The failure of the socialist promise

involved the redistribution of social power into the hands of the
working class. Rather the problems of achieving gradual social change
in the face of class opposition were effectively circumvented by a faith
in the compatibility of class interests and by a definition of socialism
that removed it from the struggle between classes.

(c) Parliamentarianism

Nowhere was this optimism in the possibilities of gradual social change
by common agreement clearer than in the Labour Party's attitude to
the opportunities presented to the working class by Parliamentary
democracy. For this is the Party which, as Miliband has said, 'has
always been one of the most dogmatic - not about socialism but about
the parliamentary system. Empirical and flexible about all else, its
leaders have always made devotion to that system their fixed point of
reference and the conditioning factor of their political behaviour.'[27]
This immense faith in and consequent commitment to Parliamentary
action was evident from the beginning. It was the whole *raison d'être*
of the Party's creation, that with popular support a Parliamentary
Labour Party with an elected majority could fulfill its entire programme, no matter what that programme might be. Thus MacDonald,
by 1919:

> A parliamentary election will give us all the power that Lenin had to
> get by a revolution, and such a majority can proceed to effect the
> transition from capitalism to Socialism with the co-operation of the
> people and not merely by edict . . . A socialist government in
> Parliament may be met by obstruction, and in the country by
> agitation. But if that Government has the country behind it, it will
> stand no humbug in Parliament.[28]

Snowden agreed.

> Though the avowed advocates of an armed revolution for the over-
> throw of the capitalist system are few in Great Britain, there is a
> fairly considerable section of the Labour and Socialist Movement
> who maintain that a conflict between the masses and the classes at
> the barricades is possible or inevitable, because a bloody revolution
> will be forced by the classes if a Labour Government attempted
> large schemes of reform, involving the expropriation of the capitalist
> class . . . The policy of a Labour Government would be determined
> by the strength of its position in Parliament. A Labour Government
> with a small majority would not be justified in attempting too
> drastic measures of economic and social change. If its majority were

large, and if it had been returned to power on a definite programme
of economic and social reconstruction, then it could proceed to
carry out that programme with the full assurance that its measures
would be supported by the country, and that the minority would
acquiesce . . . The privileged classes in Great Britain have always
shown a remarkable willingness to bow to the inevitable.[29]

This faith in the power of Parliamentary action went hand-in-hand
with a rejection (as both unnecessary and counter-productive) of extra-
Parliamentary political methods, and hence with a rejection of the
politics of the S.D.F., the Syndicalists and the Communist Party.[30] To
the latter, Labour Party leaders were particularly hostile. As Morrison
put it 'the Labour Party believes that progress to Socialism can only be
securely based upon popular understanding and popular consent
expressed in a growing measure of electoral support for the representatives of Labour. We desire Socialism by consent, whereas the
Communists desire dictatorship by imposition.'[31] And in its commitment to Parliamentarianism the Labour Party demonstrated an
antipathy (which grew over the years) to the use of industrial power
by the working class to support political demands, even where those
demands had the backing of the Parliamentary Labour Party and its
leadership. The Labour leadership's support of industrial action against
the threat of arms shipments to Poland and against war with Russia
in 1920 was the great exception; and the Party's attitude to the
General Strike was more typical. Here the deep commitment of the
Labour Party's leaders, in both the industrial and political wings of the
movement, to the inviolability of constitutional procedures was clearly
expressed by J. H. Thomas who, in his abject leadership of the Strike,
made that much quoted and telling remark: 'I know the Government's
position. I have never disguised that in a challenge to the Constitution,
God help us unless the Government won.'[32] In the light of the arguments to follow, it is essential to recognise how entrenched in both the
rank and file and in the leadership of the Party has been this faith in the
potential of Parliamentary action, and how early it came to be
established as one of the defining characteristics of Labour Party
politics.

(d) The autonomy of the State

Such a faith in the possibility of gradual but substantial change through
Parliamentary leadership has been accompanied, from the beginning of
the Labour Party's history, by an immense faith in the autonomy of the

141

The failure of the socialist promise

State machine, in its amenability to radical leadership, and in its capacity to be used as a mechanism for changing the distribution of class rewards in this society. On this view, Parliamentarianism is important precisely because the party that wins an election takes over and can control a huge State machine that is itself capable of effecting major social change. The classic statement of this Labour Party faith actually predates the party itself, in George Bernard Shaw's rejection of the anarchist critique of State power:

> Fortunately, there is . . . a fine impartiality about the policeman and the soldier, who are the cutting edge of the State power. They take their wages and obey their orders without asking questions. If those orders are to demolish the homestead of every peasant who refuses to take the bread out of his children's mouths in order that his landlord may have money to spend as an idle gentleman in London, the soldier obeys. But if his orders were to help the police to pitch his lordship into Holloway Gaol until he had paid an Income Tax of twenty shillings on every pound of his unearned income, the soldier would do that with equal devotion to duty, and perhaps with a certain private zest that might be lacking in the other case. Now these orders come ultimately from the State - meaning, in this country, the House of Commons. A House of Commons consisting of 660 gentlemen and 10 workmen will order the soldier to take money from the people for the landlords. A House of Commons consisting of 660 workmen and 10 gentlemen will probably, unless the 660 are fools, order the soldier to take money from the landlords for the people . . . the State . . . will continue to be used against the people by the classes until it is used by the people against the classes with equal ability and equal resolution.[33]

It was on this assumption and analysis that the Labour Party built its politics, placing its faith in the ability of a democratically elected Government to turn the power of the State machine against the private concentrations of class power. 'If the mass of the ordinary people are agreed upon any policy,' Ramsay MacDonald once declared, 'neither electors, privileged peers, nor reigning houses could stand in their way'.[34] The extraordinary importance which Labour parliamentarians have attributed to themselves and to their electoral success makes almost complete sense from this perspective. As Harold Wilson said, before the 1964 election,

> The State machine is neutral. It is like a car waiting to be driven. Whichever way it is steered, the machine will go. What matters

therefore is the driver. If the man behind the machine is a Labour man, the machine will move towards Labour. Not only Parliament, but the vast machinery of the State which it controls - the police force, the army, the judiciary, the educational institutions, the BBC etc. are politically neutral, loyal to their political masters.

It was on to a party of this kind - one committed to the achievement of gradual social change by the Parliamentary capture of the State machine - that for a generation was grafted a programme of substantial social reform. It took the mass militancy generated by world wars and by the debacle of prolonged depression to prompt the Party to lay down such a programme in 1918, to re-establish it in the 1930s, and to implement it after 1945 via an extensive programme of public ownership and redistributive welfare reforms. This programme was sufficiently radical to attract a whole generation of socialist militants, and to establish 'Labourism' as the political universe of the British working class. It was sufficiently radical to be anathema to sections of the Labour Party leadership in the 1920s, which made it all the more necessary for the Labour Left to be in the Party, fighting the 'backsliding' tendencies of the MacDonalds and the Snowdens. Yet it is worth stressing again that even here, at its most radical, the Party was never more than a *reformist* one; that is, one committed to the abolition of something called 'capitalism' and its replacement by something called 'the socialist commonwealth' gradually, through existing Parliamentary structures, and without recourse either to violent revolution or to the direct mass involvement of a politicised working class beyond that class's periodic visits to the ballot box. And in practice, the programme, as we have seen, was moderate and made precious little impact on the overall distribution of class power in this society. It involved no sweeping attack on the basic structures of ownership and command in the economy (beyond the taking into public ownership, with generous compensation, of a number of bankrupt industries), and amounted rather to a series of legislative initiatives to ameliorate the worst social and economic excesses of untrammeled private capitalism. It involved no sustained attack on the concentrations of class power, but only a slight redistribution of income and wealth. And it involved no fundamental challenge to the distribution of class power within industrial structures, but only the strengthening of trade union negotiating rights within the existing hierarchy of managerial authority. Yet it was out of the difficulties of implementing even so moderate a programme that the retreat from reformism within the

The failure of the socialist promise

Parliamentary Labour Party began, for it was in the implementation of the programme that the Party leadership began to experience the inadequacies of that body of political theory and practice that it had inherited from the early generation of Labour politicians.

3

At the heart of Labourism, as we have seen, has been a faith in the autonomy of the State machine, and in the reforming potential of a Parliamentary majority - a faith that by winning a Parliamentary majority the Labour Party could 'then proceed to construct a new kind of society without any serious hindrance from those whom existing society exists to benefit'.[35] The trouble with such a set of beliefs is that it seriously overestimates the power of the Parliamentary State to change class relationships in the wider society.[36] It was as if the Labour Party - in its reformist period at least, and on its left wing throughout - believed that the lines of class cleavage in a modern industrial society could be translated into the confines of a legislative assembly, and converted there into a question of majority votes between competing teams of Parliamentarians. Thus Harold Wilson, in an interview in 1965,

> The Establishment can make noises, drinking gins and tonics at their New Year Eve's parties, but that doesn't have much effect on politics. Politics is a question of power, and power has been transferred. Whatever people say, at an election, the old Establishment only have one vote each at the end of the day. So has each engineer and miner in my constituency.[37]

The inordinate importance which even the Labour Left has given to Parliamentary ritual and to the Parliamentary career of individual M.P.s suggests that they deluded themselves into thinking that a ruling class can be persuaded to voluntarily surrender its powers and prerogatives (presumably because its members hold more rigorously to the norms of Parliamentary procedure than they do to their own class interests). Certainly the essence of the Party's 'gradualist' perspective was that the privileged and powerful within a capitalist society would allow their power and privileges to be eroded bit by bit, whilst being persuaded that their experience of this gradual erosion (with its promise of more erosion to come) should be accepted out of a wider commitment to the good of the community as a whole. Yet State power cannot be used to undermine class power in that way, and ruling groups have rarely if ever surrendered their power so voluntarily. But the whole theory and

144

practice of the Labour Party at its most radical expected them to do so. It was as though, committed to Parliamentary procedures and constitutionality themselves, Labour politicians failed to see that other groups need not prove so committed; and that the power structure that they faced when in office would not hesitate to use its extra-Parliamentary power to defend its class interests if these were threatened, and in so doing, seriously reduce the freedom of manoeuvre of the Parliamentary State in which the Labour Party had placed so much of its faith.

There have been occasions of course on which the Labour Party has publicly discussed this question of ruling class response. This was particularly so in the 1930s when the collapse of Weimar Germany, the spread of Fascism, and the ignominy of the Labour Party's ejection from office in 1931 combined to prompt a brief consideration of the likely response of industrial and financial capital to a socialist political party in Parliamentary power. Sir Stafford Cripps in particular, in his pamphlet *Can Socialism Come by Constitutional Means?* came as near as any Labour Party leader to questioning the validity of Labourist assumptions on the ability of the Parliamentary State to operate unconstrained by the distribution of class power in the wider society:

> We must face the fact, [he wrote] that those who at present hold the economic power will refuse their support to any Labour Government. The idea that if the Labour Party is gentle and well-behaved it will persuade the capitalists to hand over the economic power to the Government is quite fantastic.

On the contrary, he anticipated that 'the ruling class [would] go to almost any length to defeat Parliamentary action if the issue is the direct issue as to the continuance of their financial and political control'.[38] His solution, though radical, was characteristically a constitutional one: not the counter-mobilisation of the working class but rather the passing by a Labour Government, immediately on taking office, of an Emergency Powers Act under which rapid socialist transformation could be introduced before the capitalist counter-attack could get under way. Similar doubts were raised by Labour Party intellectuals Tawney and Laski in the 1930s,[39] and even Clement Attlee discussed it at some length in his writings in that decade.[40] Here too the solution proposed was a radical but constitutional one: namely that 'the Labour Government must be armed with emergency powers for taking land and buildings without waiting for elaborate enquiries as to compensation', and the House of Lords, at least in its present form, must be abolished.

These early doubts do not however appear to have troubled either Attlee or Cripps in office, and the question of the class constraints on the Parliamentary State was kept alive thereafter only in the most sporadic fashion. For the years of the Attlee Government removed this issue from the agenda of Labour Party politics for two decades, as the young Labour politicians who were to dominate the years of Opposition drew an extremely optimistic lesson from the events of 1945-51. They noted the Labour Party achievements of those years and the lack of visible and sustained ruling class offensive, and concluded both that the constraints had been negligible (and that the fears of the 1930s had been alarmist and unwarranted) and that the Labour Party could have done even more had it so chosen. So Anthony Crosland wrote in 1956,

> the contrast with both the facts and the expectations of the 1930s was complete . . . Pre-war socialists often anticipated violent, if not unconstitutional, opposition from private business; and a whole theory of 'capitalist sabotage', ranging from a flight of capital abroad to a 'strike of capital' at home was constructed on this premiss. The event was very different. Investment proceeded briskly, and indeed had to be restrained; the opposition to nationalisation, although vocal, was never violent; firms and trade associations co-operated amicably with Labour Ministers; there was no hint of sabotage; and generally the atmosphere was one of amiable amenability, not untinged with nervousness.
>
> All this was partly, of course, a reflection of the extreme unplausibility of pre-war Marxist analysis. But it also reflected a consciousness on the part of industry that the balance of power had altered.[41]

In fact, the young Labour M.P.s left office optimistic about the potentiality of State power. As Crossman put it,

> we now know that the power of the State is not in the hands of any class. It is a power in itself, and once you hold that power, once you control the Army, once you control the instruments of coercion, and the instruments of thought control through mass communication, through radio and newspapers - once you control those you have power greater than any Capitalist under the sun.[42]

And yet he would have been more perceptive if he had noted how little the Labour administration under Attlee threatened the existing distribution of social and economic power, and how closely it co-operated

The failure of the socialist promise

with the representatives of industrial and financial capital; and if he had
then concluded that this was the reason that the Labour Government
met so little opposition. It was not the power structure that had
changed from the 1930s so much as the Labour Party itself. Indeed
when the Attlee Government began, however reluctantly, to make inroads into the profitable sectors of British capitalism (with its proposal
for steel nationalisation in 1948) then the opposition which it met was
sustained and ultimately effective. John Saville was quite right when he
wrote:

> The Labour leaders are inhibited in a fundamental way by their
> parliamentarianism: by their unshakable belief that all the British
> are gentlemen and will play the Parliamentary game according to its
> rules. They have, it must be admitted, good reason for these beliefs
> since nothing has ever been done by the Labour leadership to cause
> the gentlemen of England to abandon their acceptance of the rules;
> but the record of the same gentlemen in other parts of the world,
> and on occasion in their own country, makes it abundantly clear that
> rules are adhered to simply because there is no point in abandoning
> a system that so far has provided satisfactory answers.[43]

In choosing to ignore the question of class constraints on the Parliamentary State, the Labour Party after Attlee turned away from the
basic weakness of its whole politics. It ignored the insights of the pre-
war generation, just as they had ignored the criticisms made of Parliamentarianism even earlier, in the European sections of the pre-First
World War Labour International. For the problem of 'bourgeois
democracy' and the consequences of involvement within it, were
argued out fully within the Second International just as the Labour
Party was being formed. But, shut off from the world of Marxist
socialism, the early Labour Party leaders either failed to hear or chose
to ignore the dangers of 'Parliamentary cretinism' as these were laid
out there. For as Rosa Luxemburg noted then, a preoccupation with
Parliamentary politics has always encouraged an over-estimation of the
prospects of peaceful reform and of the co-operation between classes.
'The illusion,' she wrote, that 'parliament is the central axis of social
life and the driving force of world history . . . cannot see beyond the
complacent speechification of a few hundred parliamentary deputies . . .
to the gigantic forces of world history, forces which are at work on the
outside . . . and which are quite unconcerned with their parliamentary
law-making'.[44] * The Labour Party has never been short of this illusion.

* Elsewhere she wrote 'Parliamentarianism supports not only all the illusions of

The failure of the socialist promise

4

In their illusion of Parliamentary 'power' the Labour Party leaders have repeatedly overestimated both the degree of class neutrality that they could legitimately expect from the various sections of the State machine (the civil service, the judiciary and the armed forces) and underestimated the extent to which the close connections between the civil service and the senior managerial hierarchies of private business reduce the availability of the civil service for use in programmes that seriously challenge the social power and class prerogatives of these well-organised and class-conscious groups. The Labour Party on taking office has made no sweeping changes in its senior civil service personnel, and so when it was at its most radical (in 1945) it found itself facing civil servants who were 'apathetic and antagonistic to nationalisation' and who 'by social provenance, education and professional disposition, were bound to conceive it as one of their prime tasks to warn their Ministers against too radical a departure from their traditional Departmental policies'.[45] Not that the Party in power experienced administrative sabotage. Their policies were insufficiently radical to invite that. Rather they experienced an administrative inertia that reflected the close personal, social and ideological interconnections between the State machine and the senior personnel of those private industrial and financial organisations that the Labour Party programme ostensibly challenged.

Nor, as far as we can tell, was this 'administrative inertia' restricted to the 1945-51 Labour Government. Barbara Castle reported exactly the same kind of problem as Minister of Transport from December 1965.* As she wrote later,

> present-day opportunism . . . but also the over-estimation of reform work, of the co-operation of classes and parties, of peaceful development etc. It forms, at the same time, the soil on which these illusions can be confirmed in practice, in that the intellectuals, who as parliamentarians even in Social Democracy are still separated from the proletarian mass, are thus in the sense elevated over that mass. Finally, with the growth of the labour movement, the same parliamentarianism makes of this movement a springboard for political upstarts, and accordingly converts it into a refuge for ambitious and bankrupt bourgeois existences.' (*Leninism or Marxism*, London, I.L.P. pamphlet, n.d., pp. 5-6).

* It was presumably this kind of experience which prompted the Labour Party, in evidence to the Fulton Commission on the civil service, to say 'much more difficult to justify is the amount of information which, in some departments at least, is kept from the Minister. Of course, it is possible for the Minister to find out what is going on in his department if he asks the right questions and asks to see the right files. But an enormous amount of work goes on in a

I am suddenly moved into an atmosphere of ill-concealed hostility
... I do not believe I could have got the Transport Act through -
through the department that is, not the House of Commons - if I
had not had a political team with the same interventionist approach,
ready to do battle with the very laissez-faire philosophy that I
inherited. But is it fair or sensible that a Minister should have to go
through such an expenditure of personal nervous energy to get a
radical change in policy?

I don't know how many of those vast meetings we used to have
on transport policy. It was uphill, uphill, uphill all the way. Quantity
licensing - I might have been proposing publicly-financed sin or
something. The whole instinctive reaction of the Department was
against three-quarters of the Act. I'm not saying that anybody
sabotaged it. I'm only saying I'm the one who needed moral support,
philosophical support, physical support, by people who had gone in
with my approach to transport, instead of having to win over my
civil servants.[46]

And of an earlier encounter with a Permanent Secretary with whom she
had to work, Barbara Castle wrote,

I remember Andy Cohen, the Permanent Secretary, trying to wear
me down. He used to come in on policy points and things like
appointments. He would be in my office about seven times a day
saying: 'Minister, I know the ultimate decision is yours, but I would
be failing in my duty if I didn't tell you how unhappy your decision
makes me'. Seven times a day. One person against the vast department.[47]

For senior civil servants and businessmen shared in the 1940s, and in
the main continue to share, similar social backgrounds, similar educational training, and similar social status and life-styles; and though
none of these guarantee a total empathy of interests between the two
groups, they do mean that senior civil servants are 'part of a specific
milieu whose ideas, prejudices and outlook they are most likely to
share'.[48] More important even than this is the ever-growing

department which the Minister knows nothing of; some of it research work
which produces important results which are never shown to the Minister ... ;
some of it planning work which may be deliberately concealed from him,
either because it might lead him to support policies which the department does
not (or does not yet) approve or even because it is being done in preparation
for a future Government of a different political colour' (Labour Party
evidence to the Fulton Committee on the Civil Service, published by the
Labour Party in London, January 1967, paragraph 19).

interpenetration of State and business hierarchies which brings senior
civil servants into daily and close contacts with the problems, needs
and wider social and political orientations of the world of corporate
capital, and establishes between them and the senior managerial strata
a community of common interests which leaves the civil servants less
and less open to political orientations that are at variance with the
imperatives and class prerogatives of private financial and industrial
institutions.[49] Again, Barbara Castle was very illuminating on this inter-
connection between social background and policy propensities, when
she wrote,

> When I was at the Ministry of Transport we had a long argument
> with our department. John Morris, my Parliamentary Secretary,
> came to me and said, 'Do you know, Barbara, we are getting
> involved in a lot of industrial disputes in this department . . . there
> is nobody here who has really got any effective contact with the
> trade unions. We ought to have a labour affairs adviser.' So I called
> an office meeting.
>
> The entrenched phalanxes moved in on me. The very suggestion
> that civil servants haven't got total capacity to deal with any
> situation. And I remember one, a deputy secretary . . . He said:
> 'Well I must admit Minister it is true that we do tend quite naturally
> to have more contact and, therefore, more affinity with the
> employers' associations. It is not that we wouldn't like to have con-
> tact with the trade unions. But we just don't know how to set about
> it' . . . the . . . bias is there the whole time. It's not because anyone
> wants to help one political party against another. It's just that by
> background and association, contacts must all inevitably be one
> way.[50]

But it must not be thought that the relationship between civil
servants and Labour Ministers are always those of mutual hostility. On
the contrary, as far as can be seen from outside, many Labour Ministers
have proved vulnerable to the inertia of civil service conservatism and to
the orthodoxy of civil service routines. Indeed the more radical the
Minister, the greater that the pressures of that orthodoxy will be, and
few Ministers have been long able to withstand it, let alone been able to
bend the civil service to their initial will. As Richard Crossman reported,
after six years in high government office, 'Departments are resistant.
Departments know that they last and you don't. Departments know
that any day you may be moved somewhere else, and they can forget
you. It does not pay you to order them to change their minds on

everything. There's a limit to the quantity of change they can digest.'
Indeed his view on Whitehall pressure is worth recording here.

> The greatest danger to a Labour cabinet is that its members will be
> corrupted from being a team of socialists . . . into a collection of
> individual Departmental Ministers . . . the battle is really for the soul
> of the Minister. Is he to remain a foreign body in the Department, a
> political dynamo, sparking off things they don't want, things he
> wants and the Party wants. Or is he to become *their* Minister . . .
> That's one danger, that Ministers may become departmental spokes-
> men. The other danger we face is that the Departments get together
> and dictate to the politicians behind the scenes in Whitehall . . .
> Whitehall likes to reach an official compromise at official level
> first, so that the Ministers are all briefed in the same way . . . If
> Whitehall gangs up on you it is very difficult to get your policy
> through, or even to get a fair hearing for a new idea.[51]

This Whitehall of senior civil servants was recently described by a
Labour Minister as a body of 'permanent politicians . . . with a corpus
of politico-economic doctrines - assumptions about the economy, about
society, about Britain's role in the world, [that will] frustrate and blunt
the sharpest Ministerial cutting edge . . . with the conventional wisdom
of Whitehall'.[52] With this in mind the repeated eulogies of many ex-
Labour Ministers over the years to the 'neutrality' and 'co-operation'
of their Permanent Secretaries has a significant ring; but one that tells
us less about 'the infinite ideological and political adaptability of civil
servants' than it does about 'the infinite adaptability of Social Democratic leaders to conservative purposes'.[53]

Yet the constraints on the Labour Party in power run much deeper
even than this. For it is not simply that Labour politics never challenge
the interconnections between the State machine and the capitalist
order. It is rather that the Labour Party in power invariably *strengthens*
those interconnections. For each of the post-war Labour administrations has relied heavily on the expertise and information of private
business, and has drawn many senior business executives into the
planning and control agencies that it has established. Far from transforming capitalism, the Labour Party in power has established intimate
working relationships with that system's managerial personnel. So the
complex system of industrial controls that the Labour Party inherited
in 1945 was left in the hands of senior industrial managers, and in
1964-70 the new State agencies of 'purposive' socialism (the N.B.P.I.,
the revamped N.E.D.C., the I.R.C. and the Land Commission) were

placed in the hands of men drawn from the next generation of those same senior managers, and even (in the case of the N.B.P.I.) in the hands of an ex-Conservative Minister. With such a State bureaucracy, it is hardly surprising that twelve years of post-war Labour Government have left the personnel and institutions of the private sector largely unaffected, and have failed to dent the legal and cultural superstructure within which that private sector maintains its economic and social dominance. Nor, with such a close set of connections between the State bureaucracy and senior managerial personnel from private industry and finance, is it surprising that twelve years of post-war Labour Government have totally failed to change the imperatives (of profit maintenance and capital accummulation) under which a capitalist system functions.

Yet it is no accident that the interconnections between the State and the private capitalist sector are strengthened whenever the Labour Party takes office. For in such a situation, the Labour Party faces - more than anything else - the need to ensure the smooth running of the economy over which it formally presides and on which its electorate depend for their material subsistence. And the Party in power faces only two social groups to which in principle it could turn for detailed and regular assistance: a radicalised trade union and working class movement on the one side, or the existing hierarchies of command on the other. Yet the whole tradition of Labourism has done nothing to create the former, and has indeed fought hard against its creation whenever (as in 1926) the possibility of a radicalised proletariat arose. So the Labour Party in power has left itself with no choice but to seek the co-operation of the ruling groups that it faces in industry and finance, and the appointment of their personnel to State agencies is but one visible sign of the close contacts which the Labour Ministers *must establish* if they are to achieve even their minimum stated programme of economic growth and full employment. The pattern of appointments is also one crucial indication that, in the process, the Labour Government actually strengthens the very economic system and ruling groups that its rhetoric suggested it would control and weaken.

For though it is easy to be misled by the press-coverage, the glamour and the rhetoric of electioneering into thinking that political parties are powerful entities *sui generis*, in reality they are nothing of the kind. The Labour Party in power is some three hundred M.P.s (technically white-collar workers and normally a collection of ex-trade union officials, lawyers, teachers and academics) who assemble in Westminster,

talk to one another in public, and issue documents which we call
'legislation'. These documents, embodiments of Labour Party decisions,
are in no sense self-enforcing. True, they have an immense legitimacy
and an authority which helps to make them so, though that would not
long survive in certain quarters if they proved too radical. And it is the
case that they are buttressed by the administrative and coercive
mechanisms of the State. But even if a radical Labour Party could rely
whole-heartedly on those administrative and coercive mechanisms (and
we have just suggested that this is unlikely) even then it could not
literally dominate all the private structures of command in a capitalist
economy. Instead the Labour Party in power has to win the voluntary
co-operation of the power groups that it faces, and that co-operation
will be forthcoming only on certain terms. There is thus a general truth
in Mannie Shinwell's despairing outburst in 1947: 'We do not produce
coal at the Ministry of Power. People seem to think we do. Coal is not
produced by statistics, or by Government Departments, or even by
speeches, however eloquent they may be. Coal is produced by miners
working underground',[54] and if they won't produce it, nobody else can

It is not that the Labour Party in office faces a unified, centralised
power structure, which leaves the Party as the passive tool of an unseen
elite. It is not a situation of capitalist conspiracy - even less, one of
trade union domination. Doubtless there are, particularly at moments
of crisis, elements of conscious co-ordination between the senior
managerial personnel of the various financial and industrial institutions
that the Labour Party faces. But it is more significant for Labour Party
politics that the men who may or may not conspire are capitalists than
that capitalists may or may not conspire. For the reality of power in a
modern industrial society is an infinitely more complex and subtle
entity than any simple conspiracy theory can allow. It is rather that the
Labour Party, on taking office, faces a complicated matrix of inter-
locking class relationships which set limits on its freedom of manoeuvre,
which effectively limit its ability to redistribute class power and G.N.P.,
which possess the power to negate the impact on the distribution of
class power of any Labour Party initiative, and which on occasions
impose upon the Labour Party in power demands for the redistribution
of resources away from the Party's working class electorate. For in that
complicated matrix of class relationships are concentrations of social
power, institutions whose monopoly of certain material and ideological
resources both gives to the men who head them leverage against the
State and provides those men with a set of private imperatives which

they must defend against a reforming Government if they are to maintain their own class privileges and power.

No one institution is totally dominant. Indeed it is a feature of the social tensions and inherent instabilities of capitalism as a system that it generates no one centre of power. Rather the Labour Party in power faces an industrial process dominated by large (and of late, increasingly multi-national) corporations, whose viability ultimately turns on their ability to maintain a sufficient level of profits to sustain reinvestment and research, and who can reasonably be expected to press for the social and economic conditions that will make that possible. A Labour Government also faces a set of financial institutions that are committed to the free movement of international currencies and to the stabilisation of exchange rates around a strong pound sterling. And it faces an organised working class with a vested interest in the retention and extension of its previously achieved degree of wage levels, job security and job control. At every stage in this matrix of class relationships, the Labour Party meets blockages, obstacles and power centres which have to be ameliorated and cajoled. Precisely because the Labour Party in power has to win the voluntary co-operation of these private power groupings by harnessing their self-interest to its own, so it finds that the ways in which individual and institutional self-interests are structured by the class imperatives of a capitalist society constitute the ultimate level of constraints with which its Parliamentary leadership has to come to terms.

5

There is no doubt that the major blockage on the ability of the Labour Party to reform capitalism into socialism by the Parliamentary process, or even to sustain major programmes of social reform, comes from the institutions and representatives of corporate capital - both financial and industrial. The immediate needs which these institutions have of the State set the terms of reference within which the Labour Party in power has to act, since they determine the conditions on which Labour policies of economic growth can be achieved and co-operation with business ensured. These terms of reference have been variously described. Corporate business certainly requires of the State 'a "reasonable" attitude to key industrial and financial interests; a willingness . . . to preach to the trade unions the virtues of moderation in wage demands; a "sensible" attitude to tax reform; and a sympathetic appreciation of the general requirements of an economy geared to the profit motive'.[55] Financial institutions, and the Bank of England in particular, have shown a persistent preference for fixed exchange rates, and for the free movement of international currencies, and have argued strongly for both before Conservative and Labour Governments alike.* And these general requirements may well extend (at least as far as the multi-national corporations are concerned), as Michael Barratt Brown has argued, to a list of needs that seriously undermine the sovereignty and freedom of manoeuvre of all Governments, including those of Labour. As he put it,

A favourable environment for the development of the multi-national company will include at least the following elements:

1. legal protection for subsidiaries and joint companies operating inside each national state, as favourable as that granted to indigenous companies;

2. taxation rates and concessions for subsidiaries and joint ventures as favourable as those granted to indigenous companies;

3. equal rights with indigenous companies to raise funds in national capital markets;

4. national prices and incomes policies that make possible long term advanced cost control in each subsidiary;

5. national education and training arrangements that provide reserves of skilled and qualified labour at all levels;

6. national industrial relations systems that ensure a dependable labour force at all times;

7. national policies designed to ensure steady growth of consumption and investment expenditure;

8. at the same time, freedom to move goods and capital funds between one country and another with minimal tariff, quota and exchange restrictions.[56]

But let us be clear on what is being argued, and what is not. By arguing that the Labour Party in power has to operate within the terms of reference set by the general requirements of an economy geared to

---

* As Samuel Brittan observed, 'The Bank has always bitterly distrusted exchange controls . . . It also dislikes floating rates intensely. Most traders, whether in goods or money, prefer fixed prices, whenever they can have them, to the risks and uncertainties of price competition, and Central Bankers are no exception. Their attachment to fixed exchange rates and their dire protestations of catastrophe if they are abandoned have some resemblance to the price-ring and cartel mentality so common among ordinary businessmen, and which monopoly legislation has been designed to fight.' (S. Brittan, *Steering the Economy*, London, Secker and Warburg, 1969, p. 113).

the profit motive, this is not to deny that the Labour Government has its own power-resources, which it can use, and which give it leverage against individual firms and industries. On the contrary: many firms and industries, especially those selling large parts of their product to Government agencies, and those in need of investment grants and capital loans, will experience the Labour Government as a senior partner, able to shape their own patterns of profitability and growth directly. Moreover it is clear that the general set of relationships between a Labour Government and industry are affected, if only at the margin, by the degree of unity within the Labour Party, by the size of its Parliamentary majority, by the length of time it has been in office, and by its chances of defeat at the next general election. And all Governments, including Labour ones, possess a wide range of controls that directly affect firms, industries and even multi-national concerns.*

But the danger of stopping the analysis at this point, which is precisely where most Labour M.P.s stop when talking of what 'they' will do to business and finance when in power, is in sliding from the recognition that all Governments have some power to the assumption that that power is unlimited. It is also to forget that the Labour Party, in its more radical periods at least, is promising not simply to *manage* the economic and social system, but to *change* it. As a result, if its own experience between 1945 and 1951 is any guide, a Labour Government is likely to meet opposition 'at every point at which power interests, rather than property interests'[57] are threatened. As Rogow put it, in a classic understatement of the power reality faced by every reformist Labour Government, in such a situation, 'the continued co-operation of vested power groups in measures of social change designed to reduce their power and influence can no longer be taken for granted'.[58]

---

* 'Costs and prices are materially affected by the costs of transport and power, over both of which the government exercises a close (extra-statutory) control; profits are affected by taxation; markets by hire-purchase controls and purchase tax. Businessmen are exhorted to do this and that; they are bribed with subsidies, export services, public expenditure on research, investment allowances and the like. They are dependent on the government for protection against foreign competition and dumping, and for negotiating reductions in foreign tariffs and the removal of discriminatory restrictions put up by other countries. Their trade agreements are subject to official scrutiny and may be outlawed; they cannot enter into any agreement with a foreign undertaking affecting the management and financial control of their company without government permission if the arrangement involves the transfer of sterling. The government is a large purchaser of their products and this affects their freedom of action in many ways.' (J.W. Grove, *Government and Industry in Britain*, London, Longmans, 1962, p. 75).

The failure of the socialist promise

Moreover, even if that opposition were miraculously to be absent, any Labour Government would still inevitably experience a tension between its reforming aspirations and its related search for co-operation with senior managerial personnel in a common drive for sustained economic output. For there are *real* limits to what a Labour Government can do, and to the type of policies it can actually pursue, limits that are rooted in the general requirements of capitalist private enterprise as a system, and these limits eat away at precisely those aspects of Labour policy that the Party periodically has offered to the electorate as a way of transforming capitalism gradually into a more socialist system. It cannot equalise incomes and wealth without destroying the basis of private profit and corporate endeavour.* It cannot take over vast areas of profitable private industry without alienating future private investment and therefore economic growth. It cannot introduce major changes in the distribution of control *within* industry without inviting major ideological counter-attacks from the organs of private capital, and without driving major sources of future plant, machinery and output away to 'safer' political climates. It cannot even sustain exchange controls for any substantial period without provoking a hostile response from international financial agencies and without running the risk that the big multi-national corporations will be driven to redirect their internal resources towards its competitor economies. And as the Labour Party found in the 1960s, with the dwindling international competitiveness of British industry, it cannot avoid taking an interest in cost-effectiveness within industry and in general wage rates and earning levels in the economy as a whole. That is, it cannot avoid playing a role in the control of the working class at the point of production.

For if the Labour Party is to achieve a sustained rate of economic growth from which to pay for greater social welfare programmes, educational expansion and the like, it has to provide when in office that economic and social environment in which private corporate profits can

---

*   Here is the root of Snowden's unexpected conservatism at the Treasury under the very first Labour Government. He dropped the capital levy - the centre-piece of the Party programme, because 'it had now become an electoral millstone . . . [since] the financial and trade condition of the country was such as to make the proposal impracticable'. (Snowden, quoted in R.W. Lyman, *The First Labour Government 1924*, London, Chapman and Hall, 1957, p. 145). As Lyman said, it was clear from this first period of office that 'the private investor [had] joined the working businessman as an object of Labour's solicitude' and that, in consequence, 'the circle of persons whose wealth it would be legitimate to redistribute had become narrow indeed' (*ibid*., p. 146).

157

flourish, and in which the class prerogatives of senior managerial
personnel can remain unchallenged. This shuts off the Parliamentary
road to the socialist commonwealth; for as Raymond Williams has said,

> The very institutions that would be forced to give up their private
> interests to the will of an elected government were the only insti-
> tutions through which the economy could be managed; unless, of
> course, socialist institutions were created to replace them. And it
> was just this option of the creation of socialist institutions which
> the Labour leadership had given up in advance. What was intended
> as a working compromise became first a constraint and finally a
> capitulation. The elected government could direct and manage
> everyone and everything else, but not capital.[59]

It is in this sense that the freedom of manoeuvre of the Labour Party in
power is constrained by the 'health' of the economy in capitalist terms:
by its cost-competitiveness, its overall profit rate, its productivity and
its degree of re-investment. And here, as the politics of 'Catch-22' for
the Labour Party, the paradox occurs: that the maintenance of such
'health' invariably strengthens the very capitalist class the Labour
Government was supposed to control, and brings the Party in power
into conflict with its own industrial wing and its own working class
electorate, who then appear as a secondary blockage on the Party's
freedom of manoeuvre.

For at the heart of the capitalist system lies the tension between the
political economy of Capital and that of Labour, a tension which
throws into fundamental doubt the Labour Party's traditional commitments to social unity, a national interest, and the gradual change of
class society by consensus. That tension takes many forms: of wages
against profits, of managerial prerogatives against working class job control, of capitalist exploitation against alienated labour, of the rich
against the poor in a society divided by the class allocation of wealth,
income, life chances and power. With a Labour Party experiencing and
demonstrating the real limits on its freedom of manoeuvre imposed by
corporate capital, it is hardly surprising that the working class and its
trade unions have come (albeit slowly in its official voice, more rapidly
in sections of its rank and file) to act as a secondary limit on the
freedom of the Labour Party in power, by being reluctant to surrender
easily any of its hard-won industrial control and living standards in a
new Labour Government-inspired social contract.

The Labour Governments between the wars were not so constrained
by working class trade union activity, since the industrial power of the

class was effectively destroyed by the Depression. And even since the war, the labour movement has only been a secondary blockage, after capital, on the Labour Governments - more visible perhaps to the general newspaper reader, but in practice only making its resistance felt spasmodically, in isolated struggles - and at least until the late 1960s, doing so with a degree of reluctance that reflected the ideological ties between the Party and the class that were inherited from the 1930s. For the working class has less day-to-day leverage in the critical decision-making of capitalist enterprise, and therefore less immediate economic power against the State. It is true that its ultimate weapon - the strike - is as potent an instrument of pressure as any in the camp of capital, but it is one which is difficult to use, difficult to sustain, and open to immense ideological, legal and material counter-pressures from the State, the employers and the media. When that counter-pressure has been resisted the industrial power of the working class has been a major blockage on Labour Governments, but to deduce from its occasional use that the working class and capital balance in political terms 'is to treat as an accomplished fact' a working class industrial power that is in fact only 'an unrealised potentiality, whose realisation is beset with immense difficulties'.[60]

Even so, the industrial wing of the labour movement emerged from the war strengthened by full employment, and in the two decades that followed achieved a degree of industrial strength at the point of pro- duction in the critical growth and export sectors (over earnings, over job conditions, and over job security) that gave it something to defend against State encroachments. And the Labour Party, always inheriting in office severe international payments difficulties, found itself repeatedly having to initiate such encroachments. So that when in the late 1940s and throughout the 1964-70 administration the Labour Party in power found itself under heavy pressure from industrial and financial capital to curb the industrial power of its working class electorate, it found that electorate - in its industrial setting - a very reluctant ally in the 1940s, and by the late 1960s an almost totally unco-operative force.

For those very instabilities in Western capitalism (which were most evident in the particular weaknesses of its British section) that were forcing the Labour Party on such a path of confrontation with its working class electorate were also making themselves felt down in the factories and homes of the labour force. They were felt there in the 1960s as increasingly State-induced: at best as inflation, and at worst as

The failure of the socialist promise

the intensification of work routines, short-time working and the threat
(and reality) of redundancy. These very dislocations made sections of
the rank and file of the trade union movement (and eventually even
sections of its leadership) reluctant to surrender to the State any of its
procedural controls or its substantive agreements, since these embodied
the degree of control achieved by the working class over its living
standards and its work routines. Or, if such a surrender was contemplated by the trade union leadership, it was increasingly as part of a
package of changes that were anathema to corporate capital (including
as they invariably did profit control, food subsidies and increased
welfare payments). And so it was that the Labour Party in power
repeatedly found that the area of consensus between competing social
classes on which it predicated the whole of its politics was being
narrowed to the point of extinction by the exigencies of capitalist
instability. As Raymond Williams said, 'The middle ground of British
politics always depended on the viability of British capital in a competitive world. As soon as this viability came into question, the sharp
alternatives of cuts at the expense of one side of industry or the other
had to be faced.'[61]

The consequences of this for the internal stability of the labour
movement have been enormous. For the very failure of the Labour
Party to deliver its more radical promises has eaten away at the
relationship between itself and its working class base. That relationship
has never been very strong. Organisationally the Party structure has
never made any direct connection with the worker at the point of
production. Socially, its leaders have increasingly shed (or never had)
any working class experience or roots. And ideologically, the long-
standing separation of industrial activity from political activity in the
Labourist tradition has sustained a central ambiguity in the relationship
between the two wings of the labour movement. But even so, by 1945
the connection between the working class and the Party was close
indeed. Yet the failure thereafter of the Labour Governments to shift
substantial degrees of power and resources away from corporate capital
has left its working class electorate still subject to capitalist instability,
still dependent on its own industrial efforts to achieve that degree of
affluence, job security and job control that the Labour Party could not
guarantee, and still subject to marked inequalities of power and wealth.
And as such the working class electorate is left increasingly as, at best, a
reluctant ally of a Labour Party whose response to repeated pressure
from international and national industrial and financial capital has been

The failure of the socialist promise

to adopt a 'managerial' attitude to the trade union movement and its activities that bodes ill for the continuing close relationship between the two wings of the labour movement.

This is a theme to which we will return in chapter 8. For the moment we need note only two features of this relationship between the Labour Party and the trade union movement. We need to note first that the instabilities of Western capitalism set real limits on the freedom of manoeuvre of any Labour Government, be it seeking total social transformation or merely substantial social reforms. Those limits are set both directly, via the Labour Government's relationship with corporate capital, and also indirectly, via the resistance to Government initiatives that those instabilities generate in the rank and file of the trade union movement. And that moreover, in such a situation it is hardly surprising that a Labour Party seeking a close and co-operative relationship with organised capital has tended to see the trade union movement as a blockage on its freedom of action, and has shown a propensity to turn against the militant sections of that movement with a ferocity that might not be expected from a party created 'to represent the labour interest in Parliament'. For this is but one important consequence of the Labour Party's general experience in power that there exist real and potent limits on its capacity to legislate successfully against the imperatives of the existing social order - real limits, that is, on the possibility of peacefully transforming capitalism into a 'new social order', or even of obliging a capitalist system and its ruling strata to accept major programmes of social reform. It is this repeated experience of the limits of the possible for the State in a capitalist system that has been one major factor pulling the Labour Party leadership away from radical programmes, and one major reason for that leadership's unimpressive performance when in office.

6

Before probing the consequences of this for the Labour Party's own development, we should note how it is reinforced by a secondary and related feature of Labour Party politics, namely by the Party's relationship with its electorate. For the utter dependence of the Labour Party in power on the voluntary co-operation of senior managerial personnel in private industry reflects the absence of any alternative power base within the labour movement itself to which the Party, in any confrontation with Capital, could and would be willing to turn. It reflects the absence, that is, of a radicalised proletariat able and willing to buttress Labour Party policy initiatives by industrial action at the point of production, and of a trade union movement prepared to take on that role. There have been moments, certainly, when events external to the Party have produced signs of mass political radicalism in the British working class; and it has been at these points, and only at these points, that the Labour Party has found a radical programme both electorally vital and politically viable. But it is hardly too much to say that the 'reformism' of the Labour Party before 1970 was a temporary consequence of two wars and a prolonged depression, rather than something endemic to its whole mode of politics. For the Labour Party has never set out to create such a radicalised proletariat. On the contrary, such a radicalised proletariat has always been anathema to the Labourist tradition.

Instead the Labour Party has been committed to a theory of party-class relationships which gives the Party an educating role (between the wars, for example, as a socialist propagandist) but which restricts the Party programme at any stage to a point commensurate with existing levels of political consciousness in the Labour electorate at large. Indeed, its whole mode of politics, Parliamentarianism, has made this essential, as we shall see. And in its preoccupation with Parliamentarianism, the Labour Party has not even used Parliament, as many revolutionaries have used equivalent institutions elsewhere, primarily as a stage upon which to make agitational and propagandist statements that could connect with, generalise, and intensify the growing conflict between the classes at the point of production. On the contrary, Labour Party pronouncements on even industrial disputes have been uniformly hostile to mass radicalism, and have sought always to emasculate the class struggle by restricting it to constitutionally sanctioned channels. This is as true of its hostility to the General Strike of 1926 as it is of its reaction to working class industrial opposition to the 1971 Industrial Relations Act: that the working class should not challenge the legal powers of the State by extra-constitutional industrial means, even if those legal powers were visibly class-biased and even if the alternative is to surrender and wait for the next Labour Government. To the extent that the Labour Party has had any impact at all on patterns of consciousness in its working class electorate, it has been to constantly reinforce the illusion of the untrammelled sovereignty of the democratically elected Parliamentary State.

The failure of the socialist promise

But in fact the Labour Party has had far less impact on the general level and type of consciousness in its working class electorate than have its political opponents. There are a number of reasons for this. In part, it reflects the control which private capitalists have retained over the mass media, and their willingness to use that control to defend their class privileges by sustained propaganda against Labour radicalism. The campaign against the nationalisation of steel, sugar and chemicals at the end of the Attlee Government is a case in point. Much more importantly, it also reflects the fact that the gap between Labour promises and Labour performance in office always provides such propagandists with an enormous stick with which to beat the Party. This was particularly important in the 1950s, when the very failure of the Attlee Government to transform capitalism into socialism via public ownership, state planning and welfare provision left even Labour voters sceptical of the Party's pre-occupation with the further creation of public corporations. For the Party had promised working class emancipation and a qualitative change in human existence. It had created instead a bureaucratised public sector and a strengthened capitalist class. Here the limits of State power under a 'reformist' Government left, as an *electoral legacy* to the next generation of the Party, a generalised antipathy to nationalised industries and State planning, and a concomitant faith in a private enterprise system which had been strengthened by the Attlee Government's nationalisation policies. It left, that is, a 'conservative renaissance'[62] to which the Party leadership increasingly succumbed, and against which its counter-propaganda was increasingly defeatist and hesitant.

Yet the Labour Party could ill afford such listlessness in its propagandising, for the scales of history were, and remain, against it. It inherited a predominantly conservative electorate, with a popular culture rooted in a liberal-imperialist past. Admittedly, two world wars and the inter-war experience of capitalist instability had moved that electorate towards political radicalism, but still with a culture that contained within it the anti-socialist notions and aspirations of Victorian imperialism. It inherited also a class structure riddled with internal, subsidiary status divisions between occupational groups, and one which since 1945 has witnessed a substantial shift out of manual employment into white collar occupations that were traditionally less closely identified with 'the working class' and the Labour Party. It would have taken - and still requires - a massive ideological effort on the part of the Labour Party to have shifted that legacy. But, in the event, this was an effort which the Labour Party undertook only sporadically and with limited effect. All too often, the Party surrendered to existing levels of prejudice in an undignified search for votes on any terms, so reinforcing tendencies in popular culture that were inimical to radical social change on socialist lines. This has weakened the Party profoundly, as Anderson has observed:

> The real criticism to be made of them is . . . that they *cannot* gain power as long as they sacrifice principle for the sake of winning elections. They may well win, but under these conditions 'power' is simply permission to operate the status quo. It has no purchase whatever on the statute of the society. There is no 'mandate' for changing this. Social-democracy is thus trapped in the closed circle of electoralism. It restricts its own freedom to win a partial power which is then further curtailed by its initial restriction. The result is a profound impotence and demoralisation.[63]

The precise manifestations and consequences of this varied over time. Between the wars, when the Labour Party faced an electorate shaped by political forces stronger than itself, it encouraged the Party to tone down the radicalism of its 1918 programme, until the severity of the Depression and the rigours of war presented to it an electorate demanding radical change. In the specific conditions of capitalist prosperity in the 1950s, the repeated evidence of electoral scepticism and hostility towards public ownership that the half-heartedness of the Attlee Government had itself created, was a major force pulling the Party leadership away not simply from its old 'reformist' trilogy of nationalisation, planning and welfare, but from any 'reformist' aspirations at all. And even in the changed conditions of the 1970s, when capitalist instability has undoubtedly created again a more generalised dissatisfaction within the Labour Party's potential electorate, the Party leadership are still under 'electoral' pressures to moderate their promises.

Of course, this attempt to moderate the Party's image partly reflects the leadership's realisation of how little they can actually do in power (though Labour politicians in the past have tended to forget this all too easily as the years of Opposition have lengthened). What the Party leaders cannot forget are the electoral pressures for moderation in their programme. For the Party's Parliamentarianism effectively isolates it from the points of working class struggle, and militates against effective propaganda work by the Party there. And yet this same Parliamentarianism makes the Party totally dependent upon an electorate (whose

164

support it *must* win to be able to do anything in Parliamentary terms at all) - an electorate subject to waves of ideological pressure from the Party's political opponents. Indeed, the Labour Party's passivity and impotence before the electorate is even greater than this, for it is dependent if it is to 'win' State power, not simply on the generalised support of the electorate, but on the support of critical smaller electorates in a series of marginal constituencies. It *must* win these, and by definition these are the very constituencies in which party radicalism runs the greatest risk of voter-alienation and consequent electoral defeat. The massive Labour vote of Ebbw Vale would doubtless tolerate radicalism from the Party. Indeed the Labour Party's problem now is that its traditional vote in places like the Welsh valleys is being eroded by the Party's conservatism in office. But it dare not be more radical, lest its critical marginal vote be lost. Of course, there are those in the Party who argue that it should gamble, and educate its electorate in a radical alternative.[64] But even they have to concede that it *is* a gamble, and they have invariably gone along with a toning down of party programmes at election times that is commensurate with the political sympathies of the marginal seats. Even in power, as between 1964 and 1970, it was this sensitivity to the electoral proclivities of marginal seats and marginal voters which reinforced the tendency of the Party leadership to conservatism and moderation.[*]

7

This twin experience, of the limits of State power and the logic of electoral politics under capitalism, is the source of the growing conservatism of the Labour Party's chosen agency of social change, the Parliamentary Party and its leadership. Together, they had effectively destroyed that Parliamentary Party by 1970 as an agency of anything but its own desperate search for government office. This twin experience had whittled away the radicalism of earlier party programmes, and in the process had transformed the Parliamentary Party into a mechanism for mediating the immediate needs of the capitalist

[*] As one Minister in the 1964-70 Government, Reg Prentice, has written, the Government 'made too much of a virtue of pragmatism . . . Excessive pragmatism is not only a reaction to the pressure of events. It is sometimes a deliberate political choice . . . [the result of] an obsession with the opinion polls and a deliberate search for a consensus view, the objective being to remain in possession of the "middle ground".' (R. Prentice, 'Lessons of the Labour Government: not socialist enough', in *Political Quarterly*, 41(2) April-June 1970, pp. 148-9.'

system to the working class, rather than one that could lead the class to transform capitalism, or even one that could effectively impose upon the capitalist system social reforms of sufficient scale to make a qualitative difference to the life experience of its electorate. And it had done this by educating the Parliamentary leadership into a definition of the 'realistic' in politics that was coterminous with the maintenance of the existing distribution of social power,* and had in the process generated a set of leaders whose hypersensitivity to the imperatives of that realism left them as only pale reflections of their more radical younger selves. As a result, we are left, as Tom Nairn has observed, with a situation in which

> realism turns, in Labour leaders, into mere cowardice, a kind of timid hypnosis in the face of events; practicality turns into wilful short-sightedness, a ritual pragmatism wielded to exorcise the sort of theoretical thinking socialism requires; [in which] dignified reverence for the past becomes a depraved fetish-worship of idols which seem to change into dust at the very touch of such falsity.[65]

Now when faced with such a set of Parliamentarians, it is conveniently easy to restrict the explanation of Labour Party conservatism and failure in office to an analysis of the personalities that make up the leadership. The 'sell-out' thesis, as we saw at the beginning of this chapter, has a long pedigree in Labour Party polemic and analysis. So the Labour Party is explained and excused because some of its leaders found personal advantages in sucking up to the rich (the theory of the 'aristocratic embrace'). Or it is criticised because its constituency Parties have proved too fond of selecting M.P.s from middle class

---

* So Harold Lever could write, of the 1964-70 Labour Government of which he was a member: 'With big battalions behind him, it is felt that Mr. Wilson will be under irresistable pressure from the Left and will yield to his supposed hostility to free enterprise. But . . . Clause Four or no Clause Four, Labour's leadership plainly believes in a mixed economy . . . [it] knows as well as any business man that an engine which runs on profits cannot be made to run faster without extra fuel . . .[profits then] must and will, over a longer period, increase significantly . . . Share values will continue to reflect assets and earning powers - even after a 40% Corporation Tax and Capital Gains Tax, which at 30% can hardly be described as confiscatory . . . Profit alone is not enough. No individual or economic group works well in an atmosphere of public disapproval, and Labour leaders should understand that businessmen, too, have their susceptibilities; they are entitled to good repute as well as reasonable profit. For their part, businessmen should show less sensitivity and more sense. It is time they realised that a ringing political slogan is often used as a sop to party diehards or as an anaesthetic while doctrinal surgery is being carried out.' (Quoted in K. Coates, *The Crisis of British Socialism*, Nottingham, Spokesman Books, 1971, p. 111).

occupations (the theory of leadership 'embourgeoisification'). Or it is
excused because some of its leaders, isolated from the rank and file,
found solace in excessive sensitivity to Parliamentary procedures (the
theory of 'parliamentary socialisation'). Or the Party is condemned
because a good number of its leaders, overworked and overawed, fell
victim to the dictates of their civil servants, (the theory of 'poor quality
Ministers'). Clearly Labour Party history is rich in examples of all
these, and no explanation of Labour Party politics can ignore them.
J. H. Thomas was undoubtedly under the domination of his Permanent
Secretary, Sir Horace Wilson, whom he knew affectionately as 'Orace'.[66]
Herbert Morrison was clearly passionately committed to Parliamentary
procedures and norms. Ramsay MacDonald clearly accentuated the
trend to conservatism by his personal foibles and growing empathy with
aristocratic ladies. But the trend existed in any case, and it is no
accident that the Parliamentary leaders of the Labour Party have
succumbed to these tendencies. For the logic of their conservatism is
rooted in the general character of Labour Party politics.

For what characterises that politics is that it generates sets of leaders
who, in office, experience particular problems, and particular possibilities of success and failure. To achieve power at all, as we have seen,
they require the support of marginal voters. Then, when in power, they
need the co-operation of the hierarchies of private capitalism that
surround them. They both daily experience the potential offered to
them when that co-operation is forthcoming, and the frustration and
impotence that follows its withdrawal. And in both cases, their daily
experience of office, and their observation of it from afar when in
Opposition, underline how essential it is for the Labour Party leadership to establish their 'respectability' in the eyes of the power-groupings
that they face. So the desperate search for 'respectability' and the
repeated attempts to 'prove their fitness to rule' which characterise the
speeches and policies of Labour Ministers are no accident of Ministerial
personality (though they may be accentuated by that). They are rather
rooted in the Labour Party's need for co-operation. They are the visible
admission by the Party's leaders of the limits of State power. And given
the Labour Party's pretensions to be a party of social reform, this
'respectability' is always in doubt. Business co-operation is something
on which the Party's leadership can never automatically rely, since it is
something which the Party's radical rhetoric in Opposition has
invariably done much to put in jeopardy. And so paradoxically, the
stronger the Labour Party politically, the more radical its programme,

167

and the louder its left wing, the less secure will organised capital feel, and the more that it will demand of the Labour leadership as 'proof' of that Party's 'soundness' and suitability for co-operation. Only the peculiar situation of post-war mass radicalism eased this corporate pressure in 1945, and even then it was fully back in evidence as early as 1948. Edmund Dell has described the daily reality of this lack of confidence in Labour Governments felt by business leaders:

It would be wrong to imagine that when government talks to industry it is a conversation between institutions. It is in fact a conversation between individuals. Possibilities of misunderstanding and resentment are therefore greater when there is a Labour government. As individuals and as members of the Labour Party, Labour ministers have political presumptions and ideals which are not shared by the great majority of the leaders of industry. However enthusiastic Labour ministers may be at encouraging the development of the private sector, however much they may consult, however slow they may be in extending the public sector, there is a residuum of doubt and distrust in the minds of industrial leaders. As an unknown Junior Minister I was once taken for a civil servant by the host of a lunch party of businessmen and received condolences on having the task of serving Labour ministers. Even where Labour ministers show themselves understanding of the problems of industry there remains the question of taxation of personal income to act as an irritant in these relationships. As individuals industrial leaders objected to the level of taxation. If they were owners they objected to the close company provisions. If they were senior executives in large firms perhaps with little private capital of their own, they objected furiously to the disallowance of interest on bank borrowings. I remember one industrialist, who had been more friendly and co-operative than most, exploding about the effect of that measure on his standard of living. There was not much that a Labour government could do for industry in general or for his company in particular which would compensate him for the personal consequences of that decision.[67]

This is the paradox at the heart of Labourism - that Michael Foot has called 'the fundamental and fatal contradiction of the Labour Party'. It was a dilemma clear to Aneurin Bevan as early as 1931, that:

In opposition, the Labour Party is compelled, by the nature of the class struggle, to take up an alignment which hamstrings it when in office. A Party climbing to power by articulating the demands of the dispossessed must always wear a predatory visage to the property-owning class . . . although all the time its heart is tender with the promise of peaceful gradualism. It knows that the limited vision of the workers will behold only its outward appearance, but it hopes that the gods of private enterprise will look upon its heart. In either case, one must be deceived. To satisfy the workers the Labour Party must fulfill the threat of its face, and so destroy the political conditions necessary to economic gradualism. To calm the fears of private enterprise it must betray its promise to the workers, and so lose their support.[68]

When in power, the pressures on the Labour Party leadership to take that second option, 'to betray its promise to the workers', are enormous.* As we saw, senior managerial personnel in the major private industrial and financial agencies possess a number of potent sanctions against a recalcitrant Government which in the past they have been prepared to use. So even in the Labour Party's modest history, its leaders have known strikes by senior managerial personnel, ideological offensives against certain of its policies, flights of capital out of the country, and dictation of domestic and foreign policy terms by those in control of international lending agencies. Indeed, the very international competitive weakness of British capitalism and the legacy of an Imperial past have left every post-war British Government particularly dependent on these last mentioned financial agencies. This has given British finance capital a particular leverage on the Labour Party in power, precisely because its co-operation has been vital to stem the short-term net export of funds that would otherwise send the economy into a payments deficit with the usual crippling effects on domestic interest rates, economic growth and manufacturing investment.

Yet it is significant that the Labour Party in power has only rarely experienced these breakdowns of co-operation between its leadership and the well-organised representatives of industrial and financial capital. Instead and more normally, as we have seen, the relationship between the State and the capitalist sector has been strengthened under Labour. For the threat that a radical Labour Party poses to the existing distribution of class power has been neutralised over the years far less by class coercion and lack of co-operation, far more by the *incorporation*

---

* As Richard Crossman put it, 'A Labour Government must defend as true Socialism policies which have very little to do with it. The job of Party leaders is often to persuade their followers that the traditional policy is being carried out, even when this is demonstrably not true.' (Quoted in S.M. Lipset, *Political Man*, London, Mercury Books, 1963, pp. 405-6.)

of the Labour Party leadership into the command structures and world
view of the ruling groups that the Party once existed to bring down. It
was this process of incorporation that Labour Party militants of the
1930s, in their anticipation of open class confrontation when the Party
took office, failed to envisage; and which the later apologists for State
power under Labour, reacting as they were to the confrontationist
expectations of Cripps, failed to see.

Two sets of relationships experienced by Labour politicians are
particularly significant here. Their experience of Parliamentary procedures and atmosphere is clearly one force incorporating many M.P.s
into less radical ways. As Bevan said, the radical M.P. must really be on
his guard:

> To preserve the keen edge of his critical judgment he will find that
> he must adopt an attitude of scepticism amounting almost to
> cynicism, for Parliamentary procedure neglects nothing which might
> soften the acerbities of his class feelings. In one sense the House of
> Commons is the most unrepresentative of representative assemblies.
> It is an elaborate conspiracy to prevent the real clash of opinion
> which exists outside from finding an appropriate echo within its
> walls. It is a social shock absorber placed between privilege and the
> pressure of popular discontent.[69]

This certainly was the experience which Fenner Brockway observed in
the 1930s, that in particular the 'social life associated with Parliament
blunts the sense of identity with the working class in their struggle'. All
too often, he recorded, 'one saw Labour M.P.s falling to the glamour of
the social life of the other side, steadily leaving their own class behind
them and becoming conditioned by the amenities and atmosphere of
the class which exploited the very men and women whom they had
been sent to the House of Commons to represent'.[70] Even Nye Bevan
himself, though he was a radical on the Left of the Party for virtually
his entire Parliamentary career, fell under the spell. As his biographer
and colleague, Michael Foot, put it, the impotence of Parliament in the
1930s and his own struggles with the Party leadership might easily have
induced in Bevan

> a hostility to Parliament itself, reinforcing the old semi-syndicalist
> theories of industrial action which he had brought with him to
> Westminster in 1929. But curiously the effect was the opposite . . .
> even while the institution was failing so pitifully to mirror the
> turmoil outside, he acquired a deep respect, almost a love, for the
> House of Commons. He saw it as a place where, given a proper use of

its possibilities, poverty could win the battle against property
without bloodshed. Not that he enjoyed, as a substitute for political
action, the cosy conventions of the Parliamentary game. He never
shut his ears to the storms outside . . . Yet gradually and impercep-
tibly - and the fact was of considerable importance for his own
future and the Labour Party's - he came to regard Parliament as the
most precious potential instrument in the hands of the people.
Doubtless his own powers in the arena influenced his view. It would
be harsh to blame a great matador for upholding the virtues of bull-
fighting.[71]

Yet Parliamentary socialisation can be, and has been, resisted - at
least by those few M.P.s for whom the Commons was never more than
an arena in which to make propaganda for the class struggle going on
outside. Far more insidious, and ultimately more crucial, is a second set
of relationships of incorporation between Labour Ministers on the one
side and their senior advisers in the Ministries on the other. This seems
to have been, and to remain, the major and most potent mechanism by
which Labour Party politicians are absorbed into the ruling ideas of the
day. It is the ability of private capitalism to dominate the definitions
and policy options perceived by a Labour Government which holds the
key to the absence of more frequent and more open withdrawals of co-
operation by various sections of the British ruling class whenever the
Labour Party is in power.

For the Labour Party in office is enveloped in the 'conventional
wisdoms' of the day, operating in a 'reality' defined for it by the civil
servants of the public *and private* bureaucracies that it faces (in the
Treasury, the C.B.I., the Bank of England and so on).* Because the
Labour Party coming into power inherits a situation in which there is a
close inter-penetration of personnel, institutions and attitudes between
the State bureaucracy and the private bureaucracies of industry and
finance, so it inherits a government machine which offers it only a
limited range of policy options, and which tells it repeatedly that only a
limited range of 'solutions' are possible to 'problems' that are

---

* Even the first Labour Government met this problem. As Ramsay MacDonald
said in 1924, 'until you have been in office, until you have seen those files
warning Cabinet Ministers of the dangers of legislation, or that sort of thing,
you have not had the experience of trying to carry out what seems to be a
simple thing, but which becomes a complex, an exceedingly difficult, and a
laborious and almost heartbreaking thing when you come to be a member of a
Cabinet in a responsible Government'. (Quoted in Lyman, *The First Labour
Government 1924*, p. 138).

themselves defined by civil servants operating within a world view and set of class interests shared with the senior echelons of private capitalism. At its most extreme, no Treasury Minister has presumably faced a brief in which the policy options before him stretch from de-valuation and deflation on the one side, to workers' control at the point of production at the other. On the contrary, the choice of policy options is structured and restricted: such that,

> Only a small band of the full range of alternative policies is effectively ventilated and disputed. Indeed, on some issues the band may be so narrow that decisions seem not to be 'made' at all - they just flow automatically from the 'climate of opinion'.[72]

This is very clear in the kind of information coming to Labour Ministers from the Bank of England. Readers might compare the marked similarities between the 'doom warnings' given to (and believed by) Philip Snowden in 1931[73] and Harold Wilson's description of life with the Governor of the Bank of England. A typical example from Wilson's memoirs runs as follows:

> The Governor was in his gloomiest mood and clearly felt that the financial end of the world was near. More speculation, more trouble for the pound could only mean the collapse of the world monetary system. The dollar would be engulfed: it might even go first . . . He pressed the point further and I said that if the issue was as bad as he thought, then I would be ready to fly to America for talks with the President and the Federal Reserve Authorities.[74]

Contrary to the Governor's prophecy, of course, the financial world is still intact, but Ministers getting that on a daily basis must surely be forgiven slightly for losing touch with reality. As at least one of the 1964-70 Ministerial team has said, this kind of relationship was a crucial factor in what he termed 'the drift to the right' of the last Labour Government. It is not simply the Governor of the Bank of England. It is also that Labour Ministers

> are constantly in contact with the 'establishment' . . . higher civil servants, leaders of industry and commerce and leaders of the various pressure groups who have access to Ministers' offices. Most of them are very good people and they do not, of course, all think alike. But they tend to transmit the conventional wisdom of the upper-middle classes of the South East of England.[75]

To this enmeshing of the Labour Ministers in the ruling ideas of the day, the Labour Party makes its own contribution, by repeatedly failing to generate *alternative* definitions, detailed policies, *and* the social

172

forces on which to break through the material and ideological domination of this class of men at the top of the industrial, financial and
public bureaucracies.* As a result, so all pervasive are these orthodoxies,
so united are these bureaucracies in their definition of 'important
problems', 'policy alternatives' and 'desirable solutions' that the Labour
Party in power faces a body of ideas that appears not as the embodiment of the interests of the ruling class alone but as the embodiment of
the interests of the society as a whole. The Labour Party in power, that
is, faces a truly 'hegemonic' power structure, before which Labour
Party politicians find themselves helpless, lacking as they do a counter-
definition of reality of the same force and any alternative power base
on which to put that counter-definition into practice. And so their
very impotence without the co-operation of this hegemonic power
structure only persuades them, on a day to day basis, that they really
do face only the set of policy alternatives that they are offered by their
civil service.†

The situation has been well summed up by John Saville, an argument that is worth reproducing in full.

When a Labour administration takes over the Government they
inherit a large bureaucratic apparatus that is continuing to
administer the affairs of the country. The first thing a Labour
Government does is to carry on, using the accepted and traditional

* Paradoxically, what thinking the Labour Party did between 1951 and 1964,
in drawing upon their reading of the Attlee experience, actually anticipated
many of the 'problems' and 'solutions' that the leading sections of British
capitalism would later demand: in particular, in the areas of State planning
and wages control. In such a situation, the Labour Party approaching the 1964
Election could genuinely feel itself more 'modern' and 'progressive' than its
Conservative opponents; and could genuinely persuade itself that it was
following its own pre-election thinking when in office. The very retreat from
the class rhetoric of Labour reformism, and the abandonment of the central
policy planks of the Attlee Government during the years of Opposition
opened the way to the untrammelled absorption of the Labour Party leadership into the control structures of British capitalism after 1964. The result,
as Brian Lapping observed, was that 'where once it may have been possible to
tell a Labour M.P. from a Conservative by his accent or his clothes, it was now
no longer possible to tell for certain even by many of his views'. (B. Lapping,
The Labour Government 1964-1970, Harmondsworth, Penguin, 1970, p. 21).
† To this extent, the perennial demand, from within the labour movement, that:
Ministers use their own advisers, brought in from outside the civil service,
does touch upon one of the central problems of Labour politics. The difficulty
- as both Richard Crossman and Marcia Williams have made clear in their
recent and already cited writings, is that the established civil service is both
willing and able to destroy the effectiveness of these men and women, who so
challenge them by cutting them off from information and by organising
against them.

173

practices and procedures. Its ministers slip into the seats just vacated by their Tory predecessors, and are served by the same Civil Servants whose social background is attuned to Conservative traditions. Socialists even of a moderate kind are rare in the higher reaches of the Civil Service: left wing socialists entirely absent. Labour Ministers are for the most part men who have spent many years already in Westminster: Parliamentary practices and procedures are accepted as right and proper and fundamentally unalterable, including the fiction of the neutrality of the Civil Service. Assuming that the Government has some reforming intentions, the complicated processes begin of drafting new legislation and then getting it accepted: first from within the Civil Service and then by Parliament. The pressures on a Minister from his Civil Servants, from outside vested interests, from the Tory opposition in Parliament are intense and continuous; and the more radical the measure the greater the weight of opinion and interest with which the Minister responsible will have to contend. In the case of legislation that is genuinely reforming in intention the pressures to narrow its scope and limit its application will be unceasing and unrelenting; and the reform when it finally appears as an Act of Parliament will be a good deal more orthodox and limited than when it began its passage as a draft measure . . . It is the density and tenacity of conservative institutions in Britain that defeats the genuine reformer and when reform is finally granted, often after years of weary struggle, its significance is usually exaggerated.[76]

In such a situation, it is no accident that the 'class' content of the Labour leadership's aspirations should drain over time, not least because it is the manifestations of working class aspirations which create problems for them in their dealings with the City and with organised business. As politicians in power they depend for their success on their ability to find the common ground between opposing class forces; or, failing that, on their ability to ally with the stronger class. For the alternative for them as Parliamentarians is total ineffectiveness and likely electoral defeat. So, out of their daily experience, the Labour Party leadership are driven to a view of 'reality' which defines as 'the problem' those working class forces which make more difficult the establishment of close working relationships with the senior managerial strata of private industrial and financial capital. Out of the logic of their own politics Labour leaders are drawn away from their class perspectives and their class roots, and emerge highly sensitive to the

The failure of the socialist promise

requirements of the capitalist structure that they face, increasingly
socialised in the norms of Parliamentary gradualism, increasingly prone
to define reality from a managerial standpoint, increasingly reluctant to
mobilise or radicalise their own working class base, and increasingly
willing to use State power (at times of class crisis) directly against the
material interests of the working class that they claim to represent.*

Nor is it an accident that the Labour Government in 1931, in 1948,
and in 1964-70 seriously weakened itself defending the parity of the
pound sterling that the Conservatives calmly abandoned immediately on
taking office. For the hyper-sensitivity of international financiers to
Labour plans, and the capacity of flights of money abroad to cripple production at home, leaves the Labour Party leadership *necessarily*
sensitive to the City's demands. For the financial institutions of the
City actually possess a series of material sanctions whose short-term
impact on Labour Government policies is considerably greater and more
immediate than anything that industrial capital or the organised
working class can muster. Indeed these moments of capitalist crisis
demonstrate the bankruptcy of the Labour tradition, as the leaders of
the Party are driven to turn the power of the State machine against
their own plans and against the living standards and industrial power of
their own working class electorate. For in a very real sense the Labour
Party leaders have *no choice*, if they are to win the co-operation of
organised capital, if they are to create the economic conditions in
which organised capital can afford to co-operate, and if they are to
'prove' that they can be trusted to rule. Or rather, precisely because
they have failed to mobilise any alternative source of political power
in their own working class electorate, they have no choice. It is from
the logic of their own politics that they find themselves isolated from
their own rank and file, under the intense personal pressures of office,
and with ideological defences that are inadequate to repel conservative
orthodoxies. And so ultimately Labour Party leaders find themselves in
this ludicrous situation: formally socialist M.P.s, but in reality

* As Allen Hutt put it, 'Is it that the leaders of the movement are insincere men,
dishonest men who deliberately ignore the lessons of experience? Nothing of
the kind. They are men whose point of view has been shaped by the circumstances of their personal and political lives; and that point of view may be
summed up by saying that they have a profound lack of faith in the working
class and an equally profound, almost a superstitious awe of what they feel to
be the almighty and unshakable power of the capitalist class. Hence they take
the accommodating course.' (*The Post-War History of the British Working
Class*, p. 316).

dependent for their definition of the 'national interest' on the specifications of the central institution of British finance capital. The bankruptcy of Labourism could nowhere be more clearly demonstrated than in this.

7. The weakness of the Labour Left

Presumably many people will disagree strongly with the argument of the book so far, but surely none more so than those on the Left of the Party, whose whole political strategy is directly challenged by an argument of inevitable Labour conservatism. It would be pleasant to think that the logic of deradicalisation could be reversed from within the Party, and that it could again be transformed into a vehicle of socialist advance. Indeed, there are those within the Labour Party who believe that this has already happened, in the years of Opposition since 1970. The politics of the Labour Left therefore deserve careful and detailed study.

1

The left wing of the Labour Party has always contained two contrasting groupings. For until very recently at least, a very tiny part of the Party's left-wing activists, particularly within the constituency parties, have been revolutionary socialists of one kind or another, who were in the Party *in spite* of their realisation that it was not a suitable vehicle for the working class advance to socialism. They were Party members, officially hiding their revolutionary affiliations, because they saw that the Party was in some sense a genuine workers' organisation in need of support and defence, and more importantly because they knew that the advanced and politicised sections of the working class were also in the Party or at least could not be contacted politically without the legitimacy which Labour Party membership alone could give. Even for the revolutionary socialists, till the mid 1960s at least, to leave the Labour Party was to risk total political and social isolation from the very working class that they hoped to wean from Labourism.

The events of 1964-70 changed that and drove the majority of revolutionary socialists from the Party as working class alienation from Labour grew. And in leaving, they left behind a dwindling number of Party activists of quite a different kind, whom we might call the Labour

177

Left proper, and as such, the focus of this chapter. These activists were, and remain, men and women with a particular perspective on politics that gives them a particular role. Their perspective (one they have shared with their equivalents in each generation of the Labour Party to date) has always contained three related strands: that Parliament remained a centre of social power of sufficient weight to justify an almost total preoccupation with it; that the representative institutions of the Labour Party actually tapped the dynamic of a mass movement, such that the capture or influence of key institutions within the Labour movement actually reflected something significant in power terms; and that the Labour Party, once captured, was and always would be the most appropriate vehicle through which working class goals could be realised and socialism achieved. It was this perspective that gave to each generation of the Labour Left a role and a definition of its politics: to fight as a pressure group on the Parliamentary leadership, either directly through the Parliamentary Party or indirectly through resolutions to conference, to push the Party in a more socialist direction. The Labour Left has always seen this as its job, and it has been one which successive generations of Labour leaders, in their conservatism, have made ever more necessary and difficult.

To oblige the Party leaders to pursue more radical programmes and to offer a more militant response to its political opponents has been the common preoccupation of the Labour Left over the years. The precise issues involved have differed in each generation, the notions of socialism have mellowed, and the detailed ideology of the Left has always been uncertain and confused (both within and between generations of 'left' militants). But these men and women have shared over time this abiding belief that the Labour Party could and should be captured for socialism, since with the right leadership and the right programme it was still the Party that could create the socialist commonwealth. And in this sense, the failure of one generation of the Left merely strengthened the resolve of the next, to achieve in their lifetime that which by chance had not been achieved before. For the Left of the Party to date has shared not simply a perspective, but also an unbroken experience of failure. This is as true of the Independent Labour Party between 1900 and 1932 and of the Socialist League in the 1930s as it is of the Keep Left group of the late 1940s, of the Bevanites in the 1950s, and of the groupings around Victory For Socialism and then Tribune after 1957. To see if the current generation of the Labour Left can succeed, we must first look at why earlier generations of the Left did not; and

178

discover why they were unable to stem the rightward drift of policy, and the accommodation of the Party leadership to capitalist impera- tives, that we have documented and explained in the preceding chapters.

2

It was the I.L.P. which claimed the loyalty of the majority of those within the first and second generations of the Party who sought to transform capitalism into socialism through the collective ownership of the means of production, distribution and exchange, and who struggled to convert the Party to this end. The I.L.P. was stronger than all of the Labour Lefts that were to follow it. It had an ideology of sorts and a set of distinct programmes. It had working class roots, and these stretched down into areas like Glasgow where the class knew intense poverty and despair. It pursued its job of socialist conversion against the background of extreme class hostility and industrial confrontation. The leadership it sought to convert were often also I.L.P. members, and had had less time to become entrenched in conservative ways than later Labour leaderships. The I.L.P. had a coherent organisational structure, with separate membership, a national advisory council, an annual con- ference and local branches (on which the national Labour Party was largely dependent for constituency activity until 1918). And it gener- ated leaders like Maxton and Wheatley, of considerable political skill and intellectual prowess. No later Labour Left would combine all these assets and be so well endowed in its fight to convert the Party leader- ship to socialism. And yet the story of the I.L.P. is the story of failure and decline, and in its weaknesses, if not in its strengths, it anticipated all the left groupings that were to follow.

The Independent Labour Party was formed in 1893 with a twin preoccupation, to establish an independent working class political party in Westminster, and through that Party to achieve the common ownership of the industrial system - and hence what it understood as socialism. Yet from the beginning it was clear that on occasions at least these two aims would be incompatible, and that whenever they were, the first priority of the I.L.P. was the establishment and retention of an independent working class Parliamentary presence. So in 1893, at the founding conference of the organisation, the word 'socialist' was not included in the title lest this alienate potential support. And in 1900 I.L.P. militants did not press their socialist convictions on the new

Labour Representation Committee that they had worked so assiduously to create, lest this prevent the new Parliamentary group from gathering mass trade union support. Instead, and from the beginning, the I.L.P. compromised its political programme out of its concern to create the political party that might one day be the vehicle of its socialism; and in the process of course, it gave itself a role - that of converting the Labour Party it had helped to create into a genuinely reformist socialist organisation. But that, sadly, was more than the I.L.P. could manage, and in the end it was to be destroyed by its own uncontrollable creation.

For the Parliamentary Labour Party, as we have seen, spent its first eighteen years fully within the ideological and political universe of Liberal-Radicalism, pursuing moderate policies of discrete social reform as a palliative to the growing waves of industrial unrest that swept pre-First World War Britain. The hold of Liberal-Radicalism on even the I.L.P. Parliamentarians was unshakable, and their moderation ever more evident. The sensitivity of the Party's potential electorate to Liberal issues withstood I.L.P. propagandising, and the commitment of the large trade unions (or at least of the bulk of their leaders, their M.P.s and their activists) to non-socialist perspectives remained. And so even within the first decade of the new Party, and with growing despair at their own creation, the radical wing of the I.L.P. had to fight to tighten extra-Parliamentary control over M.P.s and to stiffen the policies that the Parliamentary group pursued. To this end, four members of the I.L.P.'s National Advisory Council wrote the Green Manifesto in 1909 (*Let Us Reform The Labour Party*) which called on the Party to stiffen its socialist resolve, to publicly associate itself with its own socialist principles, and to end its practice of tailoring its policies to satisfy its Liberal connection. In arguing this case, the Left of the I.L.P. was criticising its own leadership as well as that of the Parliamentary Party, since the two overlapped in their major personnel; and was in effect offering an alternative interpretation of I.L.P. strategy to that pursued by MacDonald, Snowden and Hardie. But the appeal did not shift the policies of these men, and radical I.L.P. branches and members defected in considerable numbers between 1910 and 1914 to the tiny Marxist sects operating on the left of the Party. But neither they nor the I.L.P. loyalists that remained in the Labour Party were able to persuade the Parliamentary leadership to adopt a socialist programme before 1914, and I.L.P. membership dropped. Nor were they able to prevent the Labour Party from giving its support to the carnage of the First World

War, though this at least gave the I.L.P. a fresh lease of life, as its principled opposition to the war attracted into its ranks the war weary, the pacifists and the radicals.

Nor could the I.L.P. claim much responsibility for the adoption of their own aim in the Labour Party constitution of 1918. As we saw, the motives for the adoption of the new constitution reflected the changing pattern of class militancy within the post-war Labour electorate, rather than any I.L.P. pressure. Indeed the adoption of the new constitution was accompanied by the removal of the I.L.P. from its privileged position on the National Executive of the Party, and by the creation of Constituency Labour Parties to replace local dependence on I.L.P. branches. I.L.P. activists spent much time and energy in 1920 and 1921 in the creation of these constituency parties, so proving again their loyalty to a Party that, in taking over the I.L.P.'s aim, was undermining I.L.P. influence and powers in favour of the more conservative trade unions.

As the Labour Party's promise of 1918 failed to materialise in the 1920s, the I.L.P. was driven into increasing opposition to the leadership of MacDonald and Snowden, even though these men had long been I.L.P. leaders, and (in MacDonald's case) had won the Party leadership only because of I.L.P. support. For the I.L.P. in the 1920s found itself in a situation of paradoxes. It was the largest of the socialist groupings in and around the growing Labour Party. It was at the height of its own growth and organisational cohesion. It had a strong local membership in the heart of the depressed working class areas, in Scotland in particular, and its own left wing was well represented at Westminster by the Clydesiders (Maxton, Wheatley, Kirkwood and company). Yet throughout the 1920s it was trapped between its own involvement in a Labour Party that would not bend to its repeated radical calls, and a small but active Communist Party on its own left, that repeatedly attacked the ambiguities of its policies, that offered a home and an alternative focus of loyalty and hope to dissident I.L.P. members frustrated by Parliamentary failure, and which questioned the validity of the Parliamentary road to socialism to which the I.L.P. was committed. The I.L.P. leadership could not go too far in accommodation to and support of the Parliamentary Labour Party and its policies without losing sections of its own rank and file to the Communist Party. Nor could the I.L.P. leadership accommodate too fully left-wing pressure within its own organisation, without losing all contact with the Parliamentarians of the Labour Party whose policies it sought to shape. Throughout the 1920s the I.L.P. thus had to tread a path between the moderate Parliamentarianism of the Social Democratic Second International and the ostensibly revolutionary politics of the Communist International; and in the end it found, as did so many left-wing social democratic groupings in inter-war Europe, that the path could not be held.

However this was not immediately clear. In 1922 the I.L.P. increased its Parliamentary representation from five M.P.s to thirty-two, and its most militant Parliamentary section was instrumental in placing MacDonald in the Party leadership. The weakness of the I.L.P. within the inter-war Party came clear only during and after the first Labour Government. The I.L.P. in 1924 pressed MacDonald to use the moment of Parliamentary power to set up commissions to take public evidence and to 'elaborate socialist legislation in detail'; but MacDonald would not. In spite of the I.L.P. having as members 129 of the 192 Labour M.P.s in 1923-4 (including five Cabinet Ministers and the Party leader), it was unable to persuade the Labour Cabinet to adopt even its most modest proposals. For as Dowse said,

> when the I.L.P. appeared at the very pinnacle of its power, when its members were in a Cabinet and Government whose leaders they had helped to select, its organisational and strategical shortcomings were obvious. The failure to win even the active sympathy of a Front Bench which, in principle, was dominated by the I.L.P. suggests a lack of commitment in I.L.P. allegiance which was remarkable. Throughout the period [of the first Labour Government] it was impossible to detect . . . 'the I.L.P. spirit' in anything the Labour Government achieved.[1]

For MacDonald, as we saw, set his face against 'the wild men' in his own Party, and sought a close and co-operative relationship in power with the very social groups to which the socialism of the radical wing of the I.L.P. was opposed.* And as the realisation of this grew, the divisions

---

* It was the old I.L.P. militant, Philip Snowden, who was MacDonald's firmest ally in this. As he said in his autobiography, 'The conversation turned upon what we might be able to do in the first session. There would be two courses open to us. We might use the opportunity for a demonstration and introduce some bold Socialist measures, knowing, of course, that we should be defeated upon them. Then we would go to the country with this illustration of what we might do if we had a Socialist majority. This was a course which had been urged by the extreme wing of the Party, but it was not a policy which commended itself to reasonable opinion. I urged very strongly to this meeting that we should not adopt an extreme policy, but should confine our legislative proposals to measures that we were likely to be able to carry.' (P. Snowden, *An Autobiography*, 1934, vol. II, pp. 595-6).

within the I.L.P. between moderates and radicals intensified; and the I.L.P., under increasingly radical leadership, became ever more the focus of opposition to MacDonald, drawing up counter-policies and proposals, attempting to discipline I.L.P. M.P.s, opposing the second Labour Government in the lobbies at Westminster, and eventually disaffiliating from the Labour Party completely.

For 'ever since the fall of the first Labour Government, and indeed before, the I.L.P. and particularly the I.L.P. left, had devoted much effort to a threefold task: firstly to formulate policies which would, in its view, be appropriate to a movement . . . pledged to the establishment of a socialist society in Britain; secondly, to persuade the Labour Party to incorporate these policies in its own programme; and thirdly, to compel the Labour leadership to *act* upon these policies'.[2] In its attempt to shape the policy of the MacDonald leadership, the I.L.P. issued its own policy manifestos: particularly *Socialism in Our Time* in 1926, and the Cook-Maxton Manifesto in 1928. Through these, the I.L.P. proposed that the next Labour Government follow a prearranged programme of socialist legislation on which, if defeated in the House, it could go to an electorate already educated in the socialist alternative available. Yet the actual policies that the I.L.P. proposed were relatively mild: the institution of a national minimum wage (a 'Living Wage' guaranteed by a system of family allowances financed by progressive taxation), price subsidisation to stimulate a general revival in trade, the nationalisation of key industries, the reorganisation of the rest, and the 'control' of the banking system. In effect, the I.L.P. was combining the language of class radicalism with specific proposals that ameliorated working class conditions by strengthening the very capitalist system that their rhetoric so vehemently condemned.* In this central ambiguity, *Socialism in Our Time* earned the I.L.P. more hostility from the Communists on its left, and total rejection from the Parliamentary leadership on its right.

---

* 'while the demand for a living wage was sometimes presented as equivalent to a demand for Socialism, at other times it appeared as a "policy of directly increasing the purchasing power of the workers as a means of turning the wheels of home industry and bringing an immediate wave of prosperity to the country, in which even the capitalists would have their share" to quote the [I.L.P.] *New Leader*. The implication that the policy was as much related to capitalist reorganisation as it was to Socialist transformation was heightened by the uncritical extolling of the "high wages" policy of American capitalism . . . "Ford versus Marx" was an alternative seriously posed by the I.L.P. in those days.' (Hutt, *The Post-War History of the British Working Class*, pp. 107-8).

The weakness of the Labour Left

Finding the Parliamentary leadership unresponsive, the I.L.P. turned again to the question of Parliamentary control, by attempting to impose its own discipline on M.P.s carrying I.L.P. membership, and Party control on the Parliamentary leadership itself. Maxton for the I.L.P. successfully urged the 1929 Labour Party conference to support a motion giving the Parliamentary Party (and not MacDonald) the right to decide the membership of the next Labour Cabinet - a victory that made no difference at all to the way in which MacDonald chose his government a few months later. With noticable reluctance, the I.L.P. was driven to a final break with MacDonald himself. Through the 1920s, they had been increasingly critical of the man and his policies, but they had proved extremely reluctant to organise seriously against him. Only in 1927 did the I.L.P. even decide not to nominate MacDonald for the Party's Treasurership. Like Labour Lefts of later generations, the I.L.P. in the 1920s showed a marked loyalty to leaders who had long abandoned their policies, and a marked failure to control even those M.P.s who carried I.L.P. cards.

In the end, in 1930, the I.L.P. felt compelled to insist that its M.P. members obey I.L.P. policy even when that clashed with the policy of the Parliamentary Labour Party. But then the I.L.P. found that only 17 of the 140 M.P.s who were also I.L.P. members were prepared to continue as I.L.P. members on those terms. The rest resigned and supported MacDonald's policies as those led inexorably to the collapse of 1931. The 17 I.L.P. stalwarts that remained could then do nothing more than offer sustained opposition in the House of Commons to this general passivity of the second Labour Government. They criticised the Government's opening policy statement for its inertia, arguing as before that MacDonald should pursue a socialist policy, and go to the country if defeated.* They continued to demand more radical measures on unemployment, more humane treatment of those out of work, and more socialist measures on public ownership. The general thrust of their critique was that the Labour Government could and should do more,

---

* Wheatley put the I.L.P. case: 'This is the day of the Government's power. Today the Government could do anything. Today the Government are not showing the courage that their supporters on these benches expect. If they displayed that courage and went on with their own policy, the parties opposite would not dare to wound them, however willing they might be to strike; but, after the Government have disappointed their friends, by twelve months of this halting, half-way legislation, as one of my friends described it, and have been discredited in the country, then, twelve months from now, there will be no party in this House poor enough to do them honour.' (Speaking in the Commons in 1929, and quoted in Skidelsky, *Politicians and the Slump*, p. 106).

and in this they spoke for the millions of the unemployed that the Labour Government betrayed.

But they spoke to no avail, and in the wake of the debacle of August 1931 the I.L.P. disaffiliated from the Party, hoping to replace the shattered Labourites with I.L.P. members as the Parliamentary leaders of the embattled working class.* But by then the Labour Party was strong enough locally to outfight I.L.P. candidates, and sufficiently entrenched in the loyalties of the working class to rise again in 1935. The final irony for the I.L.P. was that the Parliamentary Party it had created, sustained and strengthened as a vehicle for socialist advance was strong enough by the early 1930s to defeat the I.L.P. in open competition for working class loyalty and support. Having helped to establish the Labour Party as *the* political voice of the working class, the I.L.P. found that to leave and oppose the Party was to commit itself to political isolation and decline.† From 1932 onwards the Left *had* to be in the Labour Party, if it was to avoid total annihilation, and if it was to have any influence at all. This was the major legacy of the I.L.P. to later generations of the socialist Left within the Party. The irony was that the I.L.P. was the first casualty of its own handiwork. Other casualties were to follow.

3

The I.L.P.'s decision to disaffiliate from the Labour Party was not taken without much internal dissension, for it was clear to many even in 1932 that to leave the Party was to lose any hope of establishing a socialist presence as the predominant political voice of the British working class. These I.L.P. dissidents regrouped themselves within the

---

* The 1932 I.L.P. conference which disaffiliated from the Labour Party was, as its chairman Fenner Brockway put it, 'all set to replace the Labour Party by the I.L.P.'. (F. Brockway, *Inside the Left*, London, Allen and Unwin, 1940, p. 243). In its misplaced confidence, it argued that 'the class struggle which is the dynamic force in social change is nearing its decisive moment . . . there is no time now for slow processes of gradual change. The imperative need is for Socialism *now*'. And the I.L.P. publicly recognised - a little too late as it happened - that 'the approach to socialism could not be made by Parliamentary methods only . . . the critical circumstances demand that Socialists must be prepared to organise mass industrial action as an additional means to the attainment of their objectives'. (I.L.P. *Statement of Policy*, quoted in Miliband, *Parliamentary Socialism*, p. 194).

† The I.L.P.'s 16,773 members in 1932 had shrunk to 4,392 in 1935. It was against this background that 'the tendency grew in the I.L.P. to reconsider its relationship with the Labour Party' and Brockway, for one, 'reached the

Labour Party in 1932, and in alliance with other left-intellectuals
formed the Socialist League and began again to push for the adoption
by the Party of a socialist programme. In doing so, they faced a
situation that was at once more hopeful and more difficult than that
faced latterly by the I.L.P. Their situation was more hopeful, in that
the gradualism of the 1920s was everywhere discredited in the Party.
But it was also more difficult, for the League faced the conservative
influence of the big trade unions and of the majority of the Parliamentary Party with a left-wing organisation that lacked the size, the
organisational structure and the working class roots of its I.L.P. predecessor. Against the growing anti-intellectualism of the trade union
leadership, and the electoral preoccupations of sections of the Parliamentary Party, the Socialist League could mobilise only 2,000-odd
members, behind a leadership that initially spanned a political spectrum
from the centre-left to the margins of the Communist Party itself. Its
greatest strength lay in the significant position within the Parliamentary
Party and within the Party's intellectual coterie that that leadership
held, but in the end that was not to be enough to swing the Labour
Party in total behind either the domestic or the foreign policy of the
League.

The League saw itself as a 'ginger group' on the Labour Party
leadership, as a 'socialist educational and propaganda organisation',
working - as its Secretary later put it - 'for the transformation of the
Labour Party into the Party of the working class revolution' and, as
such, united in its belief 'that the only political organisation which
holds out any hope to the workers is the Labour Party'.[3] In this role, it
pressed its policies at Labour Party conferences; and in the discussions
which led to the adoption by the Party of *For Socialism and Peace* in
1934 the League formulated its own and more radical programme,
Forward to Socialism. The two programmes had much in common.
Both condemned capitalism. Both offered a socialist alternative. Both
defined socialism as including public ownership and State control, and
both saw the route to its achievement through a Labour Party electoral victory. But the tone and detail of the League's programme was
more radical. The League was preoccupied with the threat of Fascism,
and with the danger that the ruling class would desert Parliamentary

view that some sacrifice of freedom was justified in order to function within
the mass political movement of the workers' (*Inside the Left*, p. 243). The
I.L.P. and the Labour Party were on the verge of agreement on the terms of
the I.L.P.'s reaffiliation when they were divided by their attitude to the
Second World War in 1939.

procedures in defence of their class privileges, as had already happened in Germany and Austria by 1934. This questioning of the Parliamentary road to socialism went hand-in-hand with the League's belief that capitalism was in increasing and profound crisis, and that only decisive and rapid action towards socialism could avert the Fascist threat. Hence the League's proposals were far more sweeping than the Labour Party contemplated in its *For Socialism and Peace.* Indeed, for the League, the proposals of *For Socialism and Peace* were to be rushed through by a majority Labour Government, under Emergency Powers if necessary, in the first few months of office, to beat by sheer speed any capitalist counter-attack and to lay the foundations of a more extensive five-year programme. That programme was to involve wide-scale public ownership (extending into munitions and heavy chemicals, textiles, shipbuilding and health services), a coherent national plan, the reorganisation of agriculture on the basis of land nationalisation, and the introduction of workers' participation in management at the point of production. To finance this, taxation was to be heavily progressive and compensation to dispossessed capitalists severely limited; and to prevent its delayed implementation, the House of Lords was to be abolished.

But the League never managed to persuade the Labour Party at its conferences in the 1930s to adopt so radical a programme, and in this critical sense the Socialist League was no more successful as a ginger group on the Labour Party leadership than had been the I.L.P. before it. True, many of the leaders of the League played a central role in committing the Party to extensive nationalisation even before the Party adopted *For Socialism and Peace.* Stafford Cripps and Frank Wise in particular, were the movers of the resolution at the 1932 Labour Party conference to take the joint-stock banks into public ownership. And Socialist League ideas - on Emergency Powers, and on the abolition of the House of Lords - found echos in the programmes, policy statements and writings of Party leaders throughout the 1930s. So to this extent at least, the Socialist League could and did claim some credit for the undeniably leftward shift in the Party programme after 1931.

But the League's attempts to amend *For Socialism and Peace* failed. On the scope of public ownership, on the question of compensation, on the nature of Socialist State Planning, and on the importance of workers' control, the Labour Party programmes of the 1930s remained less radical than the League required. Indeed, the Labour Party's official position moved away from that of the League as the 1930s progressed. *Labour's Immediate Programme* in 1937 still left the Party committed to the creation of a Socialist Commonwealth, still prepared to resist 'obstructions from vested interests or unrepresentative bodies', still calling for socialist national planning and the public ownership of basic industries, and still intending to finance extensive welfare provision by progressive taxation. In all this, it echoed the Socialist League. But by 1937 there was no mention of workers' control. Rather the policy statement offered the public corporation as the instrument of nationalisation, watered down earlier promises on land nationalisation, and restricted the list of industries to be nationalised. Without the League, it is unlikely that the Labour Party would have spent the 1930s committed to even this programme, however moderate that programme was. But the programme was moderate, and League members knew it. But they could not push the Party further, nor provide the electoral majority which alone could have turned the programme into action.

Instead, the League fell victim to the fierce divisions within the Left in the 1930s on the strategies and tactics to be used in the fight against Fascism. For as Fascism spread across Europe and as the Nazi military machine grew, the politics of the Labour Party in the 1930s became increasingly dominated by the problems of rearmament and appeasement, by Abyssinia and critically by Spain, and by the role of the U.S.S.R. as a bulwark against Fascism, and hence of the Communist parties as possible allies in the domestic struggle. The question of socialist transformation remained an academic one for the Socialist League and the Labour Party alike, so long as the Party lacked an electoral majority. The danger of Fascism, on the other hand, was real and immediate, and threatened the very Parliamentarianism in which both the League and the Party placed their hopes. But the two increasingly diverged on how best Fascism could be fought, and in that confrontation the League discovered, like the I.L.P. before it, just how vulnerable and impotent Left groupings were in the face of Party discipline and the threat of expulsion.

The issue which divided the League from the bulk of the Parliamentary Party, and from the trade union leadership whose bloc votes dominated the Party conference, was their attitude to the Communist Party. That tiny party, which had spent the years after 1928 denouncing both Parliamentarians and Trade Union bureaucrats as social fascists, switched its policy line in 1935, and sought a broadly based coalition on the left to fight the Fascist menace. As early as 1933, the Labour Party had rejected any such alliance, arguing that communism and Fascism were both threats to Parliamentary democracy; and the Socialist League itself, in 1935, initially rejected any notion of a 'united front' with the Communists lest, as the League put it, they 'be diverted into activities definitely condemned by the Labour Party' which would 'jeopardise the League's affiliation to the Party and undermine its influence there'.[4] Yet a year later, with a Popular Front Government in France and with Spain in civil war, the Socialist League changed its mind. It supported the Communist Party's application to affiliate to the Labour Party in 1936, and in January 1937 joined the Communists and the I.L.P. in a 'unity campaign' of public meetings that brought it into direct confrontation with the N.E.C. of the Labour Party.

For by an overwhelming majority, the Labour Party conference of 1936 had rejected Communist affiliation and the 'united front' policy against Fascism, and in line with these decisions the National Executive of the Party banned any participation in joint activities with the Communist Party. By March 1937, the N.E.C. had proscribed the Socialist League, and had declared that, as from June of that year, membership of the League would be incompatible with continued membership of the Labour Party; and this again was overwhelmingly ratified by the Party conference later in the year.

The members of the Socialist League were then left with a simple if cruel choice. They could continue to defy the N.E.C. by prolonging their association with the League and the unity campaign, and face the certainty of expulsion from the Party. Or they could abandon the League and the campaign as the price of continued Party membership. The League chose the latter course, dissolving itself at its Whitsun conference in 1937, and leaving those of its members who continued to associate with the unity campaign to face the disciplinary procedures of the Labour Party alone. 'Many were to regret that decision in later years, when the Left in the Party, robbed by their own act of any effective organisation, found themselves hopelessly pitted as individuals against the Executive machine.'[5] In fact, leading League figures like Cripps, Bevan, Laski and Strauss all defied the Labour Party ban on association with the Communist Party, and only avoided expulsion by their temporary abandonment of the unity campaign later in 1937. But when in 1939, Cripps proposed a 'popular front' alliance that would have brought the Labour Party into an electoral pact with Liberals as well as with Communists, and when he took this issue to the rank and file of the Party in defiance of an intransigent N.E.C., he was expelled, and with him went those of his supporters who were not prepared to

189

abandon him under N.E.C. pressure. Though some leading ex-Leaguers did desert Cripps in 1939, others, including Bevan, Strauss, Young, Bruce and Trevelyan, all lost their Party membership because of their defiance of the N.E.C., and they returned to the Party during the war only after giving individual undertakings to obey Party rules. But by then the issue of Popular Frontism was dead. It was destroyed by the Labour Party's participation in the wartime coalition and electoral truce, and by the Communist Party's abrupt change of line after the signing of the Nazi-Soviet pact. Ten years of Left agitation within the Labour Party against the background of Fascism and Depression petered out, and had come to nothing.

4

Left opposition within the Labour Party to the policies of the Attlee Government was slow to start, was sporadic, and was almost totally preoccupied with questions of foreign policy. Moreover, unlike both the I.L.P. and the Socialist League, left-wing activity within the post-war Party was restricted almost exclusively to Parliamentary manoeuvring, in which the only significant actors were that tiny hand-ful of Labour Left M.P.s elected in the 1945 landslide. With both Cripps and Bevan in the Cabinet, the initiative passed to these new back-benchers, fifty-three of whom tabled an amendment to the King's Speech in November 1946, criticising the Government's close alliance with the United States as the cold war opened. Fifteen of them, including Michael Foot, Richard Crossman and Ian Mikardo, developed their demand for a 'third way' between American and Russian imperialism in the 1947 pamphlet *Keep Left*; and thereafter this tiny group of young Parliamentarians kept up a sporadic and wholly un-successful pressure for disengagement from the wildest excesses of American foreign policy. But they did not coalesce into a coherent group, or even gain much publicity or momentum, until they were joined by Aneurin Bevan, Harold Wilson and John Freeman, all of whom resigned from the Labour Government in 1951.* From then until the Labour Party conference of 1957, the Left of the Labour

---

* There was no regular, close and organised connection between the *Keep Left* M.P.s and Bevan before the 1951 resignations. Rather, as Crossman's diaries record, 'Nye never as a Cabinet Minister intrigued with outside groups. Indeed, the trouble was that, whereas Morrison, Shinwell, Dalton were busy organising cliques, Nye was like a bear in his corner'. (Quoted in M. Foot, *Aneurin Bevan, Volume 2 1945-1960*, London, Davis-Poynter, 1973, p. 374).

Party was inextricably linked with the political career of Nye Bevan, and the mantle of the Socialist League had passed to the Bevanites.

The sequence of events around which Bevanism focused are relatively well known. Bevan and his junior colleagues resigned in opposition to cuts imposed on the National Health Service by Bevan's political opponent, Gaitskell, in the latter's 1951 rearmament budget. In their resignation and subsequent agitation within the Party - most notably in the pamphlet *One Way Only* - the three ex-Ministers and their Parliamentary followers argued that the level of defence expenditure demanded by the American alliance would culminate in domestic retrenchment, unemployment and possibly world war. Its adoption by the Party leadership moreover, rested in their view on a basic misreading of both American and Russian intentions, and reflected the willingness of the Right of the Party to slow down the rate of socialist reform in the name of domestic consolidation and cold war politics. In the wake of the 1951 election defeat, and amid growing hysteria from their opponents in the Parliamentary Party and in the trade union leadership, the Bevanites opened a sustained campaign within the Party for the extension of nationalisation and for disengagement from the worst excesses of the American military alliance. In the columns of their paper, *Tribune*, in the brains trusts that they held in virtually every constituency between 1951 and 1956, and in the speeches that their leading Parliamentary figures made in the Commons, in the Party's N.E.C., to Conference, and at public meetings, the Labour Left attempted to persuade the Party leadership to toughen its opposition to Conservative foreign policy, and to offer a further package of 1945-style domestic reform.[*]

The struggle between the Left and the Right of the Party in the Bevanite years went on in all the representative institutions of the labour movement: in the constituency parties, in the trade union branches, at Party conference, in the N.E.C., and in the Parliamentary Party. In each (with the possible exception of the constituency parties) the Bevanites, like every Labour Left before them, were in a minority, struggling to win influence in the N.E.C. and Shadow Cabinet and hoping (via Conference resolutions) to set limits on the Parliamentary

---

[*] 'At the Bevanite meetings, as throughout earlier discussions on the National Executive, Bevan himself was always the foremost to insist that the demand for extended public ownership must retain its place at the head of any Socialist programme. Indeed, he was shocked that anyone could think otherwise. A Socialism which did not envisage a transformation in property-owning and property-relationships would be one drained of all virility.' (*ibid.*, p. 370).

leadership's drift to consolidation and revisionism. So in 1951 the Bevanite Barbara Castle defeated ex-Defence Minister Emmanuel Shinwell in the C.L.P. elections to the Party's N.E.C., to the consternation of those sections of the Party already disturbed by Bevan's resignation and half-ready to blame him for the 1951 election defeat. In March 1952 fifty-seven M.P.s, including Bevan, defied the Party whips by voting against defence estimates that the new Conservative administration had inherited from the Attlee Government. At the Morecambe conference of the Party that same year, the 'consolidationists' Morrison and Dalton were defeated in the C.L.P. elections to the N.E.C. by the Bevanites Wilson and Crossman. As a result, six of the seven constituency seats on the 27-strong N.E.C. then lay in Bevanite hands; and in spite of Bevan's own silence, a motion supporting his policies on rearmament and the American alliance won over two million votes. In the face of all this, opposition to the Bevanites from within the Parliamentary Party and from the trade union leadership grew, encouraged by the political groupings around Morrison and Gaitskell, for both of whom Bevan represented a strong potential challenger in the struggle for Attlee's succession. Under this pressure, which touched at times on hysteria, Attlee reintroduced the Party's Standing Orders, which had been in abeyance since 1946, and banned factional organisations and personal attacks on Party leaders and policies. The Bevanites were then forced to open their regular weekly meetings to all-comers, and later to abandon their brains trusts, in favour of maintaining their pressure on the Parliamentary leadership via their membership of the N.E.C., and in 1953 and 1954 via Bevan's own presence in the Parliamentary Party's Shadow Cabinet.

Their impact there was reflected in the 1953 N.E.C. policy document, *Challenge to Britain*, which made major concessions to Bevanite demands on foreign policy, and which in its ambiguous phraseology marked the high-spot of left-wing pressure for a firm Party commitment to further extensive nationalisation. Unsatisfactory as this document was when compared to Bevanite demands, Bevan gave it his full support at the 1953 Party conference. But in 1954 this temporary lull in internal Party wrangling ended when Bevan criticised Attlee directly in the Commons for Labour's inert opposition to the Conservatives' policy on South East Asia, and resigned from the Shadow Cabinet in order to campaign nationally for a change in the Party's foreign policy. In this move to mobilise the Labour rank and file, Bevan also resigned from the N.E.C. to fight Gaitskell for the Party Treasurership, but was defeated at the 1954 conference by the bloc votes of the larger trade unions. It was at this conference that left-wing opposition to the American military alliance in general, and to German rearmament in particular, brought the N.E.C. to the edge of defeat; and raised right-wing hostility to Bevan (who sat silently through the debate) to even greater heights of intensity and bitterness. So that when, early in 1955, Bevan clashed again with his Party Leader in the Commons, and joined sixty-two other Labour M.P.s in defying a three-line whip in the defence debate, he alone was censored by the Parliamentary Party and had the Party whip withdrawn. But moves to eject him completely from the Party, as had happened in 1939, came to nothing; and the whip was restored after Bevan had given a highly ambiguous apology. It was with Bevan back in the Parliamentary Party that Labour fought and lost the 1955 election.

But the internal divisions that had wracked the Party in its first five years of Opposition were not to be repeated in its second. Bevan made his uneasy peace with the new Gaitskellite leadership in 1956 and 1957, and broke with his former supporters on the issue of unilateral disarmament at the 1957 Labour Party conference. Like Cripps before him, Bevan by 1957 had moved into a political alliance with the right-wing figures whom he had once so vigorously opposed, and had joined on the front bench of the Labour Party under Gaitskell men like Harold Wilson who had made the same political journey away from the Labour Left earlier in the 1950s.* By 1957, Bevanism - though not all of the Bevanites - had made its peace with Gaitskell, and on Gaitskell's terms.

For Bevanism as a political force within the Labour Party in the 1950s carried all the weaknesses of its I.L.P. and Socialist League predecessors, and carried them in an even more accentuated form. Organisationally, the Bevanites were even weaker and more Parliamentarily

---

* His friend and biographer Michael Foot makes it clear that Bevan's *rapprochement* with Gaitskell should not be interpreted as a straightforward process of Bevan's career aspirations overriding his principles; but rather as the consequence of his recognition that some influence within the Party was better than none, and that the world in 1957 was too threatened by nuclear destruction for him to retreat into political isolation again (*ibid.*, p. 581). It is clear too that Bevan genuinely rejected the unilateralist case, and in an act of considerable personal and political courage, broke with his friends of twenty years (*ibid.*, pp. 566-84). Yet here in microcosm was the perennial dilemma of the Labour Left M.P., of needing a Labour Government and a position within it if he was not to be totally impotent, but having to pay a high price (in Bevan's case, his silence on domestic policy) for his position of influence.

based than earlier Labour Lefts. This was no 'grass roots' mass working class movement of the I.L.P. kind. Rather the Labour Left's main strength in the 1950s lay in a coterie of some fifty M.P.s, supplemented by a 'second eleven' of Parliamentary figures and prospective candidates, all of whom toured the country publicising Bevanite ideas in brains trusts, and discreetly encouraging sympathetic Constituency Parties to adopt pro-Left Parliamentary candidates when vacancies arose. The Bevanites' national organisation was rudimentary, and devolved on to the discreetly organised 'second eleven' after Standing Orders were invoked in 1952. They had no organised roots outside the constituency parties, as had the I.L.P.; nor did they manage to mobilise rank and file support in the trade union movement. True, the activists and officers of certain of the smaller trade unions gave Bevan full support at conference, but beyond this the Bevanites had no organised working class roots. And as a Parliamentary force, without massive working class rank and file membership or noticable electoral pull, the Bevanites were vulnerable to the full rigours of Party discipline. Like the Socialist League, they were obliged to dismantle their organisational structure under N.E.C. pressure, even terminating their 'second eleven' brains trusts in 1956 as N.E.C. opposition loomed.[6] Like the League, the Bevanite M.P.s ran the risk of Parliamentary discipline and ultimately the loss of Party membership; and like the I.L.P., proved particularly vulnerable to calls for unity and party loyalty as General Elections approached. In 1951 and 1955, they loyally supported Party documents on which they had strong reservations, in order to keep the Party united and to defeat the Conservative opposition.

For Bevanism did not operate, as had the I.L.P. and the Socialist League, against a backcloth of mass working class discontent, with which the Labour Left M.P.s sought connections and to which they offered political leadership. The Bevanites were concerned, far more than the Left of the 1920s and 1930s, exclusively with the requirements of Parliamentary politics, and defined 'left' and 'socialist' activity in wholly Parliamentary terms. Their one excursion into trade union politics (in which they gave their support to the N.A.S.D. in its dockland struggle with the Transport and General Workers Union) came late, and was not part of any systematic attempt to link industrial and political struggle. Rather it grew out of the Bevanites' increasingly acrimonious relationships with the Transport Workers' Leader at Party conferences, and never went beyond the sale of their paper *Tribune* in dockland and the giving of full public support to the N.A.S.D.

bureaucracy. In the quiet class conditions of the early 1950s, perhaps no Labour Left could have done more; but it is clear that the Bevanites were not frustrated industrial agitators for socialism driven to Parliamentary action by the absence of mass working class mobilisation. Rather their failure to attempt systematically to sink organisational roots in the trade union rank and file was fully in accord with their own Parliamentary preoccupations and elitism, in which their choice of issues to fight, and their staying-power on any issue chosen, was not dictated by the pattern of class struggle outside Parliament but by the passing and immediate Parliamentary requirements of their leading figures. The Party's working class electorate were *just not involved* systematically in the struggles of the Bevanite years, for by then the battle was between 'essentially undemocratic groups' within the Party,[7] engaged in a fight in which the Right had no interest in involving the mass of the Party's trade union membership, and in which the Bevanites proved incapable of doing so.

For Bevanism, more than any earlier Labour Left, reduced the whole question of the struggle for socialism to a question of Party leadership and individuals. This meant, amongst other things, that the Left in the 1950s suffered *par excellence* from the delusion that the struggle for socialism entailed nothing more than the passing of resolutions at Labour Party conferences, and the placing of key men in positions of influence within the official labour movement. And in particular, the Left in the 1950s fell victim to the undeniable magic of Nye Bevan himself, and subordinated its energies and its strategies to furthering his own political career.* Yet he was of necessity ever the 'cautious rebel', playing an intricate game of tactical manoeuvring with

---

* Nye Bevan attracted great passion in his followers, even in those close to him who knew the complexities of the man. As Peggy Duff said, 'my respect for Aneurin Bevan was always this side of idolatry. He was often autocratic. He was neither a great innovator, nor, I think, a great thinker . . . But his rhetoric was important because it highlighted, in the context of a social democratic government which had won power in 1945 and seemed capable of winning it again, an emphasis on radical change, an assault on the structures of power, on rejection of capitalism, the lack of which had doomed social democratic parties in Europe by the late 1960s . . . The Gaitskells, those who opposed Nye and, later, many of those who stood with him, saw Labour achieving power and retaining it only through a more efficient, technological management of a capitalist society. A little more gentle to the poor, a little less racist to the coloured people, a little more compliant to the United States, a little more capable of raising the G.N.P. No fire this time or next time. *Fire died with Aneurin.*' (Peggy Duff, *Left, Left, Left*, London, Allison and Busby, 1971, pp. 76-7, my emphasis).

the rest of the Party leadership. He was trapped into silence by N.E.C. and Shadow Cabinet membership (with their conventions of collective responsibility) at critical points in the debates of those years; and chose to stay silenced in the interests of his own complex search for political power. And he, of course, in the end bought influence within a Labour Party that he could not capture by forging a political alliance with his major adversary, and by deserting the old left-wing allies whose hopes and aspirations he had so embodied. So that whilst 'the controversy within the Party did not begin with Bevanism, nor did it end with the reconciliation between Bevan and Gaitskell',[8] even so, whilst the two fought, the struggle for Party leadership dominated the Labour Left, absorbed its best energies, and encouraged it to reduce all questions of programme and perspective to a choice between two men.

In that fight between the two, the Left found again that it was the weaker, unable to break out of its minority status within the Parliamentary Party, and unable to break the stranglehold of the big trade union bloc vote on the Party conferences of the early 1950s. And its weakness here was not simply an accident of the personalities of the big trade union leaders or of the average rank and file M.P., though clearly the bitterness of those years was compounded by personal animosity between the major participants and by the general hysteria of the early cold war period. The Bevanite weakness and ultimate failure also reflected ideological ambiguities and defects that put it at a disadvantage in the struggle against its revisionist opponents, by weakening the credibility of its own foreign and domestic policy alternatives.

For the Bevanite foreign policy, though the most attractive part of the Left's programme, was electorally unpopular, and made no direct connections with a working class that was traditionally preoccupied in its politics with questions of domestic reform. Nor was that policy adequately linked to any assessment of how (or to any social group by which) a Labour Government could disengage itself from the military aspects of American imperialism at a time when the economic interpenetration of American and British capitalism was going on apace - as indeed it had been under the Attlee Government also. Nor was the Left's call for disengagement from the American alliance free from an inverted chauvinism, by which the American connection was condemned as much for its restriction on British national sovereignty as for its anti-socialist consequences. That inverted chauvinism was to appear again in the Campaign for Nuclear Disarmament. In their domestic policy too, the Bevanites did little more than offer again the package of

196

1945, without coming to grips with the defects of the Attlee years, and without finding any way of effectively reversing the unmistakable electoral hostility to calls for further nationalisation. For the domestic policy of the Labour Left still failed to confront the problem of class power *within* industry, and in its silence here offered as a socialist panacea the very bureaucratic State corporation *against* which the Socialist League had fought in the 1930s.*

In its defence of the Morrisonian public corporation, the Labour Left was less well placed than the revisionists to handle the electoral unpopularity of the Attlee legacy, and was incapable of relating its domestic proposals to the emerging pattern of full employment and growing material 'affluence' in its own potential working class base. Indeed the Bevanites' very strength in the N.E.C. (and Bevan's in the Shadow Cabinet) compounded this by denying them the opportunity to break free from a defence of policy documents whose very ambiguity barred the way to a systematic left-wing critique of the bureaucratic corporation of the Attlee years. The Bevanites' willingness to remain so constrained by the niceties of collective responsibility reflected their own lack of just such a critique; and in this sense the ambiguities of their parliamentary position reflected their own theoretical lacunae and their own degree of involvement in the whole corpus of Labour orthodoxy.†

The weakness of the Labour Left did not vanish with Bevan's defection. On the contrary, the Parliamentary Left in the late 1950s and early 1960s was even weaker than in the Bevanite years. It regrouped in 1958 as the reactivated *Victory for Socialism*, but in spite of its aims‡ was again prevented by N.E.C. pressure from establishing a

---

* Bevan is on record as recognising that nationalisation in the future might require 'a wider application of the principle of industrial democracy'. (Foot, *Aneurin Bevan Volume 2 1945-1960*, p. 372). But he did not make this the centre-piece of his demands on public ownership, and his writings at times suggested a preference for the type of public corporation created by the Attlee Government of which he was a leading member. See for example his *In Place of Fear* (London, Heinemann, 1952, pp. 116-7).

† As Miliband said, 'the political ambiguities of parliamentary Bevanism were but a reflection of its ideological ambiguities. Throughout, parliamentary Bevanism was a mediation between the leadership and the rank and file opposition. But the parliamentary Bevanites, while assuming the leadership of that opposition, also served to blur and to blunt both its strengths and its extent'. (*Parliamentary Socialism*, p. 327).

‡ 'to recruit thousands of active Labour Party members, form branches, stimulate fresh discussion about the application of socialist principles, and, above all, inspire renewed faith in the power of democratic action'; so that, eventu-

sophisticated organisational structure or regular grass roots contacts on any scale. For a while the rise of C.N.D. eclipsed the Parliamentary Left, as the unilateralists, through their work amongst trade union activists, swept the union conferences and won the Labour Party conference to unilateralism in 1960. The C.N.D. story has been told elsewhere;[9] and in the history of the Labour Party stands now only as a passing moment in the break of the Parliamentary leadership from conference domination in the 1960s. Yet at the height of the Campaign's impact on the Labour Party, when the 1960 conference had repudiated the Party Leader's position on nationalisation and the Bomb, neither Wilson nor Greenwood were able to topple Gaitskell from the leadership, though both tried. Nor, as the Campaign disintegrated in the years after 1960, were the Labour Left able to save it, or to prevent the Party from adopting the technocratic policies of the ex-Bevanites and ex-Gaitskellites in Wilson's leadership. Indeed the Labour Left welcomed the new leadership, as constituting a move towards socialism, and succumbed to the general euphoria of the Wilson promise of 1963-4. As we have seen, that euphoria could not have been more misplaced. But again the Labour Left was slow to see this and even slower to respond. *Tribune*'s headlines as late as the General Election of April 1966 insisted that under Wilson 'socialism [was] right back on the agenda';[10] and the emergence of fairly systematic Left opposition within the Parliamentary Party came only in the wake of the deflationary package of July 1966. The rise of a stronger Labour Left came even later, after 1970, and whilst the 1964-70 Labour Government lasted, the Left proved incapable of altering its basic course.

5

By now it should be clear that there are deep, even intractable, problems and limitations associated with the politics of the Labour Left. Successive generations of militants within the Labour Party have found that gradualism within the Party (the slow winning of the leadership to socialism) is no more successful than gradualism as a set of Party policies (the slow transformation of capitalism into socialism) because, in each case, the attempt culminates in the strengthening of the very forces of conservatism that were the initial enemy.

---

ally, V.F.S. might 'invigorate the whole body of the Labour Movement and sweep forward to a Victory for Socialism through the Labour Party'. (*Tribune*, 21 February 1958).

The weakness of the Labour Left

This persistent dilemma of the Labour Left is ultimately explicable only by examining again that first decision of the I.L.P. to create and sustain a political party in which the majority of the initial membership did not subscribe to socialist views. For whenever histories of the Labour Party are written, this decision is rarely questioned, but is treated invariably as an inevitable and obvious strategy for socialists in the 1890s. Yet it was not. It was an *intelligible* strategy, but it was not an inevitable one. For there were a range of political strategies open to socialists in the 1890s, as they struggled to connect themselves with, and convert, the emerging working class to a socialist philosophy which they claimed embodied working class interests and a resolution of working class dilemmas. Each strategy had already found organisational expression (from the Fabians to the S.D.F. in Britain, from Bernstein to Lenin later in continental Europe) but as yet no one strategy had come to predominate.

So socialists in that generation faced a set of real choices. They had to decide to use the Parliamentary road to socialism, or to use the industrial power of the working class to challenge and destroy the Parliamentary State. They had the choice of building a widely based socialist alliance, or of restricting membership to men and women sub-scribing to a specific definition of socialist goals and political tactics. They had the choice of forging a coherent, disciplined party organisa-tion, or of creating a loosely coordinated structure in which local autonomy was honoured and in which the freedom of political leader-ship was untrammelled. And they had a choice of particular socialist philosophies: Marxist, Anarchist, Syndicalist, Christian, or just plain radical. Which of these each group of socialists chose turned on a series of factors: on their reading of the cohesion, and receptivity to change, of the ruling order that they faced; on their reading of the economic conditions of the emerging working class, and its likely set of political and industrial attitudes, institutions and patterns of behaviour; and on their own individual propensities for accommodation, for confrontation - even for prison and death. It was not an easy choice. Individual socialists often changed their minds, and hence their allegiances. And the future development of each alternative was unknown. All was potential and possibility. But the choices that were made were crucial, for they structured left-wing politics for that generation, and later ones, by establishing a definition of the socialist goal, a set of immediate targets, a set of organisational imperatives, and a set of tactics.

The weakness of the Labour Left

For perfectly intelligible reasons, the I.L.P. chose the Parliamentary road;* and to achieve that in the 1890s, they had to forge an alliance with non-socialist forces that were already strongly established among the organised sections of the working class. In their willingness to forge such an alliance, and to forego any notion of creating a theoretically rigorous, tightly disciplined socialist party operating within and outside Parliamentary procedures, the I.L.P. gave itself a role within the new Labour Party, but obliged every generation of socialists thereafter to fight in an arena in which the forces of conservatism were stronger than the Labour Left itself - one in which the non-socialist wing of the Labour Party required the Labour Left rather less than the Left needed the rest of the Party. And if the Labour Party began as a coalition of working class political orientations, institutions and men in which the socialist presence was a minority one, so it has always remained; and the very weakness of each generation of the Labour Left within the Party has been at one and the same time an index of past Labour Left failure and a guarantee of failures to come.

For having chosen to create a party in which it was a minority, and on the leadership of which strong forces of conservatism would operate, as we have seen, successive generations of the Labour Left faced a cruel dilemma of strategies. One strategy was to take a firm stand on its socialist principles, to be 'an open conspiracy'[11] for socialism within the Party, to refuse to compromise with Labourist moderation and to organise within the Labour Party to pull the leadership to its view. Yet this strategy was fraught with difficulty. The need to organise as a separate entity with its own programme was essential if the rest of the Party was to be won to a socialist position, and yet separate Left organisation created at best, the dilemma of dual loyalties and, at worst, made left-wing activists open to party disciplinary procedures and even expulsion. The very organisation of a left-wing faction within the Labour Party threatened the unity, and through that the electoral viability, of the Party to whose electoral success the Left was itself committed; and ran the risk that too vigorous a pursuit of left-wing

---

* It is conventional amongst revolutionary students these days to write the Labour Party off from the beginning as nothing but a set of knaves and fools, who failed to see - as see they should - that the Parliamentary State was but a mask for the class rule of the bourgeoisie, and as such, not open to use as a vehicle for Socialism. But it is perhaps worth saying that Marx himself thought that *perhaps* the Parliamentary road to socialism was open in Britain; and that from the vantage point of the 1890s no one could be absolutely sure. It had simply not been tried; and if it had worked, it would have been the least difficult and most peaceful of all the routes to a socialist society.

issues would, in dividing the Party and alienating the marginal voter, let
the Tories in. And of course, too explicit an organisation and an
agitation for left-wing causes invariably alienated the very Party leadership that the left wing sought to influence. For left-wing activism could
be - and invariably was - seen by the leadership of the Party as a
challenge to its authority, to its electoral success, to its freedom of
manoeuvre, and ultimately to its ability to create a co-operative
relationship in power with the institutions and personnel of industrial
and financial capital.

Yet the alternative strategy (the one urged on the Labour Left by
successive generations of Party leaders) of tolerating compromise and
fudging issues in the name of Party unity, was no better either. Here the
price of Party unity could be too high. Certainly it strengthened the
Party's electoral appeal, but it did so only by the Labour Left accepting
unity on terms it found distasteful, and so being obliged to abandon its
defining role - of pressing a socialist programme - at the very moment,
as a general election approached, when it was critical that the Party
leadership commit themselves to radical policies. At best, it obliged
Left militants to spend vast periods of their time supporting programmes they did not like, and propping up leaders that they did not
trust, and whom they knew would oppose Left policies within the
decision-making structures of the Party itself. At worst, this acceptance
of Party unity on non-socialist terms compromised the Left in the eyes
of the electorate, so that Labour Left politicians were unable to dissociate themselves from the general alienation from Labour politics that
right-wing Labour Governments generated. And by accepting co-
habitation with leaders and policies from the Right of the Party, the
Labour Left also compromised itself with parts of its own membership;
and was vulnerable to criticisms from, and defections to, revolutionary
socialist groups on its own left flank.

The Labour Left in each generation was thus faced with a series of
irresolvable dilemmas. To create a separate programme was to create a
problem of dual loyalties and party unity, but to fail to do so was to
remove any rationale for existence and to surrender any hope of
influence. To implement that programme once drawn up, required the
support of the Parliamentary Party and its leadership; and yet to win
that support invariably required that the Labour Left show its loyalty
by playing down its programme and its organisational autonomy. If it
failed to win that support, as invariably was the case, it had the choice
of accepting defeat (and therefore at least temporary impotence and

201

compromise) or of refusing to back the Party line (so alienating the leadership, and reducing their likely openness to left-wing pressure later). And in the end, as Michael Foot said, the Labour Left faced 'a perpetual dilemma' of how to 'do everything in [its] power to persuade or urge the Labour Party to take a different course' without going so far as to 'tear the Labour Party to pieces'.[12]

In consequence, trapped between two equally unattractive and problematic strategies, the Labour Left waxed alternatively hot and cold. It fought in public to strengthen a Party in which it was only a minority, and in which it was forced to cohabit with leaders, activists and programmes that offended its socialist principles. But when co-habitation proved too much, as periodically it did, then the Labour Left campaigned, criticised and threatened defection as periods of Opposition began, only to voluntarily tone down its critique as elections loomed. For in a sense it had no choice. The prerequisite of any implementation of any part of its programme was the return of a Labour Party majority, and thus unity on any terms almost invariably proved preferable to letting the Tories in. But in the process of fighting election after election behind programmes and leaders that were not satisfactory to it, the Labour Left became progressively weaker. For this electoral activity *strengthened* within the Party a leadership hostile to Left policies, and gave to that leadership an electoral credibility and support which the Labour Left could never claim. Indeed, by going to the electorate time and again behind non-socialist programmes, the Labour Left repeatedly missed its major opportunity to educate its class and to create a groundswell of electoral support for its own pro-gramme. And in its repeated compromises with right-wing Party leaders, it tended also to alienate its own membership - the defection of parts of which to more radical groupings outside the Party (or out of politics altogether) left those behind in the Party still weaker, and still less representative of anyone but themselves. As Raymond Williams observed,

> the Labour Left has been a kind of shadow reproduction of the whole official Labour Party and its perspectives. Just as the Labour Party has been a compromise between working class objectives and the existing power structures at the national level, so the traditional Labour Left has been a compromise between socialist objectives and the existing power structure, at the party level. It has made important efforts to reform this party power structure, but with the odds continually against it. Alternatively, it has had to choose

between what are in effect electoral campaigns within the party, and political campaigns which can stand in their own right. When it chooses the electoral campaign it becomes of necessity involved in the same kind of machine politics, the same manipulation of committee votes in the names of thousands, the same confusion of the emptying institutions of the movement with the people in whose names they are conducted, as that of the leaders and managers whom it seeks to affect or displace. It is then not only that in the game of manipulation it is always likely to lose; it is also that it is directing energy into the very machines and methods which socialists should fight.[13]

Only when forces external to the Labour Left itself radicalised the electorate, and only when the right-wing leadership temporarily discredited itself by policies which culminated in its electoral defeat, was the Labour Left in the past able to exert any sustained leverage on the Party. And then it has always met an additional set of problems associated with its inability to control the Parliamentarians, no matter how strongly entrenched it has been in the extra-Parliamentary organs of the labour movement.

This has been a critical weakness for socialists who have always insisted that the Parliamentary road to a socialist commonwealth is open, and that therefore the crucial actors in the process of socialist transformation are Parliamentarians themselves. Even the I.L.P. found that it could not control its large bloc of M.P.s, or turn its membership sanction into a political resource of sufficient weight to offset the other pressures to conservatism acting on the Parliamentary Party. Instead 123 of its 140 M.P.s in 1930 chose to remain loyal to their Parliamentary leadership, within a Parliamentary Party in which the leader's control of Governmental posts was invariably sufficient to discipline all but the most intransigent M.P., and was certainly enough to hold the loyalty of the careerist majority within Labour's Parliamentary ranks. When a Party leader under challenge from his own left wing added to the disciplinary force of his potential patronage an appeal for unity as the General Election approached, and pointed out how crucial it was to win marginal seats in which left-wing ideas had little currency, then it was rare for the bulk of M.P.s to persist in their loyalty to what was only an organised faction or tendency within the wider labour movement. And if they did, it was always open to the Parliamentary leadership to proscribe the Left faction, and to discipline or expel its leading members, who were then in danger of losing their own seats at the next election, should (as was likely in all but a few constituencies) the legitimacy of the Party ticket be more electorally popular than a simple reputation for rebelliousness. Ironically, to the degree that the Labour Left M.P.s in previous elections had striven to cement the legitimacy of the Party leadership against which they now rebelled, they actually left themselves more vulnerable to the permanent loss of the Party Whip. This was a lesson which could not have been lost on many a potential rebel within the Parliamentary Party.

Even at the Party conference where, in Opposition at least, the prestige of the Parliamentary leadership was less overpowering, and where electoral considerations often operated at a second remove, the left-wing activists invariably met frustration and failure. For large periods of the Labour Party's history, the bloc votes of the big trade unions cemented the dominance of the right-wing leadership. And when this was not the case, the willingness of the Party leaders to manipulate the conference proceedings and to build paper compromises and ambiguous verbal formulas undermined the reality of conference control. The left wing of the Party has always talked of the labour movement as though it was a genuine mass phenomenon, whose representative institutions did tap the electoral and industrial attitudes, behaviour and aspirations of the working class; and accordingly the Left has attached enormous significance to the wording of resolutions and to the winning of conference motions. Yet the extra-Parliamentary institutions of the labour movement have only rarely approximated to this, and in their bureaucratisation have often demanded courses of action at variance with the electoral imperatives of the Parliamentary group, who have in their turn sought ways to ignore them. For the very dependence of the labour movement on the Parliamentary Party as its vehicle of action has meant that the ultimate veto on conference policy has lain in the Parliamentary group; and there have been moments - in the 1960s in particular - when the Parliamentary leadership has been able simply to *ignore* conference rulings. Thus, in both the Parliamentary Party and in the extra-Parliamentary centres of decision-making within the labour movement, the left wing of the Party has thus far always found either that its influence has been negligible, or where it has been formally powerful, it has been ignored.

For this persistent weakness the Labour Left is itself much to blame, for its theories and associated political practice have always carried the deficiencies of traditional Labourism. Like the wider Party, the Labour Left has always resisted the temptation to offer a coherent, detailed

and sophisticated analysis of the character, potential and internal con-
tradictions of capitalism, or to go beyond the vaguest generalisations on
the nature of its socialist alternative. Like the wider Party, the Labour
Left has always subscribed to a faith in Parliamentary supremacy,[*] and
its leaders have never fully confronted the significance for socialist
politics of the limited potential of the Parliamentary State as a vehicle
of qualitative social transformation.[†] In its programmes and in the
public utterances of its leaders, it too has shown itself repeatedly
subject to the wider Party's incompatible dualism: of seeking, on the
one hand, to abolish capitalism and all its works whilst, on the other,
offering programmes and demands that ameliorated working class dis-
contents by strengthening capitalism as a system. The Labour Left too
has suffered from the elitism of the wider Party. For though it alone
has kept alive within the Labourist tradition the issue of workers'
control, it too has tended (and did so especially in the 1950s) to define
socialism as bureaucratic public ownership; and (after Maxton had gone)
to show an antipathy (or at best, to attach no significance) to mass
industrial action by the working class. Instead the Labour Left has
repeatedly put its faith in Parliamentary leadership, arguing that if this
was strong and socialist enough, it could by its own efforts squeeze
more for the working class and for the dispossessed out of capitalism
to a point at which the system itself would be transformed; without
providing that leadership with any real leverage with which to repel the
pressures of accommodation and conservatism discussed in chapter 6.

Moreover, left-wing members of the Labour Party have persistently
subscribed to a theory of the dynamics of class consciousness under

[*] Bevan's *In Place of Fear* is a classic statement of this faith, and of the alternatives consciously foregone. Bevan reminds us of the militancy of the
syndicalists: 'Going to Parliament seemed a roundabout and tedious way of
realising what seemed already within our grasp by more direct means. As . . .
Noah Abblet put it, "why cross the river to fill the pail?" ' (p. 19). Yet,
Bevan wrote 'these dreams of easy success did not survive the industrial
depression of the twenties. Mass unemployment was a grim school. Industrial
power was just what the unemployed did not possess' (p. 19). And so Bevan
reasserts the potential of Parliamentary action. *'The function of parliamentary
democracy, under universal franchise, historically considered, is to expose
wealth-privilege to the attack of the people. It is a sword pointed at the heart
of property power. The arena where the issues are joined is Parliament'* (p. 5).

[†] The I.L.P., it will be remembered, discussed this seriously only after its
disaffiliation from the Labour Party; and then ironically became increasingly
opposed to Parliamentary action at the very time when the rest of the left -
including the Communist Party - were busy defending Parliamentary politics
against the threat of Fascism. (On this, see J. Jupp, *The Left in Britain,
1931-41*, M.Sc. Thesis, University of London, 1956, pp. 303-36).

capitalism that suggested that socialism could and would win its way into the hearts of men and women if only the Party educated, preached and proselytised; and that this could be done successfully *without* forging a disciplined Party presence within the working class in its industrial setting that might connect socialist politics with the daily reality of the class struggle occurring there. Accordingly the Labour Left has been unable to avoid the wider Party's electoral dilemma: of the gap between its socialist aspirations and the uneven and even hostile patterns of attitude and belief found repeatedly in sections of the working class and so in parts of the Party's electorate. The Labour Left, like the wider Party, has had no way of bridging that gap except by risking electoral defeat or toning down the Party's programme to win electoral support at whatever level of consciousness the Party currently faced. By doing that, of course, the Labour Left has made its own contribution to buttressing strands in popular culture that were inimicable to the very growth of socialist consciousness that it so avidly sought.

In other words, and hitherto at least, the Parliamentary preoccupation of the Labour Left has rendered its politics particularly ineffective. That preoccupation has meant that left-wing activists within the Labour Party have always been vulnerable to appeals for Party unity as elections approached. The preoccupation with Parliament has encouraged them to fudge issues and policies, and to reject working class industrial militancy if and when that might endanger the electoral success of the Party. It has generated, especially in left-wing M.P.s and since the loss of the I.L.P., an elitism which has tended to reduce all the problems of class politics to the single question of who leads the Labour Party, and which has accordingly meant that left-wing militants have proved particularly vulnerable to the appeals of individual leaders (like Wilson in one generation and MacDonald in another) who in their youth occupied leftish political positions that they have long since abandoned.

Indeed the history of the Labour Left is characterised by the systematic defection of its leaders as they, faced with the insoluble dilemmas of left-wing Parliamentary agitation and committed to their search for Parliamentary power above all else, have each, in their own time and place, eventually accommodated themselves to right-wing policies and colleagues. This is as true of Castle and Greenwood in this generation as it was of Bevan in the 1950s, of Cripps in the 1940s, and of Snowden and MacDonald before 1931. This pattern of defection must not be thought the cause of Left impotence. It is, and always has been, merely the most visible index of the sterility of the particular mould into which Labour Left politics has fallen. As Raymond Williams has said, amid the impotence of its Parliamentarianism, the Labour Left always

> reacts . . . in familiar ways: tabling resolutions for the party conference; campaigning for this or that man to be elected to the National Executive Committee; calling on 'Left' ministers to be loyal to their socialism; making hopeful demands on the [Labour]. government for 'an immediate change of course'. All these actions are clearly based on a strategy of giving political priority to Labour in parliament, and of thinking organisationally in terms of the existing structure of the Labour Party . . . What has happened . . . is a materialisation of the Labour Left around certain personalities, certain M.P.s and certain short-term issues. And this has prevented the outward-looking and independent long-term campaign which would carry forward the politics of the many thousands of people . . . in a general political campaign.[14]

For most crucial of all, the Parliamentarianism of the Labour Left has militated against such socialists moving outside their position of structured impotence within the Labour Party, by preventing them from building connections with, and offering leadership to, the working class in struggle at the point of production itself. 'No Left M.P.', as Michael Foot himself said, 'can be effective if there are no mass movements outside' Parliament.[15] And yet the Labour Left, in its Parliamentary preoccupation, has never gone out - at least since the days of the I.L.P. - to build a mass working class movement that could give it some leverage with Party leaders and capitalists alike. This self-adopted isolation from its potential class base, and its insistence that the relationship between the socialist wing of the Labour Party and working class socialist militants should be almost exclusively an electoral one, has had far-reaching repercussions on the character and degree of success of the Labour Left. The absence of a mass base of support for its policies has denied the Labour Left any leverage within the Labour Party, since it has meant that the Left represented nothing more than a minority strand even in electoral terms. By not going out to create such a mass base for itself, the Labour Left has had precious little impact on general levels of consciousness in the class that it seeks to represent and lead. By isolating itself from daily involvement in class struggle, the Labour Left M.P.s have cut themselves off from their major source of evaluation of their own theory and policies; and in their Parliamentary isolation, have continued to articulate an old theoretical package - of public ownership, planning and welfare - in which they (and not the working class) would again be the major actors but whose bankruptcy was already visible to large sections of the Party's electorate by the mid 1950s.

Yet it is no accident that the Labour Left has not created such mass support for itself. For the only way in which that mass support could have been created would have been if the Labour Left had been pre-pared to take up unambiguously hostile positions against its own Party leadership when in office, by acting outside Parliament to defeat the leadership by mobilising the industrial power of the working class for political ends. There can be no guarantee that even if the Labour Left had tried this, it would have succeeded. In certain periods, like the early 1950s, any call for mass working class mobilisation might have fallen on unresponsive ears. In the inter-war years and in the late 1960s, prospects were better. But the Labour Left has never been willing to try such a form of socialist politics on a systematic and prolonged basis, and so it has remained trapped: blocked by its own Parliamentarianism from adopting a form of behaviour that alone could permit it to shape patterns of working class consciousness on a mass scale; and blocked, by the absence of such mass support, from being influential within Parliament itself. The Labour Left has, instead, remained wrapped in the rhetoric of the 'Labour Movement' whilst failing to act in any way which might have turned this rhetoric into a reality. The result has been a dismal and unbroken record of failures.

6

The revival of socialist militancy within the depleted ranks of the Labour Party must be seen in this context, and its significance under-stood in the light of this perennial weakness of the Labour Left. For as in the years of Opposition after 1931, so after 1970, Left agitation within the Party shifted the whole terms of reference for Labour Party policy and perspective away from the technocratic preoccupations of office. The Party is now (in 1974) experiencing the full impact of the strongest Labour Left in forty years. It is a Left whose strength within the decision-making structures of the Party is partly based, as in 1931-4, on the total (if temporary) discrediting of the policies which the Party leadership pursued in their previous period of office. Not that the events of the early 1930s are being mechanically repeated. For after

The weakness of the Labour Left

1931, when last a Left revival happened so rapidly and violently, it was accompanied by the Party's rejection of the old leadership as well. In the four years since 1970, it has been accompanied only by the rediscovery, by the leaders of the 1960s, of the old rhetoric and socialist aspirations that they systematically ignored when in power. But even so, and for the moment, no one in the Labour Party leadership is defending with any great enthusiasm the 'white heat of the technological revolution' or arguing again for that unbridled pursuit of economic growth under private control that characterised the early Wilson years. The tone and rhetoric of Labour Party debate have altered; and with them the policies to which the Labour Party in Opposition committed itself, and which in Government it is purporting to seek.

But old leaders have been discredited before without a Left revival of this scale, and so the events of 1970-4 within the Labour Party cannot be explained simply in terms of the 1970 electoral defeat. There is more. For the current Labour Left, unlike any before it, is not simply or even mainly a Parliamentary force. Indeed its Parliamentary weakness, as we shall argue, will doubtless be its undoing. For it is a Left which captured control of the Party conference by mobilising an alliance between Left M.P.s, constituency activists and, crucially, the votes of the delegations from the big trade unions. For the first time, the Labour Left activists in Parliament and in the constituencies established a firm organisational connection, through their alliance with the leaders of the large unions, with the groundswell of working class industrial militancy. That militancy, prompted as it was by the industrial relations policies of the 1964-70 Wilson Government, was sustained and intensified by the Heath Administration's attempts to resolve the central tension between wages and profits in a weak capitalist economy; and was reflected in the personnel and policies of the trade union delegations who made their way to recent Labour Party conferences. It was trade union support for, and indeed their insistence upon, left-wing policies that gave the Labour Left its leverage, by breaking the hold of more moderate leadership on the Party conference and N.E.C., and which brought the Party by 1973 to the point at which it adopted as its programme the radical call laid out in chapter 1.

This left-wing revival began in the late 1960s. In Parliament, a tiny group of Left M.P.s maintained fairly consistent opposition after 1966 to the Wilson Government's policy on prices and incomes. They opposed the Government's support for American action in Vietnam.

The weakness of the Labour Left

They offered an alternative economic strategy that included public ownership and exchange controls.* They opposed the January 1968 cuts in the welfare and education services. And, of course, amid a much wider alliance of M.P.s, they opposed *In Place of Strife* and blocked the Labour Government's intended bill on industrial relations legislation.[16] Parallel opposition to the Labour Government's policies grew at conference after 1966. Hostile resolutions were passed on Vietnam and military spending in 1966, and on Vietnam and Greece in 1967. In 1968 conference, by a massive majority, rejected statutorily based incomes policies, and rejected Government plans on Rhodesia, fuel policy and prescription charges. In 1969, the T.U.C.'s alternative economic policy received the full backing of a conference that was otherwise keen to avoid a party row in the build up to a closely fought General Election. And after the election, conference reaffirmed its right to control M.P.s, reversed Labour Government policy on the Common Market, and began the shift leftwards that culminated in the 1973 conference's acceptance of *Labour's Programme*, arguably the most radical socialist document to be endorsed by a Labour conference since *For Socialism and Peace* in 1934.

Understandably then, the Tribune meeting at the 1973 Labour Party conference was a jubilant gathering. Though mindful of the tragic events in Chile that hung over the Labour Party conference that year, Tribunites were able legitimately to claim that Left agitation within the Party had shifted the axis of party debate back into a 'reformist' perspective. Yet as many who were there were aware, and as Eric Heffer said, between conference resolutions and Labour Government action lay all the pitfalls and problems of Left Labourism. Heffer, at that Tribune meeting, was optimistic that they could be overcome. But nothing in the Labour Party past supports his optimism. Sadly, this Labour Left looks as vulnerable as every Labour Left before it; and this is clear from the moment that we examine closely the detail of the 1973 programme, the character of the Parliamentary Party that was asked to implement it, and the nature of the economy within which, if

---

* 'To close the balance of payments gap, by a rapid expansion of the economy, which is what Labour promised at the election and what *Tribune* and the T.U.C. advocates today, requires measures to protect us from the pressures of the speculators, the capital exporters and the bankers in the meantime. And that means exchange controls, export directives, extended public ownership, maybe import controls and the mobilisation of some of the country's immense financial reserves'. (*Tribune*, 17 May 1968).

it continues in office, the newly elected Labour Government will be obliged to operate.

The 1973 *Programme* is a mixture of radical promise and verbal ambiguity. It certainly marks a break with Labour Government policy in the 1960s, as was argued in chapter 1. It reaffirms the Labour Party's prior commitment to the poor and dispossessed.* It reasserts the need for widespread public ownership. It states, as so often in the Labour Party's more radical past, that a Labour Government *will control* the private economy that it chooses not to nationalise. And it re-establishes a 'social contract' between the Party and the trade union movement that commits the next Labour Government to introduce price controls, increased pensions, progressive taxation, public ownership of the land, and 'real moves towards industrial democracy'.[17] It is adamant that the full programme cannot be completed in one five year period, and that the Party's priorities should be price control, the reform of housing, health and education, the extension of industrial democracy, the achievement of full employment, the massive redistribution of wealth and incomes, and the extension of the public sector.[18]

But when the document goes on to say *how* this will be achieved, and to specify exactly *what* it will involve, the old ambiguities and dilemmas reappear. The Party is committed to full employment (and therefore to economic growth) without saying how it will resolve the tension in a private economy between the incentive structures required for economic growth and the Party's promises on income redistribution and industrial democracy. We have seen how that tension has been resolved - against the working class - by every Labour Government to date, and there is little in the programme to suggest that things will be different the next time. On the contrary, the Labour *Programme* is still saying that social reform and capitalist prosperity can be achieved at the same time, and is still implying that social inequality is a *barrier* to

---

* It is worth quoting on this. 'Socialism is about helping the poor and eliminating poverty. It is also about achieving a massive and irreversible shift in the distribution of wealth and income in favour of working people. For Socialists, the creation of wealth is seen above all else as a *social* process - one which involves the co-operation of countless individual men and women, and of the community as a whole. No one person - or indeed any family or group of shareholders - can be said to 'create' wealth, great companies or great estates. It is the people who create; it is the fortunate few, blessed by the custom and law of the land, who are deemed to own. It is time, we believe, to change these customs and laws. We must begin to load the scales in favour of equality. And this can only mean radical *Socialist* measures.' (*Labour's Programme 1973*, pp. 8-9).

the growth and prosperity of an economy in private hands, rather than - as in fact appears to be the case - a prerequisite for its ability to function at all. Only on these assumptions is the *Programme* able to mix its socialist radicalism with its assertion that State planning can generate greater industrial efficiency in the private as well as the public sector.

That unresolved dilemma - of economic management against social reform - runs through the whole document. For the radical tone of the *Programme* rests again on the Labour Party's promise of State intervention and control. It proposes the creation of a National Enterprise Board as a State Holding Company that will buy controlling interests in firms in the profitable manufacturing sector. It makes clear that the Industry Act will this time have teeth, in that the State will invest in companies, and on occasion purchase them outright, to guarantee that their performance is 'in the national interest'. But that national interest is still seen as conterminous with the strengthening of the competitive position and growth potential of an economy that will remain predominantly in private hands and that will still be subject to the imperatives of survival amid the harsh realities of international capitalist competition.

So the detail of the Party's proposals on State 'control' of industry suggest that, as before, the Labour Party in power will be involved in a collaborative exercise with the senior managerial personnel of the very largest private companies, on whose co-operation the Party's proposed Industry Act will depend for its effective gathering of data and policing of growth targets. The Party is not even proposing to take these large companies into public ownership, though on its own recognition they dominate the economy. Instead, in the *Programme* and in the voting at the 1973 conference, nationalisation is again to be restricted to 'basic' industries that are incapable of surviving in private hands, and which in public hands can be used to service and strengthen a private capitalist sector. So the incorporation of the State and a private economy will go on apace if the new Labour Government survives. That much is certain. And it will do so in the name of a radical, even a socialist national interest. But there is no guarantee in the *Programme* - there is only the assumption - that in that merger the 'socialist' aspirations of the Ministers will survive, and prove stronger than, the managerial ethos and capitalist imperatives of the large and increasingly multi-national corporate structure. But how can that assumption be believed when all the Labour Party's record stands witness to its negation?

The weakness of the Labour Left

For the detail of *Labour's Programme* is unconvincing at its critical points. On the question of incomes control, we are offered again the promise of a socially just incomes policy, in which wages and salary increases will be voluntarily tied to the rate of increase of national productivity because of a Labour Government's ability to create an environment of social equality. But that was the Party's promise in 1964, and look what happened. The *Programme*'s optimism for a better and more successful performance this time seems to be based solely on an assertion that now the Party leadership's resolve is tougher, and its proposed controls (on the movement of money in particular) tighter. But the economic imperatives that structured Labour Party performance after 1964 remain to constrain this new Administration of the Left; and on how the Party will prevent these from destroying its ability and its will to create a socially just environment, the *Programme* is silent.

Nor is it particularly clear on the question of industrial democracy. It is a measure of the radicalism within the Labour Party ranks that this item is on the agenda again, that - as Tony Benn said to the 1973 conference - 'we have had enough experience to know that national-isation plus Lord Robens does not add up to socialism'.[19] But the Party's commitment to a radical shift in class power *within* industry is ambiguous. The *Programme* proposes a stronger legal code of rights for individual workers and for collective bargaining and all this is subsumed under its general rubric of industrial democracy. But the Party is not proposing workers' control. It is considering direct trade union representation on Boards of Directors, and permissive legislation for the creation of joint control committees. But it is not intending to dis-mantle managerial hierarchies. Rather, as the *Programme* put it, 'industrial democracy in this country is something of an uncharted continent' in which the Party hopes to make only 'the beginnings of a new start'. That 'new start' will, the *Programme* hopes, simply involve 'experiments in new forms of workers' participation . . . especially in the public sector';[20] and for the rest, industrial democracy is to be understood as the extension of trade union rights within the existing structures of private managerial control. As usual, between the heady rhetoric and the actual concrete reality will lie the corpse of qualitative socialist change.

The Party's 'new social order' will not then be built on the direct control of the industrial process by its working class electorate. As ever, all that Labour is offering is public control of the industrial system by Ministers who characteristically succumb to the very managerialism that they are supposed to control, plus big public corporations which do not qualitatively alter the life-style, living standards or industrial control of the Labour Party's working class electorate. Should the Party retain power, the scene appears set for another period in which Labour Governments will strengthen national capitalism by nationalising its weaker units and subsidising its investment programmes, will use its managerial personnel to plan its central processes in a close and working relationship with the State bureaucracy, and will subordinate the Party's promise of social reform to the more powerful imperatives of economic growth, capital accumulation and international payments. The best that the 1973 Programme appears to offer is a repetition of the Attlee Government, and its reality is likely to be a repetition of 1964-70.

Even if this is a particularly pessimistic interpretation of the possibilities of the 1973 *Programme*, it is clear that there are strong forces at work within the Labour Party that will argue against any more radical interpretation of the Party's policy. For the Labour Left is still weak where ultimately - in its form of politics - it matters: in the Parliamentary Party itself. There the new found socialist militancy of the Party leadership is visibly skin-deep, and the old technocratic pre-occupations with growth and efficiency remain. Harold Wilson's recent and favourable statements on strikes in general, and on militant miners in particular, must be compared with the man's record when in office, when he regularly indulged in vitriolic attacks on working class industrial militancy, and tolerated and supported Ministers (like Ray Gunter at the Ministry of Labour) who were even more hostile to manifestations of working class industrial power. For the leadership of the Party now is still dominated by the personnel of the 1964-70 Government, and during their period in Opposition they mostly looked embarrassed by the radicalism of their rank and file. This was particularly clear in the handling of the nationalisation issue at the 1973 Labour Party conference. There, Harold Wilson and the N.E.C. would not support the call to nationalise either the largest 25 or the largest 250 companies - a call which at least made some attempt to give the Party power over increasingly concentrated economic structures. Instead, public ownership was redefined as a policy instrument with a different application, which would *not* be applied to the growth points of British manufacturing capital.*

* Though the Party rhetoric promises once again to capture the commanding heights of the economy, the industries that were specifically mentioned by

The weakness of the Labour Left

In his handling of the nationalisation issue at conference, the Party Leader clearly spoke for the bulk of the Parliamentary Party, which was way to the Right of its own conference on questions of domestic reform. Even the widely popular Michael Foot was defeated for the Deputy Leadership by the moderate candidature of Edward Short, for the bulk of the Parliamentary Party could apparently see neither the electoral advantage nor the practical possibilities of sweeping social change. As Reg Prentice said in 1973 - in an open attack on the Labour Left - 'if Labour won the next election it would provide a moderate, left of centre, reforming administration', since the Parliamentary Party, in his view, was 'not hell-bent on nationalising everything'.[21] Significantly, Prentice came lower only than Callaghan and Foot in the Shadow Cabinet elections in November 1973. Here the true sympathies of the bulk of the Parliamentary Party were made clear, within a month of the Party's most radical conference in forty years. Of the top 12 M.P.s elected to the Shadow Cabinet by their fellow Labour Parliamentarians, only two were 'to the Left' of the Party, and all the rest had in the past been identified with either the Gaitskellite wing or the Centre of the Party. As Miliband said earlier, of just these men: 'it is absurd to think that the men who now rule the Labour Party . . . will ever want, or would agree under pressure, to push the Labour Party in socialist directions, and to show the resolution, the single-mindedness and staying power which such reorientation would require. Carthorses should not be expected to win the Derby'.[22]

So the Labour Left's capture of the Party conference must be recognised as of limited significance for future patterns of Labour Party performance. Conference domination did not survive the last period of Labour Government, and it is hard to see why history should not repeat itself. For the Left captured a conference that was attended only by representatives of highly bureaucratised trade unions and of sparsely attended constituency parties, who collectively are no longer representative of the Party's wider electorate. For though trade union radicalism at conference undoubtedly reflects the upsurge of industrial militancy amongst large sections of the working class, that industrial militancy has not been accompanied by any comparable resurgence of

Harold Wilson at the conference did not extend to the finance sector, or to the major export industries. The list was extensive, but was limited to fuel industries (particularly oil), to transport and distribution (road haulage and ports), to industries that are already heavily dependent on state subsidies and orders (aircraft and shipbuilding) plus 'identifiable sections' or individual firms in the drug, machine tool and construction industries.

215

support for the Labour Party and its programme. On the contrary, at the very moment at which the Labour Party conference was discussing its most socialist programme since 1934, the opinion polls were only giving Labour 38% of the vote, and the by-elections were underlining the rising tide of Liberalism. In such a situation, the Labour leadership was again under heavy electoral pressure to tone down its programme - which it did, by 'simplifying' it in its election manifesto. And though returned to office in the wake of the General Election in February 1974, the Labour leaders found themselves insufficiently popular this time even to command a majority in the new House of Commons.

In any case, the new Labour Government seems doomed to experience once again the limits that exist on the use of State power for 'reformist' ends. If the Parliamentary Labour Party can retain office, and eventually win a Parliamentary majority, it will doubtless take a number of basic and derelict industries into public ownership, create its planning machinery and price controls, and must surely persist in its early days in the reforms in State pensions, welfare provision and trade union legislation to which it is so publicly committed. But of its promise to 'bring about a fundamental and irreversible shift in the balance of power and wealth in favour of working people and their families',[23] there seems little hope; and already (by July 1974) there are ominous signs that the events of 1964-70 could well be repeated. The Chancellor of the Exchequer has already arranged what Dennis Healey believed to be 'the largest loan ever raised in the international capital markets'.[24] Labour Ministers at the Treasury in particular have already publicly reassured senior industrialists that the new Labour Government, like its predecessors, understands the need for reasonable profits and high investment, and 'has no intention of destroying the private sector or encouraging its decay'.[25] The Labour Government has already had to face strikes by its own employees in the National Health Service and in the London teaching system against pay policies which appear to perpetuate low pay in the public sector. The newspapers are full of reports of struggles within the Cabinet between Treasury orthodoxy and the 'Left radicalism' of Benn, Hart, Foot, Shore and Castle.[26] And the level of inflation persists, and the already enormous balance of payments deficit worsens.[27]

For the persistent weakness of British capitalism remains, to deny the economic base for radical policies of the Labour Party kind. Any Labour Government that survives into the mid 1970s seems fated to live with a truly enormous balance of payments deficit, with an economy that is investing an insufficient percentage of G.N.P. in new machinery and plant, and that is still insufficiently competitive in its exports to offset the enormously increased bill for imports (and especially for oil), and with a strongly entrenched working class that is willing and able to resist State-led encroachments on its living standards and industrial power. Yet whether the Labour Government's promised social contract can be achieved will turn, as always, on the health of the capitalist economy over which the Labour Party presides, and all the signs suggest that a Labour Government in the second half of the 1970s will face once more immediate and pressing economic and financial difficulties that will drown its promised social reforms.

In such a situation, the culmination of the Left revival in the Party will not be a move towards a socialist society, but simply the ever greater incorporation of the State into the economy and the strengthening of the relationships between the public and private bureaucracies that will reduce even further the freedom of manoeuvre of Labour Governments to come. And in the process, the Labour Party in power seems doomed to succumb to this managerial embrace, and to turn once more against the industrial power of its own working class electorate in a desperate search for economic growth and balance of payments surplus. If that is the likely scenario for the Labour Party in the next decade, then the experience of further Labour Governments will not bring us any nearer socialism or a 'new social order'. It will merely mark yet another stage in the decay of the British labour movement. When the heady euphoria of Labour Party rhetoric subsides, this seems the inescapable if unattractive verdict on the Left revival since 1970.

8. The exhaustion of a tradition

Hitherto at least, the central economic, social and political features of British capitalism have proved surprisingly immune to the impact of Labour in power. After more than seven decades of Labour Party politics, and after two six-year periods of post-war Labour Government, the social fabric of this society - which Labour politicians have periodically promised to transform - shows only limited signs of the Party's long presence and past performance. Reforms there have undoubtedly been: in the provision of welfare services, in the ownership of basic industries, and in the maintenance of higher living standards and employment levels. And since these have affected and eased the lives of each and every one of us, they rightly figure in the public justification of the Labour Party by its leadership. Yet that leadership often claims too much. For these reforms have often come from, and been maintained by, Conservative Governments no less than by Labour; and more important, even the reforms to which the Labour Party can lay full claim have not seriously diminished the pattern of inequality in British society. Indeed the current revival of left-wing radicalism within the Labour Party is but one measure of the failure of past reforms to radically transform a highly inegalitarian social order and its capitalist economic base.

So by now it should be clear how I at least would answer the questions that were set out in chapter 1, of the Labour Party's potential as a vehicle for socialist change and therefore as a focal point for the loyalty and activism of aspiring socialist militants. For if the arguments of the earlier chapters have any force, they suggest that the Labour Party cannot and will not transform capitalism into a socialist order, or even in the present economic conditions make any noticable progress in its promised attempts to ameliorate capitalism's worst social excesses. But let us be quite clear on the nature of the argument that has been offered. In making this critique of the Labour Party and its politics, the thrust of the argument has *not* been that what has gone wrong is that

218

the Party has abandoned its revolutionary socialist past for its moderate and technocratic present. Rather I have argued that what we have witnessed over the years is the periodic upsurge of a *reformist* impulse within a Party totally committed to constitutional modes of political activity. This reformism. I have argued, should be understood as the periodic reappearance within the Labour Party of the promise to transform capitalism gradually and peacefully, the Parliamentary way, into a new and a socialist society. Yet in power, Labour Governments have persistently allowed that reformist impulse to come to nothing, and necessarily so. For my argument has been that the Labour Party is not only *not* a revolutionary party, but that it is not a successful reformist party either; and that its reformism has not and will not work precisely because in its mode of activity, in its programme, and in its impact on the consciousness of its own working class, the Labour Party has not been revolutionary enough.

Paradoxical as this view may be, it has been reached by the following argument: that the Labour Party, in its gradualism, has neither created nor sustained the one social force, namely a radicalised working class, which alone could provide it with the power base on which to effect a socialist transformation. It has consistently rejected any view of socialism that was conterminous with the establishment of workers' control at the point of production and with the dismantling of the managerial hierarchies and authority structures generated by a private capitalist economy. It has been reluctant to countenance the mass mobilisation of the working class in open (and doubtless bitter and bloody) class war that such a view of socialism would inevitably entail. Instead the Labour Party has chosen to define socialism, even in its most radical periods, as public ownership, state planning and welfare provision - as a set of social changes, that is, which could be implemented (and only implemented) by its own Parliamentarians, capturing and using the Parliamentary State and its bureaucracy in open electoral battle with the Conservative and Liberal political oppositions. And as a corollary of that, the Labour Party has always relied, in its pursuit of its notion of socialism, on the voluntary co-operation of the very social forces (the managerial strata who head the private bureaucracies of industrial and financial capital, and their class allies in the State administrative machine) whose powers and privileges would be undermined by any serious attempt 'to bring about a fundamental and irreversible shift in the balance of power and wealth in favour of working people and their families'.[1]

The exhaustion of a tradition

Yet this Labour Party dependence on such co-operation has effectively denied to it the ability to achieve its socialist transformation. For not surprisingly, when in office the Labour Party has found that these groups could not be relied upon for the implementation of (nor would they co-operate in) policies which made substantial inroads into their own class prerogatives and power. Instead, these entrenched capitalist social formations have pressed upon Labour Governments, by the systematic deployment of the massive ideological and material sanctions that they control, sets of social changes which strengthened national capitalist forces, and which did not either markedly shift class power or alter qualitatively the life-experience of the working class sections of the Labour Party's electorate. The resulting disaffection of that electorate, which appears in part at least to have grown out of the gap between Labour promise and performance, has now come to act as a secondary barrier on Labour Party power: both by prompting organised sections of the working class to resist by industrial action Labour Governments only slightly less than Conservative ones; and by leading the working class sections of the Party's electorate to vote with less and less enthusiasm, and in ever shrinking numbers, for the Labour alternative to Conservatism. In such a situation, as we have seen, the Labour Party itself has changed, particularly in its Parliamentary wing. For in response to the repeated experience of office and opposition has come a steady erosion of socialist purpose in the Labour Party leadership, and a steady diminution of the ideological, programmatic and personal connections between that leadership and the working class sections of its electorate.* [2] It is these trends which have left the Labour Party even more unwilling and unable to mobilise the industrial power of that working class to strengthen its hand against capitalist forces on those very occasions - as in 1974 - when once again the extra-Parliamentary sections of the Party have set its Parliamentarians the task of creating a new and a socialist order.

2

That process of conservatism, and of the weakening of the links between the Labour Party leadership and its working class roots, has

---

* The percentage of Labour M.P.s with working class backgrounds fell from 87% in 1918 to 27% in 1970. By 1970 half of all Labour Party candidates were from the professions, and in the Parliamentary Party elected in 1970, the largest occupational categories were teachers (56), barristers (34), and journalists (27). There were only 22 miners, 33 skilled and 17 semi-skilled gone on systematically since 1945, and has been accelerated by the Party's experience of and reaction to its two periods of post-war majority government. For in office the Labour Party experienced in full the dilemma of its 'reformist' aspirations. The paradox of Labour politics was clear in the Party's experience after 1945. For the desire within the Party ranks to create a socialist society had been fed by the inter-war experience of the particular weaknesses of British capitalism, and had been a response by sections of the Party's activists and leaders to their own observations of the social dislocation, injustices, hardships and human waste brought on by a private capitalist economy in crisis. The Labour Party in the 1930s was a stern critic of untrammelled capitalism, and expected to take office amid an economic crisis which its leaders believed they could exploit for their own socialist ends. Yet their reformist impulse was actually defeated by the very weakness of the capitalist system that Labour policy was supposed to transcend. For because the Labour Party in 1945 did take power, as so far it always has, at a time of immense difficulties for British capitalism, the incoming Labour Government found that its ability to introduce what it under-stood as a socialist transformation was particularly undermined by the economic context and power structure that it inherited. For it is precisely at moments like 1945, when for whatever reason the domestic economy's inability to capture a sufficient percentage of world trade is undermining the ability of any government to maintain an adequate flow of essential imports and a sustained rate of industrial production, that Labour Governments experience the most severe constraints on their own freedom of manoeuvre, and come under the heaviest and most effective pressure to strengthen the national capitalism at the cost of their own socialist programme. Yet hitherto at least, the Labour Party has been elected into power *only* at these moments of capitalist crisis. For only then apparently do sufficient sections of its opponents' electorate abstain, or abandon their previous political allegiances, in the hope of a better deal from Labour; and there is no reason to suppose that the Party will be any more fortunate in the future.

The Wilson Government's experience between 1964 and 1970 brought home this dilemma clearly. For that Government, even though its members had by then long abandoned the policies and reformist aspirations of the Attlee generation, found itself dependent for the effectiveness of its policies on the voluntary co-operation of the power

---

workers. (On this, see M. Stewart, *Protest or Power*, London, Allen and Unwin, 1974, pp. 67-8).

structure that it faced, and hence on the support of the hierarchies of industrial and financial capital, and of the organised unions of the working class. The concentration of power in the hands of private capital gave to the senior managerial strata of industrial and financial institutions enormous leverage over the Labour Government; and since they were themselves under intense and growing product market and labour market pressures, that leverage was used to prevent the State from adding to those pressures by its own programme of social reform. Indeed, so intense were the economic difficulties of the leading sections of British capitalism by the second half of the 1960s that the Labour Government was under severe pressure, not simply to abandon its social programme, but also to use State power to whittle away the degree of social reform already granted, and to curtail, if only at the margin, the industrial power of the organised working class that was adding to the competitive difficulties of critical export sectors.

So, as a 'reformist party' after 1945 and as a 'party of social reform' after 1964, successive Labour Governments found that they were pushed inexorably towards a situation in which the weakness of the capitalist economy over which they formally presided required a direct State-initiated confrontation either with the imperatives of organised business and finance or with the organised working class that the Labour Government was elected to represent. Yet in each case, and in spite of the Party's aspirations when in Opposition, the Labour leadership were not prepared ideologically, organisationally or politically for the massive dislocations associated with a confrontation with organised capital. For that confrontation would have been traumatic, constituting as it would nothing less than a social revolution. Instead, and out of the logic of its own politics, each Labour Government moved - slowly after 1945, rapidly after 1964 - to abandon its policies of social reform in order to use State power to undercut the industrial power and living standards of its own working class electorate. Indeed, there seems to be a general lesson here: namely that in situations in which the national capitalism is too competitively weak to pay the price of ambitious programmes of social reform, Labour Governments that depend on the voluntary co-operation of the senior echelons of the capitalist command structure will fail to deliver that which they promised, and in the process undermine their credibility with their own electorate at the very moment that they strengthen the political power of groups who stand to suffer most from Labour Party reformism. In such situations, Labour Governments destroy themselves. That is what happened in

1970; and will doubtless happen again if the Labour Government elected in February 1974 continues in office. The easier relationships between the Labour Party and the trade union movement that were re-established in the years of Opposition after 1970 were almost entirely the accidental by-product of Conservative Government policies; and with Labour back in power, and the common Conservative enemy removed, the scene appears set for a growing confrontation between the Labour Party and its own trade union working class base. And this will surely occur unless there are rapid and qualitative changes in either the pattern of class militancy now prevalent or in the state of British capitalism as a competitive economic system. Neither of these changes seems likely.

To take the latter first. The economy that the 1974 Labour Government has inherited is so far showing no signs of resolving significantly the weakness of its competitive position; and must in any case continue to increase its exporting potential if only to offset an apparently long-term tendency for the price of world commodities to increase. In addition, the economy is dominated increasingly by the large multi-national corporations and banking networks, whose ability to redirect investment and money flows on a global scale has already noticably eroded the freedom of manoeuvre of the national State and its bureaucracy. That State bureaucracy is, in any case, ever more involved in close daily connections with the managerial structures of private capitalism, as the State machine comes to play an ever more central role in the planning, subsidising and protection of a national capitalist structure under international competitive challenge. Accordingly, the Labour Party in power will again be subject to a coherent, pressing and institutionally buttressed set of capitalist imperatives, that will push it once more to subordinate its policies of social reform, and of the re-distribution of wealth, income and power between the classes, to the prior needs of the social groups on whose co-operation the State machine relies for its effectiveness.

In such a situation, the Labour Party will doubtless be brought up against, and be obliged to challenge, the industrial power and degree of job control of its own working class electorate. And it will come to that confrontation not as the passive tool of an unseen capitalist elite, but on its own initiative and out of the logic of its own dependence on State power. To achieve economic growth in a capitalist world, to ease the balance of payments pressure on a weak economy, to guarantee the flow of essential raw materials, Labour Governments to come will again

223

have to abandon any set of proposals that undermine the incentives and managerial structures of private capitalism, and will again have to confront those manifestations of trade union power - on wages and on job control - that add to manufacturing costs, reduce competitiveness, and absorb imported goods from international competitors.

But as the Labour Government found in the latter part of 1969 and 1970, and as the Conservative Government found later, such State initiatives against trade union industrial power and working class living standards can now expect stiff resistance from the groups of workers concerned. The voluntary restraint of the working class in the face of Labour Party appeals for national unity and common sacrifice, of the kind that Labour Governments successfully made in 1948 and in 1966, are unlikely to be effective in the present climate of tenser class relationships. For the visible involvement of the State, under both Labour and Conservative leaders, in the policing of industrial relations, in the setting of incomes norms and in the drive to intensify work routines, is now too regular and too all pervasive to be presented as a crisis measure, deserving of special consideration and working class restraint.

Instead, a generation of workers is emerging who have seen the State deploying its vast ideological and material resources to cut employment, to set limits on living standards and to effect industrial reorganisation and increased labour productivity amid continuing social inequality. That same generation of workers has also witnessed regular and protracted strikes against State policy by large and growing numbers of workers: by miners, railwaymen, post-office workers, local government manual workers, ambulancemen, and dockers; and even by white collar workers such as teachers and airline pilots. They have seen State attempts to encroach upon job control and earning levels resisted by shop floor militancy across the engineering industry, as well as by set-piece confrontations of an official kind between public sector unions and the State. And they have seen even their own trade union bureaucracies obliged to give a lead to those struggles, and to demand an extensive package of social reforms as their price for income restraint.

The Labour Party in Opposition promised that it would deliver that package: on pensions, income redistribution, welfare services and employment. But there is nothing in the state of the economy that the Labour Party has inherited, and even less in the record of the men it has put into positions of Government leadership, to suggest that that package will in fact be implemented. And if it is not, then the whole

224

The exhaustion of a tradition

experience of the last five years - of sustained working class industrial militancy in opposition to State policies of encroachment on living standards, job security and industrial control - stands as a model for future working class response to a Labour Government that has returned to its true colours: those of a technocratic managerialism in the unbridled pursuit of economic growth.*

If that confrontation comes, the Labour Party will continue (in an accelerated fashion) its already well-established process of internal decay. There are many signs of the internal malaise of the political wing of the labour movement. The Labour Party vote in 1970 was 1.8 million down on the total of 1951, in an electorate that had

---

* It is here that the anti-trade union arguments offered by apologists for the 1964-70 Wilson Government are both fundamentally misleading, and also indicative of the managerial ethos that divides the Labour leadership in power from its class base. The case is made strongly by Beckerman *et al.*, in the work already cited, where trade union 'irresponsibility' is blamed for the failure of the Government's incomes policy. To quote Beckerman: 'Of course most trade union leaders are responsible people who realise fully how much harm the trade union movement is doing to its public image; and many of them may even recognise how much damage excessive increases in earnings may do to the longer term interests of the men they are supposed to represent ... Mr Jack Jones and Mr Hugh Scanlon are either incapable of understanding this, or are guilty of cynical betrayal of the interests of their members' (pp. 70 & 72).

Yet the argument is bizarre. The belief of these right-wing Labour economists that the Labour Party's 'pro equality' perspective was blocked only by trade union opposition is simply ludicrous. It is not clear that any of the Labour Government's proposed industrial relations reforms were prompted by, or were likely to create, greater equality between the classes. On the contrary, all the evidence is that the industrial relations reforms aimed to undercut working class power at the point of production, to ease the pressure on profits and to redistribute wealth upwards. It is equally clear that the Labour Government made no serious attempt to use its prices and incomes policy to favour the lower paid, even amongst those it directly employed; and indeed its period of office ended with massive strikes by low paid workers in the public sector against six years of income discrimination.

It is illuminating that, on this argument, the trade unions act 'responsibly' if they endorse prevailing patterns of inequality in the distribution of wealth, income, power and life-experience between the classes; and if they reduce questions of income inequality to those of its distribution between sections of the working class itself. Yet it was precisely because of the Labour Government's refusal and inability to markedly reduce wider class inequalities (and indeed because of the Government's pursuit of policies, particularly of productivity bargaining, that intensified non-monetary class inequalities) that trade union leaders were ultimately unable - try as most of them did - to 'sell' Labour Party policy to their own rank and file.

To 'blame' the trade union movement for the Labour Government's difficulties is then to operate within tightly blinkered parameters, in which the aspirations of the Party have already been reduced to those of servicing a

225

increased in size by almost five million;* and there are as yet few signs of any permanent and major reversal of that electoral trend. Indeed, in the February 1974 General Election, the Party could only take 37.5% of the poll, where once (in 1951) it had taken 48.8%; and there is some evidence that in 1970 at least, 'the swing against Labour was highest amongst unskilled workers and the poor'[3] - highest, that is, amongst the traditional bedrock of Labour support. Labour Party individual membership and levels of activity are also in long term decline. Between 1951 and 1970 individual membership of the Party probably fell by nearly 200,000;[4] and as far as can be seen the number of paid up and active members has only slightly increased during the recent period of Opposition. There is some evidence too that what membership remains is older and more middle class than Labour Party membership in the immediate post-war period.[5] And it is certainly the case that, in a predominantly young labour force, the bulk of workers now have known a Labour Government, if they have experienced one at all, as something against which workers strike, and with whose policies workers need feel no automatic sympathy.

3

Of course loyalties and habits die hard, and the Labour Party still has a strong hold on working class voting loyalties at least. It would be ludicrous to write the Labour Party off, and foolish to underestimate its potential for regeneration and for electoral survival, particularly in any second general election in 1974. All that can be said is that there is real evidence that the *total domination* of working class political loyalties by the Labour Party is beginning to break down; and that there is every reason to expect that that fragmentation of the Party's hold over its working class will go on apace. It is in this sense

---

high-growth capitalism. For it is true that wage pressure added to the competitive difficulties of British capitalism in the second half of the 1960s; and that the politics of men like Jack Jones appear to carry all the dilemmas of Left Labourism. But to maintain the pretence that Labour reformism is possible if only the trade unions behave is to fail to make clear that the trade unions are a blockage on the Labour Party only because of the failure of Labour reformism; and that the growing tension between the trade unions and the Labour Party in power is not the 'cause' of Labour's problem, but the central manifestation of the bankruptcy of Labourism as a political force of the working class.

* The Labour vote in 1951 was 13,948,605 in an electorate of 34,645,573. In 1970 the Labour vote was 12,178,295 in an electorate of 39,342,013.

that the recent and rapid growth of the still miniscule revolutionary socialist Left is significant, for its growth suggests that socialist alternatives to Labour are no longer doomed to extinction if they operate outside the Party. It also indicates the arena to which socialists must turn, and in which they must act, in the face of the irretrievable nature of the Labour Party's conservatism.

For the options facing socialists now are realistically wider than at any time since the 1930s. For so long as Labour domination of working class political loyalties was total, there was nowhere else for the socialist Left to go but the Party itself, and nothing for socialists to do except to work inside the Labour Party to stem the rightward tide. But as Labour hegemony begins to disintegrate, there is a real possibility of breaking the hold of Labourism on the political perspectives of the working class; and that requires activity outside the Labour Party by socialist groupings able to explain the limitations of Labour politics to workers who are themselves exposed to Labour Party irrelevance in Opposition and to its managerialism when in power. We need be under no illusions as to the difficulties, problems and even dangers that this forging of a socialist alternative will entail. But if the argument of the above chapters is correct, it is this strategy which must be pursued if there is to be any hope on the Left. For this current Labour Left, and later ones, will not be able to transcend the limitations of their own weak position, and no Labour Party leadership now or later will be able and willing to transcend the limitations operative on Parliamentary power under capitalism. So activity within the Labour Party is pointless.

Of course, hope springs eternal on the Left, as elsewhere, and this gloom may be misplaced. But it seems unlikely. For if the Labour Party is to become again a serious force for socialism, its leadership must be willing to abandon their Parliamentary preoccupations, and unite with other Left groupings in a common endeavour to mobilise the industrial power of the working class for socialist ends. But that requires them to break totally with the whole defining tradition of Labourism, and to endure the social dislocations and personal hardships of revolutionary socialist politics. It is inconceivable that the Labour Party leadership will do that; and it is ludicrous to ask or expect socialist militants to waste their time attempting to make them try.

This is a very sweeping decision to take, to make a clean break with the political organisation to which the majority of British workers have given their allegiance over seventy years, and it is as well to remember the degree of controversy that still surrounds this issue on the Left in

227

Britain today. The view expressed here is very much a minority one, and there are many socialists who argue that, like it or not, activity still has to go on inside the Labour Party. The argument of the Labour Left, that socialists should be in the Party, fighting to hold it to its socialist potential, has been restated recently by Eric Heffer. He argued in his book *The Class Struggle in Parliament* that the Labour Party is a working class party capable of achieving socialist change by Parliamentary action, such that 'those socialists who refuse to join the Labour Party and assist in this great effort are in practice being divisive and give great comfort to those who are the enemies of socialist advance'.[6] Ken Coates has equally argued, in a timely and impressive article,[7] that the Labour Party is still the only arena in which active socialists should be engaged. His argument differs from Heffer's, in being more hostile to the current Party leadership, in laying greater stress on the left-wing revival in the trade union movement, and in dismissing the revolutionary socialist Left as inevitably sectarian, miniscule, and barren. He explicitly rejects the premiss of this book, saying that 'it is no use at all to claim that the dispersion of illusions about the Labour Party will produce a climate in which new organisations may take root'.[8]

Both men are worth reading and considering carefully. But it seems to me that Eric Heffer's politics carry all the dilemmas of the Labour Left, and already in his few months as a junior minister, he is showing signs that this Labour Left will be no more successful than earlier ones. Ken Coates' argument is more telling; and in the end his pessimism on the revolutionary Left may be justified. It may be too late to start afresh a mass revolutionary socialist party in Britain, and the Labour Party may be all that we ever know. But that is a dismal prospect. Just because the odds are long against success, that is not necessarily sufficient reason for failing to make the attempt. Certainly there will never be a genuine socialist party with mass working class support unless active socialists are prepared to attempt its creation; and there are signs that suggest that as the Labour Party runs into ever greater difficulties, and gives daily testimony when in power to its own bankruptcy as a vehicle of working class interests and socialist change, that the possibility of creating a viable alternative to Labourism is emerging in this generation as it did not in earlier ones. Here indeed lies my basic disagreement with the kind of argument that Ken Coates makes so well. For it is clear that to work inside the Labour Party is, whether we like it or not, to lend support to those seeking to cement the hold of Labourism on the minds and political loyalties of working people and their families, when it is this very hold of Labourist illusions which must be shed if a genuinely socialist presence is to be established in Britain in the last quarter of this century. Indeed there is a major problem in Ken Coates' argument, in that he rejects strategies that involve leaving the Labour Party apparently because of the *difficulties* of creating alternative political parties. Yet if that task is difficult, the task of winning the Labour Party to socialism seems *impossible*. There is either no road to a socialist Britain left to this generation, or there is a new one, to be made against and in spite of the Labour Party and its politics.

For with hindsight it is clear that the Labour tradition as a vehicle for socialism contained at its outset the seeds of its own failure. At the heart of the recurrent emergence of conservatism in the history of the Labour Party stands the impossibility of the Parliamentary road to socialism. For as the international history of the working class, from the rise of Hitler to the bloody overthrow of Salvador Allende all too bitterly demonstrates, the power of the Parliamentary State is apparently not open to those who seek fundamental social transformation of a socialist kind. It would be pleasant, easier, convenient and gratifying to think that this were not so - that there was a peaceful and constitutional route to a socialist society of free and equal men; and it is easy to see why early Labour Party politicians thought that they had found it. For they had watched for so long Conservative and Liberal Governments in power, implementing policies by receiving the obedience of senior administrators and the loyal co-operation of powerfully placed groups in industry and finance. And if they could do it, why not Labour also? But these early Labour Party politicians failed to see that there is a fundamental incompatibility between the goal of socialism and the basis of power of the Parliamentary State. The power of the Parliamentary State depends precisely on this obedience of administrators and on this loyal co-operation of powerfully placed citizens. Yet socialism involves nothing less than a sustained assault on the powers and privileges of the very class of men who head the administration, and who control the private hierarchies of business and finance; and the one thing in which they will be neither loyal, obedient nor co-operative is their own social demise.

For the men who capture the Parliamentary State will not receive loyalty, obedience and co-operation from the private power-centres that surround them if the implementation of socialism is their goal. No ruling class in history has voluntarily surrendered its prerogatives and

The exhaustion of a tradition

power. Rather such a class has (and invariably will) deploy the full
range of its sanctions against any set of Parliamentarians bent on its
destruction: sanctions rooted in its class position under capitalism, and
stretching from administrative obstructionism through economic dislocation, financial movements, and ultimately to the use of force itself.
If the extremities of these sanctions have not been seen in Britain, this
is not because the ruling class here is more constitutionalist than sane.
It is because the Labour Party has never seriously challenged its fundamental powers and prerogatives.

The Parliamentary State would offer a road to socialism only if the
men entering government were able and were willing to turn to an
alternative power base for co-operation and support - only, that is, if
they were willing and able to 'walk on two legs' by using the industrial
power of the working class at the point of production as a counter-
weight to the obstructionism and resistance of the privileged classes
under challenge. But tragically, those who have subscribed to the
Parliamentary road to socialism have made it *the* article of their
political faith never to encourage, and always to oppose, the emergence
of such a potentially radicalised proletariat. They have understood the
Parliamentary road to socialism as precisely the *alternative* to this more
violent confrontation of class with class, and have accepted a definition
of constitutionality in politics which denied to the working class the
right to use their industrial power to support their political ends - a
right which industrial and financial capital exercise themselves daily in
their dealings with the Parliamentary State. In consequence, the Parliamentary road to socialism, in seeking to avoid a confrontation of
classes 'on the terrain of class' (in the factories and on the streets) has
invariably, and must always, be abandoned in the face of ruling class
opposition or maintained at the cost of socialism itself. Sadly, there is
no Parliamentary road to socialism where that road is seen as an
alternative to the mass mobilisation of the working class to break the
dominance of the industrial and financial bourgeoisie. This is the unavoidable lesson of the Labour Party's repeated retreats from its
socialist promise in the twentieth century.

Notes

Preface

1 J. H. Westergaard, 'The rediscovery of the cash nexus' in R. Miliband and
  J. Saville (editors), *The Socialist Register 1970* (London, Merlin Press,
  1970) pp. 111-38.
2 J. Griffiths, *Pages From Memory* (London, J. M. Dent and Sons Ltd., 1969)
  pp. 51-2.
3 E. P. Thompson, *The Making of the English Working Class* (London, Gollancz,
  1963).

1. The socialist promise

1 *Labour's Programme 1973*, pp. 7 and 30.

2. The early Labour Party

1 J. Saville, 'The ideology of Labourism', in R. Benewick *et al.*, *Knowledge and
  Belief in Politics* (London, Allen and Unwin, 1973) p. 215.
2 E. P. Thompson, 'The peculiarities of the English', in R. Miliband and J. Saville
  (editors), *The Socialist Register 1965* (London, Merlin Press, 1965) p. 343.
3 *Ibid.*, p. 343.
4 J. Cowley, 'Idealist tendencies in British Marxism', in *Studies on the Left*, vol.
  7(2) Spring 1967, p. 114.
5 Thompson, 'The peculiarities of the English', pp. 343-4.
6 *Ibid.*, p. 344.
7 M. Beer, *A History of British Socialism*, (London, Allen and Unwin, 1940)
  vol. 2, p. 327.
8 Quoted in C. F. Brand, *The British Labour Party* (London, Oxford University
  Press, 1965) p. 11.
9 H. Pelling, *The Origins of the Labour Party 1880-1900* (Oxford, Clarendon
  Press, 1965) p. 225.
10 Quoted in S. H. Beer, *Modern British Politics*, (London, Faber, 1965) p. 125.
11 R. Barker, *Education and Politics 1900-1951* (Oxford, Clarendon Press, 1972)
   p. 8.
12 Beer, *Modern British Politics*, p. 114.
13 R. Miliband, *Parliamentary Socialism* (London, Merlin Press, 1973) p. 30.
14 *The Labour Year Book 1919*, p. 18.
15 P. Snowden, *Socialism and Syndicalism* (London, Collins, 1913) pp. 167-9.
16 *Labour and the New Social Order*, p. 12.
17 Quoted in T. Nairn, 'The Nature of the Labour Party', in P. Anderson (editor),
   Towards Socialism (London, Fontana, 1965) p. 184.

18 Miliband, *Parliamentary Socialism*, p. 62.
19 Quoted in E. Eldon Barry, *Nationalisation in British Politics*, (London, Cape, 1965) p. 267.
20 Quoted in Miliband, *Parliamentary Socialism*, pp. 154-5.
21 *Labour and the Nation*, p. 6.
22 *National Reconstruction and Reform*, quoted in Eldon Barry, *Nationalisation in British Politics*, p. 267.
23 Quoted in A. Hutt, *The Post-War History of the British Working Class*, (London, Gollancz, 1937) p. 190 (my emphasis - D.C.).
24 *Labour and the Nation*, p. 20.
25 Quoted in Hutt, *The Post-War History of the British Working Class*, p. 152.
26 Quoted in A. Bullock, *The Life and Times of Ernest Bevin*, vol. 1 (London, Heinemann, 1960) p. 249.
27 Quoted in Barry, *Nationalisation in British Politics*, p. 279.
28 In their 1920 edition of *History of Trade Unionism*, as quoted by Hutt, *The Post-War History of the British Working Class*, p. 165.
29 *Ibid.*, p. 79.
30 Quoted in Miliband, *Parliamentary Socialism*, p. 38.
31 Quoted in Hutt, *The Post-War History of the British Working Class*, p. 84 (my emphasis - D.C.).
32 Quoted in Bullock, *The Life and Times of Ernest Bevin*, p. 241.
33 Quoted in Miliband, *Parliamentary Socialism*, p. 69.
34 *Ibid.*, p. 72.
35 Quoted in Hutt, *The Post-War History of the British Working Class*, pp. 85-6.
36 Quoted in R. T. McKenzie, *British Political Parties* (London, Mercury Books, 1963) p. 375.
37 Quoted in Bullock, *The Life and Times of Ernest Bevin*, p. 257.
38 Quoted in McKenzie, *British Political Parties*, pp. 370 & 372.
39 Quoted in Hutt, *The Post-War History of the British Working Class*, p. 77.
40 Harold Nicholson, quoted in H. R. G. Greaves 'Complacency or Challenge', *Political Quarterly*, vol. 32(1) January-March 1961, p. 65.
41 R. Skidelsky, *Politicians and the Slump* (Harmondsworth, Penguin, 1970) p. 173.
42 *Ibid.*, p. 171.
43 Quoted in R. Harrison, 'Labour Government: then and now', *Political Quarterly*, vol. 41(1) January-March 1970, p. 75.
44 Skidelsky, *Politicians and the Slump*, p. 87.
45 On this, see C. Cross, *Philip Snowden*, (London, Barrie and Rockliff, 1966) p. 202.
46 Bullock, *The Life and Times of Ernest Bevin*, p. 452.
47 A. Bevan, *In Place of Fear*, (London, Heinemann, 1952) pp. 27 and 28.
48 Hutt, *The Post-War History of the British Working Class*, p. 200.
49 Skidelsky, *Politicians and the Slump*, p. 25.
50 Harrison, 'Labour Government: then and now', p. 73.
51 R. Bassett, *Nineteen Thirty-One: Political Crisis* (London, Macmillan, 1958) p. 340.
52 Miliband, *Parliamentary Socialism*, p. 175.
53 Skidelsky, *Politicians and the Slump*, p. 425.
54 See, for example, Miliband, *Parliamentary Socialism*, p. 193.
55 Quoted in Hutt, *The Post-War History of the British Working Class*, p. 237.
56 Quoted in Miliband, *Parliamentary Socialism*, p. 193.
57 *Ibid.*, p. 201.
58 *Ibid.*

59 *Ibid.*
60 The N.E.C. resolution to the 1933 Labour Party conference, quoted in Hutt, *The Post-War History of the British Working Class*, p. 239.
61 K. L. Shell, 'Industrial democracy and the British Labour Movement', *Political Science Quarterly*, vol. 72(4) December 1957, p. 519.
62 Snowden, *Socialism and Syndicalism*, p. 241.
63 Quoted in R. A. Dahl, 'Workers' control of industry and the British Labour Party', *American Political Science Review*, vol. XLI, 1947, p. 888.
64 Quoted in Eldon Barry, *Nationalisation in British Politics*, p. 292.
65 Quoted in Dahl, 'Workers' control of industry and the British Labour Party', p. 889.
66 *Ibid.*
67 *Ibid.*, p. 887.
68 Eldon Barry, *Nationalisation in British Politics*, pp. 310-11.
69 *For Socialism and Peace*, pp. 5, 6-7, 11, & 26.
70 Summarised in Eldon Barry, *Nationalisation in British Politics*, pp. 35-6.
71 *For Socialism and Peace*, p. 29.
72 Quoted in Eldon Barry, *Nationalisation in British Politics*, p. 316.
73 *Ibid.*, p. 315.
74 *Ibid.*, p. 341.
75 *Ibid.*
76 C. R. Attlee, *The Labour Party in Perspective* (London, Gollancz, 1937) p. 16.

3. The Labour Governments of 1945-51

1 *Let Us Face The Future*, p. 6.
2 Miliband, *Parliamentary Socialism*, p. 274.
3 Quotations from *Let Us Face The Future*, *passim*.
4 H. Dalton, *High Tide and After* (London, Frederick Muller, 1962) p. 3.
5 R. Brady, *Crisis in Britain* (Cambridge University Press, 1950) p. 509.
6 Bevan, *In Place of Fear*, p. 10.
7 A. Rogow (& P. Shore) *The Labour Government and British Industry* (Oxford, Basil Blackwell, 1955) p. 13.
8 *Ibid.*, p. 151.
9 *Ibid.*, p. 16 (quoting Sir Stafford Cripps).
10 Quoted in Miliband, *Parliamentary Socialism*, p. 286.
11 *Ibid.*
12 Quoted in Brady, *Crisis in Britain*, pp. 58-9.
13 *Ibid.*, p. 564.
14 D. N. Pritt, *The Labour Government 1945-51* (London, Lawrence and Wishart, 1963) p. 41.
15 Quoted in Dahl, 'Workers' control of industry and the British Labour Party', p. 897.
16 Quoted in Rogow, *The Labour Government and British Industry*, p. 104.
17 Shell, 'Industrial democracy and the British Labour Movement', p. 519.
18 *Let Us Face The Future*, p. 6.
19 Quoted in Dahl, 'Workers' control of industry and the British Labour Party', p. 899.
20 J. W. Grove, *Government and Industry in Britain* (London, Longmans, 1962) p. 250.
21 Brady, *Crisis in Britain*, p. 246.
22 *Ibid.*, p. 659.

Notes to pages 53-70

23 Quoted in R. Miliband, *The State in Capitalist Society* (London, Weidenfeld and Nicolson, 1972) p. 108.
24 Quoted in Rogow, *The Labour Government and British Industry*, p. 156.
25 Quoted in Brady, *Crisis in Britain*, p. 119.
26 Rogow, *The Labour Government and British Industry*, p. 73.
27 *Ibid.*, p. 170.
28 Trade union leaders and academics, quoted in Shell, 'Industrial democracy and the British Labour Movement', p. 521.
29 *Ibid.*
30 Rogow, *The Labour Government and British Industry*, pp. 25-6.
31 The *Economist*, quoted in S. Brittan, *Steering the Economy* (London, Secker and Warburg, 1969) p. 108.
32 Rogow, *The Labour Government and British Industry*, p. 42.
33 *Ibid.*, p. 121.
34 *Ibid.*, p. 122.
35 *Challenge to Britain* (London, The Labour Party, 1953) p. 6.
36 Quoted in Rogow, *The Labour Government and British Industry*, p. 52.
37 *Ibid.*, pp. 61-4.
38 *Ibid.*, p. 44 (my emphasis - D.C.).
39 *Ibid.*, pp. 24-5.
40 Quoted in Beer, *Modern British Politics*, p. 192.
41 J. A. Schumpeter, *Capitalism, Socialism and Democracy* (New York, Harper, 1950) p. 410.
42 T. Balogh, 'The drift towards planning', in Anderson (editor), *Towards Socialism*, p. 54.
43 Quoted in Pritt, *The Labour Government 1945-51*, pp. 184-5.
44 D. Marquand, 'Sir Stafford Cripps: the dollar crisis and devaluation', in M. Sissons and P. French (editors), *Age of Austerity 1945-51* (Harmondsworth, Penguin, 1964) pp. 190 & 191.
45 Rogow, *The Labour Government and British Industry*, p. 39 .
46 Quoted in A. Howard, 'We are the masters now', in Sissons and French (editors), *Age of Austerity 1945-51*, p. 25.
47 Brady, *Crisis in Britain*, p. 565.
48 *Ibid.*, pp. 19-20.
49 *Ibid.*, p. 564.
50 *Ibid.*, pp. 562-3 (my emphasis - D.C.).
51 Quoted in Beer, *Modern British Politics*, p. 193, n. 1.
52 Quoted in F. Bealey (editor) *The Social and Political Thought of the British Labour Party* (London, Weidenfeld and Nicolson, 1970) pp. 173-4.
53 See Brady, *Crisis in Britain*, p. 6.
54 A. Glyn and B. Sutcliffe, *British Capitalism, Workers and the Profit Squeeze* (Harmondsworth, Penguin, 1972) p. 35.
55 Quoted in P. Jenkins, 'Bevan's fight with the B.M.A.', in Sissons and French (editors), *Age of Austerity 1945-51*, p. 262.
56 Quoted in Pritt, *The Labour Government 1945-51*, p. 186.
57 Rogow, *The Labour Government and British Industry*, p. 164.
58 Dalton, *High Tide and After*, p. 138.
59 See G. Hodgson, 'The Steel Debates', in Sissons and French (editors), *Age of Austerity 1945-51*, p. 313.
60 Dalton, *High Tide and After*, p. 136.
61 Hodgson, 'The Steel Debates', in Sissons and French (editors), *Age of Austerity 1945-51*, p. 315.
62 Quoted in Brady, *Crisis in Britain*, p. 189.

63 Miliband, *Parliamentary Socialism*, p. 311.
64 *Labour and the New Society*, p. 18.
65 L. Epstein, 'Socialism and the British Labour Party', *Political Science Quarterly*, December 1951, pp. 559-60.
66 Miliband, *Parliamentary Socialism*, p. 310.
67 See V. L. Allen, *Trade Unions and the Government* (London, Longmans, 1960) pp. 273-4.
68 R. H. S. Crossman, 'Towards a philosophy of socialism', in R. H. S. Crossman (editor), *New Fabian Essays* (London, Turnstile Press, 1952) pp. 26-7.

4. The Labour Party in Opposition 1951-64

1 S. Haseler, *The Gaitskellites* (London, Macmillan, 1969) p. 55.
2 *Britain Belongs To You*, p. 3.
3 Quoted in V. Bogdanor, 'The Labour Party in Opposition', in V. Bogdanor and R. Skidelsky (editors), *The Age of Affluence* (London, Macmillan, 1970) p. 84.
4 *Ibid.*, p. 80.
5 On the roots of revisionist theory, and the specific writings associated with revisionism, see Haseler, *The Gaitskellites*, pp. 61-111.
6 See in particular A. Crosland, *The Conservative Enemy* (London, Cape, 1962) pp. 84-90.
7 A. Crosland, *The Future of Socialism* (London, Cape, 1956) p. 504.
8 *Ibid.*, p. 505.
9 Haseler, *The Gaitskellites*, p. 59.
10 *Ibid.*, p. 90.
11 J. Kincaid, 'The decline of the welfare state', in N. Harris and J. Palmer (editors), *World Crisis* (London, Hutchinson, 1971) pp. 36-7.
12 J. Jupp, 'Socialist rethinking in Britain and Australia', *Australian Journal of Politics and History*, vol. 4(2) November 1958, p. 203.
13 *Labour Party Annual Conference Report 1960*, p. 201.
14 The point is well established in L. Minkin's unpublished Ph.D. thesis, *The Labour Party Conference and Intra-Party Democracy, 1956-1970* (University of York, 1975).
15 *Labour Believes in Britain*, p. 12.
16 *Industry and Society*, pp. 48-9.
17 *Ibid.*, p. 46.
18 Quoted in Bogdanor, 'The Labour Party in Opposition', p. 89.
19 *Industry and Society*, p. 27.
20 Hugh Gaitskell, *Socialism and Nationalisation* (Fabian Pamphlet, 1956) p. 42.
21 *Industry and Society*, p. 57.
22 *Labour Party Annual Conference Report 1957*, p. 140.
23 *Plan for Progress*, pp. 5, 7, 10, 12, 15, 18 & 21.
24 *Labour's Aims* (N.E.C. Statement 1960) p. 4.
25 P. Sedgwick, 'The End of Labourism', *New Politics* vol. 8(3) 1970, p. 80.
26 *Signposts for the Sixties*, p. 10.
27 *Ibid.*, p. 35.

5. The Labour Governments of 1964-70

1 Haseler, *The Gaitskellites*, p. 246.

2 *The New Britain*, p. 6.

3 *Ibid.*, p. 8.

4 Harold Wilson, quoted in Foot, 'Parliamentary Socialism', in Harris and Palmer (editors), *World Crisis*, p. 86.

5 *Labour Party Annual Conference Report 1963*, extracts from pp. 134-40.

6 Quoted in P. Foot, *The Politics of Harold Wilson* (Harmondsworth, Penguin, 1968) p. 148.

7 H. Wilson, *The New Britain* (Harmondsworth, Penguin, 1964) p. 23.

8 Quoted in Foot, *The Politics of Harold Wilson*, p. 135.

9 *Ibid.*, p. 139.

10 *The New Britain*, p. 8.

11 *Ibid.*, p. 5.

12 *Labour Party Annual Conference Report 1963*, p. 199.

13 *The New Britain*, p. 3.

14 R. Pryke, 'The predictable crisis', *New Left Review*, 39 September-October 1966, p. 3.

15 Bogdanor, 'The Labour Party in Opposition', p. 112.

16 *Labour Party Annual Conference Report 1957*, p. 129.

17 Both men are quoted in W. Beckerman (editor), *The Labour Government's Economic Record 1964-1970* (London, Duckworth, 1972) p. 59.

18 Brittan, *Steering the Economy*, p. 253.

19 Marcia Williams, *Inside Number 10* (London, Weidenfeld and Nicolson, 1972, p. 360).

20 Brittan, *Steering the Economy*, p. 218.

21 See for example Beckerman, *The Labour Government's Economic Record 1964-1970*, p. 61.

22 H. Wilson, *The Labour Government: a Personal Record* (London, Weidenfeld and Nicolson and Michael Joseph, 1971) pp. 34-5 & 37.

23 For the events of February 1965, see H. Brandon, *In The Red* (London, Andre Deutsch, 1966) p. 79.

24 Brittan, *Steering the Economy*, p. 194.

25 Brandon, *In The Red*, pp. 100 & 106-7.

26 *House of Commons Debates*, vol. 755, 30.11.1967, col. 651 (my emphasis - D.C.).

27 B. Lapping, *The Labour Government 1964-1970* (Harmondsworth, Penguin, 1970) p. 50.

28 Quoted in Harrison, 'Labour Government: then and now', p. 75.

29 See Brandon, *In The Red*, p. 91.

30 Quoted in K. Coates, *The Crisis of British Socialism* (Nottingham, Spokesman Books, 1971) p. 45.

31 Wilson, *The Labour Government: a Personal Record*, pp. 587, 691 & 588.

32 See M. Barratt Brown, *From Labourism to Socialism* (Nottingham, Spokesman Books, 1972) p. 115.

33 P. Shore, *Entitled to Know* (London, MacGibbon and Kee, 1966) p. 121.

34 As Shore himself stressed (*ibid.*, p. 118).

35 This growth of shop-floor power throughout the engineering industry is documented in S. W. Lerner and J. Marquand 'Workshop bargaining, wage drift and productivity in the British engineering industry', *Manchester School*, vol. 30, pp. 15-54; and in chapter 3 of the *Report of the Royal Commission on Trade Unions and Employers' Associations 1965-1968* (Cmnd 3623).

36 The figures on this are in Glyn and Sutcliffe, *British Capitalism, Workers and the Profit Squeeze*, p. 66. It should be noted in passing that their interpretation and calculation of the declining rate of profit has been challenged in many quarters; but significantly for our purposes what has been in dispute is

the precise severity and permanence of the profit fall. There appears to be
widespread agreement amongst economists that profits did fall, and fall
markedly, towards the end of the 1960s. For critical reviews of the Glyn and
Sutcliffe thesis from totally opposed viewpoints, see W. Beckerman's article in
The New Statesman of 8 December 1972, and D. Yaffe, 'The Crisis of
Profitability: a critique of the Glyn-Sutcliffe thesis' *New Left Review*, 80,
July-August 1973, pp. 45-63.

37 For examples of this, see Glyn and Sutcliffe, pp. 19-20, 41, 47 and 171.
38 J. A. Kincaid, *Poverty and Equality in England* (Harmondsworth, Penguin,
  1973) p. 74.
39 *Ibid.*, p. 104.
40 *The National Plan*, (London, H.M.S.O., 1965) p. 204.
41 P. Townsend (editor), *Labour and Inequality* (London, Fabian Society, 1972)
  p. 298.
42 A. Graham, 'Industrial Policy', in Beckerman, *The Labour Government's
  Economic Record 1964-1970*, p. 184.
43 Wilson, *The Labour Government: a Personal Record*, p. 202.
44 For details of I.R.C. activity, see E. Dell, *Political Responsibility and Industry*
  (London, Allen and Unwin, 1973) pp. 74-84; F. Broadway, *State Intervention
  in British Industry 1964-1968* (London, Kaye and Ward, 1969) p. 129; and
  G. Bannock, *The Juggernauts* (Harmondsworth, Penguin, 1973) pp. 143-4.
45 Brittan, *Steering the Economy*, p. 206.
46 Wilson, *The Labour Government: a Personal Record*, p. 561.
47 Particularly with reference to the rights of stewards. For the treatment of a
  Halewood shop steward by the Ford management in 1971, see J. Mathews,
  Ford Strike (London, Panther, 1972), or R. Hyman, *Strikes* (London, Fontana,
  1972) pp. 11-16.
48 T. Cliff, *The Employers' Offensive* (London, Pluto Press, 1970) p. 19.
49 A. Fels, *The British Prices and Incomes Board* (Cambridge University Press,
  1972) p. 31.
50 *Ibid.*, pp. 13-14.
51 *Prices and Incomes Policy after June 1967* (Cmnd 3235) para. 20.
52 R. Collins, 'Trends in Productivity Bargaining', *Trade Union Register 1970*,
  (London, Merlin Press, 1970) p. 87.
53 Fels, *The British Prices and Incomes Board*, p. 135.
54 H. Clegg, 'The substance of productivity agreements', in A. Flanders (editor),
  Collective Bargaining (Harmondsworth, Penguin, 1969) p. 353.
55 Collins, 'Trends in Productivity Bargaining', p. 88.
56 T. Topham, 'Productivity Bargaining', *Trade Union Register 1969* (London,
  Merlin Press, 1969) pp. 75-6.
57 *N.B.P.I. Report 123* (Cmnd 4136) paras. 11-13.
58 Topham, 'Productivity Bargaining', p. 84.
59 Glyn and Sutcliffe, *British Capitalism, Workers and the Profit Squeeze*, p. 108.
60 Fels, *The British Prices and Incomes Board*, pp. 138-9.
61 See K. Hawkins, *Conflict and Change: Aspects of Industrial Relations*
  (London, Holt, Rinehart and Winston, 1972) pp. 180-2; and T. Topham, 'New
  types of Bargaining', in R. Blackburn and A. Cockburn (editors), *The
  Incompatibles* (Harmondsworth, Penguin, 1967) p. 152.
62 Quoted in Fels, *The British Prices and Incomes Board*, p. 30.
63 See P. Jenkins, *The Battle of Downing Street* (London, Charles Knight, 1970).
64 This was particularly so with the seamen's strike in 1966. For this, see Foot,
  'The seamen's struggle', in Blackburn and Cockburn (editors), *The
  Incompatibles*, pp. 169-209.

65 Broadway, *State Intervention in British Industry 1964-1968*, pp. 79-80.
66 Raymond Williams (editor), *May Day Manifesto 1968* (Harmondsworth, Penguin, 1968) p. 156.

6. The failure of the socialist promise

1 The leading revisionist intellectuals of the 1950s have now qualified their initial optimism in the light of their later experience of high government office. See in particular A. Crosland, *Socialism Now* (London, Cape, 1973) and R. Jenkins, *What Matters Now* (London, Fontana, 1972).
2 The argument had wide currency in the early 1960s in particular. It can be found in D. Butler and R. Rose, *The British General Election of 1959* (London, Macmillan, 1960) pp. 15-16; in M. Abrams and R. Rose, *Must Labour Lose?* (Harmondsworth, Penguin, 1960); and J. Vaizey, 'Socialism in the New Europe', *Socialist Commentary*, December 1959.
3 'Although the appeal to de-radicalise or "modernise" socialist parties drew upon a number of assumptions regarding the social and political outlook of affluent workers, the validity of these assumptions has been shown to be highly questionable . . . Studies of voting behaviour have established fairly conclusively that working class support for parties of the Left does not decline as income rises; many of the most affluent workers - for example, those employed in automobile plants - show higher than average support for the Left.' (F. Parkin, *Class Inequality and Political Order*, London, Paladin, 1971, p. 129).
4 *Ibid.*, pp. 129-30.
5 For example, see Harold Wilson's attack on communist agitators in the 1966 seamen's strike.
6 This is a central thesis of Beckerman's chapter in his *The Labour Government's Economic Record 1964-1970*, pp. 70-4.
7 For example, see Williams, *Inside Number 10*, pp. 344-59.
8 As the 'gnomes of Zurich' they became notorious after the 1964 election.
9 The clearest example of this is M. Foot's argument in 'Credo of the Left', *New Left Review*, 49 May-June 1968, pp. 19-34. Asked then whether Parliament could be used for socialist purposes he said that it could, and that it had not been hitherto because 'the determination of the leaders and the Labour Party itself to take over other institutions and bring them under the control of the elected parliament . . . is lacking' (p. 28).
10 R. McKenzie, *British Political Parties* (London, Mercury Books, 1963) p. 644.
11 B. Hindess, *The Decline of Working Class Politics* (London, MacGibbon and Kee, 1971) p. 170.
12 Miliband, *Parliamentary Socialism, passim*.
13 Though the argument is carried much further in Miliband's later book, *The State in Capitalist Society*, pp. 96-118; and this chapter draws heavily on the arguments to be found there.
14 For a general survey of the emerging labour movements in Europe and the United States after 1870, See G. Lichtheim, *A Short History of Socialism* (London, Weidenfeld and Nicolson, 1970), J. Braunthal, *History of the International 1864-1914* (London, Nelson, 1967), or W. Abendroth, *A Short History of the European Working Class* (London, New Left Books, 1972).
15 Miliband, *Parliamentary Socialism*, p. 18.
16 Quoted in B. Barker (editor), *Ramsay MacDonald's Political Writings* (London, Allen Lane, 1972) pp. 80-1 and 83.

17 *Ibid.*, pp. 93 and 47-8.
18 Quoted in Hutt, *The Post-War History of the British Working Class*, p. 118.
19 Quoted in Nairn, 'The Nature of the Labour Party', in Anderson (editor), *Towards Socialism*, p. 195.
20 Quoted in C. Cross, *Philip Snowden* (London, Barrie and Rockliff, 1966) pp. 177-8.
21 Quoted in Barker, *Ramsay MacDonald's Political Writings*, p. 47.
22 *Ibid.*, p. 45.
23 *Ibid.*, pp. 153 and 225.
24 Quoted in Hutt, *The Post-War History of the British Working Class*, p. 71.
25 Quoted in Barker, *Ramsay MacDonald's Political Writings*, p. 44.
26 Quoted in Foot, *The Politics of Harold Wilson*, p. 331.
27 Miliband, *Parliamentary Socialism*, p. 13.
28 Quoted in Barker, *Ramsay MacDonald's Political Writings*, p. 232.
29 P. Snowden, *Labour and the New World* (London, Cassell, 1921) pp. 58-60.
30 For the debate between the Labour Party and these groups on the use of extra-Parliamentary tactics, see Brand, *The British Labour Party: a Short History*, pp. 85-8; and Miliband, *Parliamentary Socialism*, pp. 59-82.
31 Quoted in B. Donoughue and G. W. Jones, *Herbert Morrison: Portrait of a Politician* (London, Weidenfeld and Nicolson, 1973) p. 103.
32 Quoted in V. L. Allen, *Militant Trade Unionism* (London, Merlin Press, 1966) p. 33.
33 Quoted in J. Saville, 'Labourism and the Labour Government', in R. Miliband and J. Saville (editors), *Socialist Register 1967* (London, Merlin Press, 1967) pp. 55-6.
34 Quoted in Miliband, *Parliamentary Socialism*, p. 19.
35 Saville, 'Labourism and the Labour Government', pp. 57-8.
36 There already exists a considerable literature on this question of the power of the democratic state in a modern industrial society, and the argument offered here on the Labour Party reflects a particular position within that wider debate. The literature of the 1950s that dominated the academic discussion of state power was predominantly American in origin, and reflected an optimism (which the Gaitskellite leadership of the Labour Party shared) that the democratic state enjoyed a high degree of autonomy and an immense freedom of manoeuvre, such that in the hands of a democratically elected socialist elite the state could be used for programmes of extensive social reform and economic regeneration. This literature asserted that the state faced a pluralistic power structure in which the major institutional centres of power were in some kind of rough balance; and as a result creative political leadership by electorally sensitive politicians was all that was required to enable the state to fulfill its unique role of embodying, initiating and implementing the interests of the community as a whole. This is the thrust of R. Dahl's argument in his *Who Governs?* (New Haven, Yale University Press, 1961) and S. M. Lipset's in his collection of essays, *Political Man* (London, Mercury Books, 1963). In academic terms, this pluralist orthodoxy was challenged initially only by a relatively unsophisticated elitism, which asserted that behind the facade of Parliamentary democracy power lay in the hands of well-organised conspiratorial elites, and that this power elite (the term is C. Wright Mills' in his *The Power Elite*, London, Oxford University Press, 1956) of which the executive arm of the state was a crucial part, was free to initiate whatever set of policies it so chose.
But the experience of the 1960s (from Vietnam and the American race riots to balance of payments crises, inflation and unemployment) has re-

emphasised the *constraints* within which the state operates, and has provided yet more evidence that the limits on the freedom of action of even the democratically elected state are both tight and firmly rooted in the imperatives of international capitalism as a system. It is at least arguable that state power has to operate within limits established by the economic and social needs of the class of men who head the major financial and industrial corporations which themselves own the means of production, distribution and exchange in the Western economies. For it seems that the earlier pluralist view that capitalism has been replaced by a new system of economic relationships which are more open to democratic state control is wrong. States still face a capitalist system of enormous instability, which is anarchic in the way that Marx described in *The Communist Manifesto* and in *Capital*. For it is at least possible that the pluralist writers of the 1950s misread as a permanent feature of life a degree of state autonomy that was but a reflection of the degree of stability enjoyed by Western capitalism in that period. Certainly as capitalist instability intensified in the 1960s, the freedom of the state to respond to democratic pressures fell away, and politicians seeking major programmes of social reform found themselves constrained by weak capitalist economies. It is with this in mind that the reader might compare the writings of Dahl and Lipset with R. Miliband's *The State in Capitalist Society*, with N. Poulantzas, *Political Power and Social Classes* (London, New Left Books and Sheed and Ward, 1973), and with the debate between Miliband and Poulantzas that is reprinted in R. Blackburn (editor), *Ideology in Social Science* (London, Fontana, 1972) pp. 238-64.

37 Quoted in Foot, *The Politics of Harold Wilson*, p. 337.
38 Quoted in Miliband, *Parliamentary Socialism*, pp. 197-8.
39 Laski wrote in his *The Crisis and the Constitution* in 1932 that 'the road to power is far harder than Labour has so far been led to imagine'; and writing at much the same time Tawney wrote of the Party's gradualism, 'onions can be eaten leaf by leaf, but you cannot skin a live tiger claw by claw. Vivisection is its trade and it does the skinning first.'
40 See his *The Labour Party in Perspective*, pp. 115-23.
41 Crosland *The Future of Socialism*, p. 29.
42 Quoted in Bealey, *The Social and Political Thought of the British Labour Party*, p. 182.
43 Saville, 'Labourism and the Labour Government', p. 57.
44 Quoted in R. Looker (editor), *Rosa Luxemburg: selected political writings* (London, Cape, 1972) p. 107.
45 Miliband, *Parliamentary Socialism*, pp. 293-4.
46 B. Castle, 'Mandarin Power', *The Sunday Times*, 10 June 1973, pp. 17 and 19.
47 *Ibid.*, p. 19.
48 Miliband, *The State in Capitalist Society*, p. 123.
49 This interpenetration of the state bureaucracy and private industry goes on at many levels and in many formal and informal ways. It is perhaps clearest in the large number of directors of nationalised industries who hold or have held directorships in private firms. (On this, see C. Jenkins, 'Retreat: the Labour Party and the Public Corporations', in *The Insiders*, Universities and Left Review pamphlet, 1958). It is perhaps most potent in the daily working contacts between senior civil servants at the economic ministries and senior managerial personnel in private industry and finance. (On this, see J. W. Grove, *Government and Industry in Britain*, London, Longmans, 1962, pp. 141-61).
50 Castle, 'Mandarin Power', p. 19.
51 R. Crossman, *Inside View* (London, Cape, 1972) pp. 72-3.

52 Quoted in Williams (editor), *May Day Manifesto 1968*, p. 119.
53 Miliband, *The State in Capitalist Society*, p. 121.
54 Quoted in Sissons and French (editors), *Age of Austerity 1945-1951*, p. 258.
55 R. Miliband and J. Saville, 'Labour Policy and the Labour Left', in their jointly edited *The Socialist Register 1964* (New York, Monthly Review Press, 1964) pp. 152-3.
56 Barratt Brown, *From Labourism to Socialism*, pp. 59-60.
57 Rogow, *The Labour Government and British Industry*, p. 179.
58 *Ibid.*, p. 176.
59 Williams, *May Day Manifesto 1968*, p. 124.
60 Miliband, *The State in Capitalist Society*, p. 155.
61 Williams, *May Day Manifesto 1968*, p. 120.
62 Nairn, 'The Nature of the Labour Party', p. 196.
63 Anderson, 'Problems of Socialist Strategy', in his *Towards Socialism*, p. 237.
64 The call for the 'gamble' to be attempted is very persuasively argued in J. Goldthorpe *et al.*, *The Affluent Worker in the Class Structure* (Cambridge University Press, 1969) pp. 192-5.
65 Nairn, 'The Nature of the Labour Party', p. 179.
66 Skidelsky, *Politicians and the Slump*, p. 112.
67 E. Dell, *Political Responsibility and Industry*, (London, Allen and Unwin, 1973) p. 137.
68 M. Foot, *Aneurin Bevan, Volume 1 1897-1945* (London, Four Square Illustrated, 1966) pp. 130-1.
69 Bevan, *In Place of Fear*, pp. 6-7.
70 F. Brockway, *Inside the Left* (London, Allen and Unwin, 1942) pp. 201 & 222-3.
71 Foot, *Aneurin Bevan, Volume 1 1897-1945*, pp. 227-8.
72 Anderson, 'Problems of Socialist Strategy', p. 236.
73 Above, p. 31.
74 Wilson, *The Labour Government: a Personal Record*, pp. 128-9.
75 R. Prentice, 'Lessons of the Labour Government: not socialist enough', *Political Quarterly*, vol. 41(2) April-June 1970, p. 149.
76 Saville, 'Labourism and the Labour Government', pp. 56-7.

7. The weakness of the Labour Left

1 R. Dowse, *Left in the Centre* (London, Longmans, 1966) p. 115.
2 Miliband, *Parliamentary Socialism*, p. 152.
3 Quoted in J. Jupp, *The Left in Britain 1931-41* (M.Sc. thesis, University of London, 1956) pp. 169, 171 & 172.
4 *Ibid.*, p. 175.
5 Foot, *Aneurin Bevan, Volume 1 1897-1945*, p. 229.
6 On this, see Peggy Duff, *Left, Left, Left*, (London, Allison and Busby, 1971) p. 47.
7 R. Williams, 'The British Left' *New Left Review*, 30 March-April 1965, p. 21.
8 Beer, *Modern British Politics*, pp. 220-1.
9 See Duff, *Left, Left, Left*, pp. 113-257.
10 *Tribune*, 8 April 1966.
11 The phrase is H. G. Wells', and was taken by men like I.L.P. leader Clifford Allen to mean that 'one should not refrain from action just because one is in a minority, and that by acting openly along bold constructive scientific lines one would quickly gain the support of the majority'. A. Marwick, *Clifford Allen:*

the *Open Conspirator* (London, Oliver and Boyd, 1964) p. 96.
12 Foot, 'Credo of the Left', p. 22.
13 Williams, *May Day Manifesto 1968*, p. 173.
14 *Ibid.*, pp. 172-4.
15 Foot, 'Credo of the Left', p. 27.
16 For a defence of the Labour Left M.P.s after 1966, see E. Heffer, *The Class Struggle in Parliament* (London, Gollancz, 1973) pp. 268-9 & *passim*.
17 *Labour's Programme 1973*, p. 14.
18 *Ibid.*, pp. 10-11.
19 *The Times*, 3 October 1973, p. 5.
20 *Labour's Programme 1973*, pp. 27 & 28.
21 *The Guardian*, 24 November 1973, p. 1.
22 Miliband, 'The Labour Government and Beyond', in Miliband and Saville (editors), *The Socialist Register 1966*, p. 23.
23 *Labour's Programme 1973*, p. 7.
24 In his budget speech, quoted in *The Guardian*, 27 March 1974, p. 9.
25 Dennis Healey, quoted in *The Times*, 15 May 1974, p. 1.
26 See for example *The Observer*, 7 July 1974, p. 1.
27 The O.E.C.D. estimated a deficit on Britain's balance of overseas payments of £4,500 million in 1974, which is the largest deficit estimated for any industrial country in that year. (See *The Observer*, 23 June 1974, p. 1.)

8. The exhaustion of a tradition

1 *Labour's Programme 1973*, p. 7.
2 On the 'embourgeoisification' of the Parliamentary Labour Party over time, see W. L. Guttsman, *The British Political Elite* (London, MacGibbon and Kee, 1968) pp. 225-77, Z. Bauman, *Between Class and Elite* (Manchester University Press, 1972) pp. 193-229 & 302-22; and W. L. Guttsman, 'The British political elite and the class structure', in P. Stanworth and A. Giddens, *Elites and Power in British Society* (Cambridge University Press, 1974) p. 33.
3 Crosland, *Socialism Now*, p. 101.
4 See M. Stewart, *Protest or Power* (London, Allen and Unwin, 1974) p. 129.
5 See Hindess, *The Decline of Working Class Politics, passim.*
6 Heffer, *The Class Struggle in Parliament*, p. 266. The whole argument is presented on pp. 264-79 of Heffer's book.
7 K. Coates, 'Socialists and the Labour Party', in R. Miliband and J. Saville (editors), *The Socialist Register 1973* (London, Merlin Press, 1974) pp. 155-78.
8 *Ibid.*, p. 155.

Bibliography

A study of this kind is heavily dependent on secondary material drawn from many branches of political history, political science, economics, sociology and industrial relations. It also rests on material published by Government departments and by the Labour Party. The bibliography that follows is intended to indicate the main secondary material used, in order to provide a starting point for those wishing to read more widely in the field of British Labour politics.

Abrams, M. and Rose, R. *Must Labour Lose?* (Harmondsworth, Penguin, 1960)
Alderman, A. K. 'Discipline in the Parliamentary Labour Party 1945-51', *Parliamentary Affairs*, vol. XVIII (3) Summer 1965, pp. 293-305
'The Conscience Clause of the Parliamentary Labour Party', *Parliamentary Affairs*, vol. XIX (2) Spring 1966, pp. 224-32
'Parliamentary Party discipline in Opposition: The P.L.P. 1951-64' *Parliamentary Affairs*, vol. XXI (2) Spring 1968, pp. 124-32
Allen, V. L. *Trade Unions and the Government* (London, Longmans, 1960)
Militant Trade Unionism (London, Merlin Press, 1966)
Anderson, P. 'The Left in the 1950s', *New Left Review*, 29 January-February 1965, pp. 3-18
'Problems of socialist strategy', in P. Anderson (editor), *Towards Socialism* (London, Fontana, 1965) pp. 221-90
Attlee, C. R. *The Labour Party in Perspective* (London, Gollancz, 1937)
As It Happened (London, Heinemann, 1954)
Balogh, T. 'The drift towards planning', in P. Anderson (editor), *Towards Socialism* (London, Fontana, 1965) pp. 53-76
Barker, B. (editor). *Ramsay MacDonald's Political Writings* (London, Allen Lane, 1972)
Barker, C. 'The British Labour Movement: aspects of current experience', *International Socialism*, 61, pp. 40-8
Barker, R. *Education and Politics 1900-1951: a Study of the Labour Party* (Oxford, Clarendon Press, 1972)

Bibliography

Barratt Brown, M. *From Labourism to Socialism* (Nottingham, Spokesman Books, 1972)

Bassett, R. *Nineteen Thirty-One: Political Crisis* (London, Macmillan, 1958)

Bauman, Z. *Between Class and Elite: the Evolution of the British Labour Movement* (Manchester, University Press, 1972)

Bealey, F. (editor). *The Social and Political Thought of the British Labour Party* (London, Weidenfeld and Nicolson, 1970)

Beckerman, W. (editor). *The Labour Government's Economic Record 1964-1970* (London, Duckworth, 1972)

Beer, M. *A History of British Socialism* (London, Allen and Unwin, 1940)

Beer, S. *Modern British Politics* (London, Faber, 1965)

Berry, D. R. *The Sociology of Grass Roots Politics: a Study of Party Membership* (London, Macmillan, 1970)

Bevan, A. *In Place of Fear* (London, Heinemann, 1952)

Bogdanor, V. 'The Labour Party in Opposition', in V. Bogdanor and R. Skidelsky (editors), *The Age of Affluence* (London, Macmillan, 1970)

Brady, R. *Crisis in Britain* (Cambridge University Press, 1950)

Brand, C. F. *The British Labour Party: a Short History* (London, Oxford University Press, 1965)

Brandon, H. *In The Red* (London, André Deutsch, 1966)

Brittan, S. *Steering the Economy* (London, Secker and Warburg, 1969)

Broadway, F. *State Intervention in British Industry 1964-68* (London, Kaye and Ward, 1969)

Brockway, F. *Inside the Left* (London, Allen and Unwin, 1940)
Socialism over Sixty Years (London, Allen and Unwin, 1946)

Brown, G. *In My Way* (Harmondsworth, Penguin, 1972)

Bullock, A. *The Life and Times of Ernest Bevin, Volume 1: Trade Union Leader 1881-1940* (London, Heinemann, 1960); *Volume 2: Minister of Labour 1940-1945* (London, Heinemann, 1967)

Burgess, T. *et al. Matters of Principle: Labour's Last Chance* (Harmondsworth, Penguin, 1968)

Castle, B. 'Mandarin Power', *The Sunday Times*, 10 June 1973

Caves, R. *et al. Britain's Economic Prospects* (London, Allen and Unwin, 1968)

Challinor, R. 'Incomes Policy and the Left', *International Socialism*, 27, pp. 26-30

Bibliography

'Labour and the Parliamentary Road', *International Socialism*, 52, pp. 9-15

Clegg, H. *et al. A History of British Trade Unionism: Volume 1, 1889-1910* (Oxford University Press, 1964)

Clegg, H. 'The substance of productivity agreements' in A. Flanders (editor), *Collective Bargaining* (Harmondsworth, Penguin, 1969) pp. 352-68

The System of Industrial Relations in Great Britain (Oxford, Basil Blackwell, 1970)

Cliff, T. *The Employers' Offensive* (London, Pluto Press, 1970)

Coates K. and Silburn, R. *Poverty: the forgotten Englishmen* (Harmondsworth, Penguin, 1970)

Coates, K. *The Crisis of British Socialism* (Nottingham, Spokesman Books, 1971)

'Socialists and the Labour Party', in R. Miliband and J. Saville (editors), *The Socialist Register 1973* (London, Merlin Press, 1974) pp. 155-78

Coates, K. and Topham, T. *The New Unionism: the Case for Workers' Control* (London, Peter Owen, 1972)

Cohen, C. D. *British Economic Policy 1960-1969* (London, Butterworths, 1971)

Cole, M. *The Story of Fabian Socialism* (London, Mercury Books, 1961)

Collins, R. 'Trends in productivity bargaining', in *Trade Union Register 1970* (London, Merlin Press, 1970) pp. 86-108

Cowley, J. 'Idealist tendencies in British Marxism', *Studies on the Left*, vol. 7(2) Spring 1967, pp. 109-18

Crick, B. 'Socialist literature in the 1950's', *Political Quarterly*, vol. 31(3) July-September 1960, pp. 361-73

Cripps, S. *Why this socialism?* (London, Gollancz, 1934)

Crosland, A. *The Future of Socialism* (London, Cape, 1956)

The Conservative Enemy (London, Cape, 1962)

A Social Democratic Britain (Fabian Tract 404, 1971)

Socialism Now (London, Cape, 1973)

Cross, C. *Philip Snowden* (London, Barrie and Rockliff, 1966)

Crossman, R. H. S. (editor). *New Fabian Essays* (London, Turnstile Press, 1952)

'The lessons of 1945', in P. Anderson (editor), *Towards Socialism* (London, Fontana, 1965)

Inside View (London, Cape, 1972)

Bibliography

Dahl, R. 'Workers' control of industry and the British Labour Party' *American Political Science Review*, vol. XLI 1947, pp. 875-900

Dalton, H. *High Tide and After* (London, Muller, 1962)

Dell, E. *Political Responsibility and Industry* (London, Allen and Unwin, 1973)

Donoughue, B. and Jones, G. W. *Herbert Morrison: Portrait of a Politician* (London, Weidenfeld and Nicolson, 1973)

Dowse, R. E. *Left in the Centre* (London, Longmans, 1966)

Duff, P. *Left, Left, Left* (London, Allison and Busby, 1971)

Durbin, E. *The Politics of Democratic Socialism* (London, The Labour Book Service, 1940)

Eldon Barry, E. *Nationalisation in British Politics* (London, Cape, 1965)

Epstein, L. 'Socialism and the British Labour Party', *Political Science Quarterly*, December 1951, pp. 556-75

Fairlie, H. 'Aneurin Bevan and the art of politics', *History Today*, vol. X(10) October 1960, pp. 661-7

Fels, A. *The British Prices and Incomes Board* (Cambridge University Press, 1972)

Finer, S. E., Berrington, H. B. and Bartholomew, D. J. *Backbench Opinion in the House of Commons 1955-59* (London, Pergamon, 1961)

Foot, M. *Aneurin Bevan, Volume 1* (London, Four Square Illustrated, 1966); *Volume 2* (London, Davis-Poynter, 1973)

'Credo of the Left', *New Left Review* 49, May-June 1968, pp. 19-34

Foot, P. 'The seamen's struggle', in R. Blackburn and A. Cockburn (editors), *The Incompatibles* (Harmondsworth, Penguin, 1967) pp. 169-209

The Politics of Harold Wilson (Harmondsworth, Penguin, 1968)

'Parliamentary Socialism', in N. Harris and J. Palmer (editors), *World Crisis* (London, Hutchinson, 1971)

Gelman, N. I. 'Bevanism: a philosophy for British Labour', *Journal of Politics*, vol. 16(4) November 1954, pp. 645-63

Glyn, A. and Sutcliffe, B. 'The collapse of U.K. profits', *New Left Review*, 66 March-April 1971, pp. 3-34

British Capitalism, Workers and the Profit Squeeze (Harmondsworth, Penguin, 1972)

'Wilson's Economic Record', *New Left Review* 76, November-December 1972, pp. 91-6

Goldthorpe, J. *et al. The Affluent Worker* (three volumes, Cambridge University Press, 1968 and 1969)

Bibliography

Greaves, H. R. G. 'Complacency or Challenge', *Political Quarterly*, vol. 32(1) January-March 1961, pp. 53-65

Gregory, R. *The Miners and British Politics 1906-14* (Oxford, Clarendon Press, 1968)

Griffiths, J. *Pages from Memory* (London, Dent, 1969)

Grove, J. W. *Government and Industry in Britain* (London, Longmans, 1962)

Guttsman, W. L. *The British Political Elite* (London, MacGibbon and Kee, 1968)

Gyford, J. and Haseler, S. *Social Democracy: Beyond Revisionism* (Fabian Research Series 292, March 1971)

Hanson, A. H. 'The future of the Labour Party', *Political Quarterly*, vol. 41(4) October-December 1970, pp. 375-86

Harman, C. 'Tribune of the People', *International Socialism*, 21 and 24

Harrison, M. *Trade Unions and the Labour Party since 1945* (London, Allen and Unwin, 1960)

Harrison, R. 'Labour Government: then and now', *Political Quarterly*, vol. 41(1) January-March 1970, pp. 67-82

Haseler, S. *The Gaitskellites* (London, Macmillan, 1969)

Heffer, E. *The Class Struggle in Parliament* (London, Gollancz, 1973)

Hindall, K. and Williams, P. 'Scarborough and Blackpool', *Political Quarterly*, vol. 33(3), July-September 1962, pp. 306-320

Hindess, B. *The Decline of Working Class Politics* (London, MacGibbon and Kee, 1971)

Hunter, L. *The Road to Brighton Pier* (London, Arthur Barker, 1959)

Hutt, A. *The Post-War History of the British Working Class* (London, Gollancz, 1937)

Hyman, R. *Strikes* (London, Fontana, 1972)
    'Industrial conflict and the political economy', in R. Miliband and J. Saville (editors), *The Socialist Register 1973* (London, Merlin Press, 1974) pp. 101-54

Irving, C. 'Whitehall: the other opposition', *New Statesman*, 22 March 1974, pp. 383-4

Jackson, R. J. *Rebels and Whips* (London, Macmillan, 1968)

Janosik, E. G. *Constituency Labour Parties in Britain* (London, Pall Mall Press, 1968)

Jenkins, P. *The Battle of Downing Street* (London, Charles Knight, 1970)

Jenkins, R. *The Labour Case* (Harmondsworth, Penguin, 1959)
    What Matters Now (London, Fontana, 1972)

Bibliography

Jupp, J. *The Left in Britain 1931-41* (unpublished M.Sc. thesis, University of London, 1956)

'Socialist rethinking in Britain and Australia', *Australian Journal of Politics and History*, vol. 4(2) November 1958, pp. 193-206

Kaufmann, G. (editor). *The Left* (London, Anthony Blond, 1966)

Kelf-Cohen, R. *Nationalisation in Britain: the End of a Dogma* (London, Macmillan, 1959)

Kendall, W. *The Revolutionary Movement in Britain 1900-1921* (London, Weidenfeld and Nicolson, 1969)

Kincaid, J. *Poverty and Equality in England* (Harmondsworth, Penguin, 1973)

Krug, M. *Aneurin Bevan: Cautious Rebel* (New York, Thomas Yoseloff, 1961)

Lapping, B. *The Labour Government 1964-70* (Harmondsworth, Penguin, 1970)

Looker, R. 'The future of the Left', *Studies on the Left*, vol. 7(2) Spring 1967 pp. 49-68

Lyman, R. W. *The First Labour Government* (London, Chapman and Hall, 1957)

Mackintosh, J. P. 'The problem of the Labour Party', *Political Quarterly*, vol. 43(1) January-March 1972, pp. 2-19

Marwick, A. *Clifford Allen: the Open Conspirator* (London, Oliver and Boyd, 1964)

Mathews, J. *Ford Strike* (London, Panther, 1972)

McBriar, A. M. *Fabian Socialism and English Politics* (Cambridge University Press, 1966)

McCallum, R. B. and Readman, A. *The British General Election of 1945* (London, Oxford University Press, 1947)

McDermott, N. *Leader Lost - a Biography of Hugh Gaitskell* (London, Leslie Frewin, 1972)

McKenzie, R. *British Political Parties* (London, Mercury Books, 1963)

McKitterick, T. E. M. 'The membership of the party', *Political Quarterly*, vol. 31(3) July-September 1960, pp. 312-23

McNair, J. *James Maxton: the Beloved Rebel* (London, Allen and Unwin, 1955)

Melitz, J. 'The trade unions and Fabian Socialism', *Industrial and Labour Relations Review*, vol. 12(4) July 1959, pp. 544-67

Miliband, R. 'Socialism and the myth of the golden past', in R. Miliband and J. Saville (editors), *The Socialist Register 1964* (New York, Monthly Review Press, 1964) pp. 92-103

Bibliography

'Marx and the State', in R. Miliband and J. Saville (editors), *The Socialist Register 1965* (London, Merlin Press, 1965) pp. 278-96

'The Labour Government and Beyond', in R. Miliband and J. Saville (editors), *The Socialist Register 1966* (London, Merlin Press, 1966) pp. 11-26

The State in Capitalist Society (London, Weidenfeld and Nicolson, 1972)

Parliamentary Socialism (London, Merlin Press, 1973)

Miliband, R. and Poulantzas, N. 'The problem of the Capitalist State' in R. Blackburn (editor), *Ideology in Social Science* (London, Fontana, 1972) pp. 238-64

Miliband, R. and Saville, J. 'Labour Policy and the Labour Left', in R. Miliband and J. Saville (editors), *The Socialist Register 1964* (New York, Monthly Review Press, 1964) pp. 149-56

Mitchell, H. and Stearns, P. N. *Workers and Protest: the European Labour Movement, the Working Classes and the Origins of Social Democracy 1890-1914* (Itasca, Illinois, F. E. Peacock, 1971)

Nairn, T. 'The nature of the Labour Party', in P. Anderson (editor), *Towards Socialism* (London, Fontana, 1965) pp. 159-220

'The Left against Europe' *New Left Review*, 75 September-October 1972, pp. 5-120

Newens, S. 'Mergers and modern capitalist development' in *The Trade Union Register 1970* (London, Merlin Press, 1970) pp. 25-44

The Nuffield Election Studies

Parkin, F. 'Inequality and political ideology: social democracy in capitalist societies' in F. Parkin, *Class Inequality and Political Order* (London, Paladin, 1971) pp. 103-36

Pelling, H. 'Governing without power', *Political Quarterly*, vol. 32(1) January-March 1961, pp. 45-52

The Origins of the Labour Party 1880-1900 (Oxford, Clarendon Press, 1965)

Social Geography of British Elections 1885-1910 (London, Macmillan, 1967)

Popular Politics and Society in Late Victorian England (London, Macmillan, 1968)

A Short History of the Labour Party (London, Macmillan, 1972)

Pimlott, B. 'The Socialist League: intellectuals and the Labour Left in the 1930's', *Journal of Contemporary History*, vol. 6, 1971, pp. 12-39

Bibliography

Poulantzas, N. *Political Power and Social Classes* (London, New Left
Books and Sheed and Ward, 1973)

Prentice, R. 'Lessons of the Labour Government: not socialist enough'
Political Quarterly, vol. 41(2) April-June 1970, pp. 146-50

Pritt, D. N. *The Labour Government 1945-51* (London, Lawrence and
Wishart, 1963)

Rawson, D. W. 'The lifespan of Labour Parties', *Political Studies*, vol.
XVII September 1969, pp. 313-33

Richter, W. *Political Purpose in Trade Unions* (London, Allen and
Unwin, 1973)

Roberts, E. *Workers' Control* (London, Allen and Unwin, 1973)

Rogow, A. (and Shore, P.). *The Labour Government and British
Industry* (Oxford, Basil Blackwell, 1955)

Rubenstein, D. (editor). *People for the People* (London, Ithaca Press,
1973)

Rustin, M. and Waltzer, M. 'Labour in Britain: victory and beyond',
Dissent vol. 12(1) Winter 1965, pp. 21-31

Saville, J. 'Labour and Income Redistribution', in R. Miliband and
J. Saville (editors), *The Socialist Register 1965* (London, Merlin
Press, 1965) pp. 147-62

'Labourism and the Labour Government', in R. Miliband and
J. Saville (editors), *The Socialist Register 1967* (London, Merlin
Press, 1967) pp. 43-72

'The ideology of Labourism', in R. Benewick, R. N. Berki and
B. Parekh (editors), *Knowledge and Belief in Politics* (London,
Allen and Unwin, 1973) pp. 213-26

Sedgwick, P. 'Varieties of Socialist thought', in B. Crick and W. A.
Robson (editors), *Protest and Discontent* (Harmondsworth,
Penguin, 1970) pp. 37-67

'The End of Labourism', *New Politics*, vol. 8(3) 1970, pp. 77-86

Shanks, M. 'Labour Philosophy and the current position', *Political
Quarterly*, vol. 31(3) July-September 1960, pp. 241-54

Shell, K. L. 'Industrial democracy and the British Labour Movement',
Political Science Quarterly, vol. 72(4) December 1957, pp. 513-
39

Shore, P. *Entitled to Know* (London, MacGibbon and Kee, 1966)

Simpson, B. *Labour: the Unions and the Party* (London, Allen and
Unwin, 1973)

Sissons, M. and French, P. (editors). *Age of Austerity 1945-51.*
(Harmondsworth, Penguin, 1964)

Bibliography

Skidelsky, R. *Politicians and the Slump* (Harmondsworth, Penguin, 1970)

Snowden, P. *Socialism and Syndicalism* (London, Collins, 1913)
Labour and the New World (London, Cassell, 1921)

Stansky, P. (editor). *The Left and War: the British Labour Party and World War One* (London, Oxford University Press, 1969)

Stanworth, P. and Giddens, A. (editors). *Elites and Power in British Society* (Cambridge University Press, 1974)

Steck, H. J. 'Grass roots militants and ideology: the Bevanite revolt', *Polity*, vol. 2(4) 1970, pp. 426-42

Stewart, M. *Protest or Power: a study of the Labour Party* (London, Allen and Unwin, 1974)

Symons, J. *The General Strike* (London, The Cresset Press, 1957)

Taverne, D. *The Future of the Left* (London, Cape, 1974)

Thompson, E. P. 'The peculiarities of the English', in R. Miliband and J. Saville (editors), *The Socialist Register 1965* (London, Merlin Press, 1965) pp. 311-62

Topham, T. 'Productivity Bargaining', in *The Trade Union Register 1969* (London, Merlin Press, 1969) pp. 68-95

Townsend, P. (editor). *Labour and Inequality* (London, Fabian Society, 1972)

Tugendhat, C. *The Multinationals* (Harmondsworth, Penguin, 1973)

Urry, J. and Wakeford, J. (editors). *Power in Britain: Sociological Readings* (London, Heinemann, 1973)

Vaizey, J. *Social Democracy* (London, Weidenfeld and Nicolson, 1971)

Webb, S. 'The first Labour Government', *Political Quarterly*, vol. 32(1) January-March 1961, pp. 6-44

Wedgwood Benn, A. *The New Politics: a Socialist Reconnaissance* (Fabian Tract 402)

Westergaard, J. 'The rediscovery of the cash nexus', in R. Miliband and J. Saville (editors), *The Socialist Register 1970* (London, Merlin Press, 1970) pp. 111-38

Williams, M. *Inside Number 10* (London, Weidenfeld and Nicolson, 1972)

Williams, R. 'The British Left', *New Left Review*, 30 March-April 1965, pp. 18-26

Williams, R. (editor). *The May Day Manifesto 1968* (Harmondsworth, Penguin, 1968)

Wilson, H. *The New Britain: Labour's Plan Outlined* (Harmondsworth, Penguin, 1964)

Bibliography

The Labour Government: a Personal Record (London, Weidenfeld and Nicolson and Michael Joseph, 1971)

Index

Index

Index

Index

Parliamentarianism, 22-3, 25, 134,
140-1, 142, 147, 164-5, 170-1,
205-8
parliamentary road to socialism, 39,
40, 228-9
Place, Francis, 5
poverty, 29, 115-6
power structure, 30-1, 74, 106-8,
109-13, 121, 132, 148-61,
219-22
Prentice, Reg, 165n, 215
private industry, 44, 65, 153, 154-8,
169
productivity, 48
productivity bargaining, 123-7
profits, 66n, 73, 111, 112

reformism, 143, 219
revisionism, 78-9, 80-6, 88, 89-96,
113, 130-1, 173n, 197
revolutionary politics, 6, 12, 134, 177,
227-8
Rogow, A., 54, 56, 58, 156
Rose R., and Abrams M., 84n
Russell, Bertrand, 28

Saville, J., 147, 173
Scanlon, Hugh, 225n
science, 97-9
Second International, 147, 182
Sedgwick, P., 94, 128n
Shaw, George Bernard, 142
Shawcross, Hartley, 44
Shinwell, Emanuel, 77, 79, 80, 91,
153, 192
shipbuilding industry, 120
shop stewards, 119-20
Shore, Peter, 216
Skidelsky, R., 30
Snowden, Philip, 11, 15-16, 19, 25,
28, 29, 31, 32, 35, 72n, 137-8n,
139, 140, 157n, 172, 180-1,
182n, 206
Social Democratic Federation, 9, 136,
141, 199
Social Democracy, 68, 135, 164
social insurance, 46
social reforms, 11-12, 14, 38, 47, 60-2,
81-6, 113-15
socialism, Labour Party view of, 2, 12,
13, 18, 19, 33-7, 40-2, 62-3,
78, 93, 95, 99, 139-40

socialist commonwealth, 21, 43, 75,
143
Socialist League, 39, 178, 186-90,
193-5
state controls, 45-6, 54-9, 91
state planning
1945-51, 43, 44-5, 54-9
1964-70, 99-100, 116-19
state power
extent of, 141-3, 144-7, 156
constraints on, 30-1, 74, 106-8,
109-13, 121, 132, 148-61, 167,
219-22
Labour Party view of, 141-7
steel nationalisation, 69-71, 77, 79,
91, 100
sterling convertibility, 69
Strachey, J., 80
strikes
by managers, 70
by workers, 73, 120, 158-60
Labour Party attitude to, 21, 73,
137, 138n, 141, 162, 214, 219
political, 141, 162
syndicalists, 12, 21, 39, 134, 141

Taff Vale, 12
taxation, 14, 43, 46, 61
Third International, 182
Thomas, J.H., 24, 25, 27, 28, 29, 32,
142, 167
Thompson, E.P., 7
Townsend, P., 114n
trade unions, 7, 9, 11-13, 48-9, 50n,
61-2, 73, 79, 85, 87, 88, 107,
132, 158-61, 209, 223-4, 225n
Trades Disputes Act, 12
Trades Union Congress, 7, 31, 32, 62,
70, 107
Transport and General Workers' Union,
22, 194
Treasury, the, 28, 29, 31, 108, 216
Tribune, 178, 191, 194, 210
troops, use of, 21-2, 73, 138n
Tugendhat, C., 110n, 111n

unemployment, 26, 68, 80, 126
unilateral disarmament, 87, 88
Unilever, 57

Victory For Socialism, 178, 197-8

256

Index